The Collected
Correspondence
of
Allen Ginsberg
and
Neal Cassady

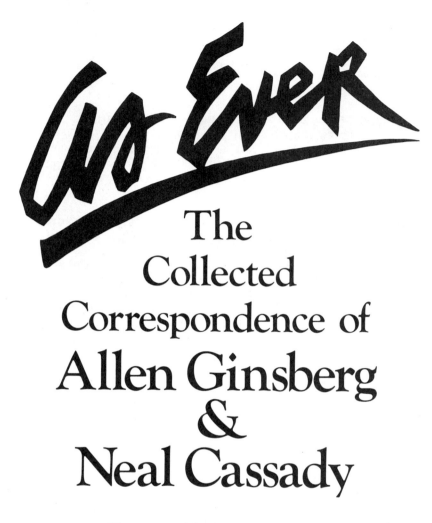

As Ever

The
Collected
Correspondence of
Allen Ginsberg
&
Neal Cassady

Foreword by Carolyn Cassady
Edited with an Introduction by Barry Gifford
Afterword by Allen Ginsberg

Creative Arts Book Company

Letters of Allen Ginsberg, Neal Cassady, Carolyn Cassady,
Gregory Corso and Peter Orlovsky appear through the courtesy of
the Special Collections Division of Butler Library, Columbia University, New York; the Humanities Research Center of the University of Texas at Austin; Carolyn Cassady; and Allen Ginsberg.

Allen Ginsberg's use of the closing 'As ever' began in the early
1950s in imitation of William S. Burroughs. Grateful acknowledg-
ment is hereby extended to Mr. Burroughs for the genesis of
the title of this book.

Designed by Michael Patrick Cronan
Typeset by Ruth Berling
Cover print "Bodh Ghaya Busokuseki footprint left on the rock
where Shakyamuni first elucidated the turning of the wheel
Dharma" by Michael Corr.
ISBN 0-916870-08-1 (paper)
       0-916870-09-X (cloth)
Library of Congress Card Catalog Number 77-082182

Published by Creative Arts Book Company
833 Bancroft Way, Berkeley, California 94710

Contents

Dear Allen, et al: CASSIDY. A-47667

The lights have failed in the cell-block so am writing this last S.Q. line in semi-darkness making my scribble excusable for once, assuming I get thru this 787th straight nite behind bars just as I assume you missed the Chile — got your great letter from the Earthquake & are still alive; I shall leave here in the morning & go to a job at Con. Lithograph Corp & my home at 1823 Bancroft ave., Los Gatos to begin a 6 mo parole. Love To all — (Write). Neal.

Postcard from Neal in San Quentin, 1959.

Read by Page Numbers
(tho They are mixed up.) ①
                                                        Jan 18, 54

Dear Neal & Jack & Caroline: Palenque, Chiapas, Mx.

        Since I last wrote I have been from
Merida to Uxmal to Campeche (a port on the
Peninsula on the way) to Palenque where I am
now.

        I am beginning to really hate mexico
& almost wish I were out of it as travelling with
so little money I am Continually obsessed
with saving it, and Consequently making
mistakes in spending what I have & building
up great reservoirs of ~~desire~~ anger at whoever
gets in my way - usually a mexican —
when I spend it. As it is I have about 34
bucks left to get to D.F. on where (I presume)
I have more waiting from the Telegram and
it better be true - though with dear old
Bill Garver around I suppose I won't
become a public charge. However I ~~as~~ ain't
going to hit a lot of ~~cit~~ cities on the way
that I wanted to - partly no money to get
there (San Cristobal de Las Casas way down
South Chiapas) or time + $ to find out how

Letter from Allen in Mexico, 1954.

Editor's Note & Acknowledgments

Original spelling and punctuation have been preserved throughout. The letters are dated as accurately as possible and reproduced complete with the exception of material deemed extraneous by Carolyn Cassady or Allen Ginsberg.

I wish to thank Donald Allen for his advice and counsel, and David Farmer of the University of Texas Humanities Research Center for his efforts in making the material in that collection available. Thanks also to Kenneth Lohf of the Special Collections Division of Butler Library, Columbia University for allowing the use of materials in their archives. Special thanks to Carolyn Cassady for suggesting the possibility of the project, and to Allen Ginsberg for his time and courtesy.

Finally, my constant gratitude to Mary Louise Nelson and Marshall Clements, whose understanding makes anything possible.

B.G.

Foreword

Had it been left to Neal, this book would never have come into existence. Neal viewed most of his "past"—even if only yesterday—as a likely mistake or cause for guilt, and best it be forgotten as quickly as possible. He seldom analyzed former errors to improve future behavior or to find reasons for the present. It was through his friendship with Allen Ginsberg and Jack Kerouac that he was urged to look within and behind and to consciously express in words his past actions and associations as well as his present thoughts and feelings.

In an effort to keep everyone happy, Neal tried to juggle several relationships simultaneously and felt it advisable to keep them separate and secret from one another; it was best to destroy the evidence or change it with a lie . . . just in case. Consequently, in this correspondence, we have Neal's letters to Allen in 1947 but none of Allen's to Neal. At that time Neal was courting me and told me nothing of his true relationship with Allen. These letters from Neal, as well as some others, I now see for the first time. I value all such private communications, since they provide me with an added dimension of objectivity in my attempt to understand Neal's complex character.

After Neal and I were married Neal shared Allen's letters with me and I was able to save them. This I did with care, not only because I'm a pack-rat by nature, but also because I was convinced Allen was a genius, and I clearly foresaw the time that has now arrived when these chronicles of Allen's struggle for growth would help to document his development and illuminate his published works. What I couldn't have foretold is this testimony to the tenacity of deep and enduring love.

Carolyn Cassady

Note: It will be evident that as Neal's friendship with Allen grew, along with their correspondence, he became far more particular about spelling and grammar; his two-finger typing technique persisted, however, as did the typographical errors.

C.C.

Introduction

"I don't know what I am when I speak like this but it is near my true speech," Allen wrote Neal in 1947—and in 1948 recognized his "phantasies [as] shadows of the truth . . . which will one day emerge in all its power and intensity." These letters thus prove prophesy—less than a decade from that date Allen Ginsberg had shown himself to be the most pervasive poet of his age. He'd written "Howl" and "Kaddish", classics certain as his progenitor Whitman's "Leaves", Blake's "Sunflower"—A decade further the poet emerged as counsellor to two generations, a public conscience intense and powerful enough to be crowned King of the May, father-figure for half the world's youth. "I have genius," he'd written Neal, ". . . my every act is a trial of the soul."

Here is the record of that trial, the twenty-year odyssey Denver-New York-San Francisco-Central & South America-Alaska-India-Dakar-"on the road to Texas in [an] old Ford in the rain in Oklahoma"—letters from Allen exploring ancient Chiapas ruins, Neal wheeling to railroad brakeman job fifty miles San Jose to Frisco "filling up all the weeded air my lungs will hold and just before and during release of the minute and some seconds held breath, which has been exhausted of its vegetable qualities by my eager sacs extended lips, at which instant the mystic spin develops at the heads peak and dives downward to the toes traveling along the nerves with a relaxing rush and the floodgates of amazement are open and every sight astounds and mystifies to manufacture a thought that startles one into exclaiming aloud a big soft 'Oooooohhhh!' "

Beginning with the tender heart-talk of forties love letters, through vicissitudinous lifetimes of the fifties and eventual sixties sadness and death, Allen and Neal chronicled the emotional and political passage of an era. Peopled by a variety of active, vital participants—Jack Kerouac, William Burroughs, Gregory Corso, Ezra Pound, William Carlos Williams, Bertrand Russell, et al—whose impact on life in the western world was considerable, their universe was (and for Allen still is) dynamic and ever-changing—"Amazing how truly ageing is a process of horror and disillusioning," said Allen, ". . . I never dreamed it would be like this. We create our own world and world-delight and romance out of our own hearts . . . . After all the dross of history is washed down the drain . . . you emerge pristine . . . shining and triumphant like an angel rejoicing in the strength of your own imagination."

Included here is Allen's surprising uncomprehending first reaction to Kerouac's epic *Visions of Cody*—"a holy mess"—and Neal's discovery of his *On the Road* "Dean Moriarty" character'd life-to-be; Neal's prison notes—"Assuming I get thru this 787th straight nite behind bars . . .''; Allen's Christmas 1960 message after first Harvard mushroom highs: "Stop hiding yr light in a bushel", rushing to telephone Jack *"The revolution has begun—"*; up to Neal's frantic "serious-top secret" scribbled plea to meet at JFK Dallas assasination site, ten months left to live.

"Save from the grave!" Allen entreated in "Fragment 1957" from Calcutta '63—"O Neal I love you I bring this Lamb into the middle of the world happily—O tenderness—to see you again—to recognise you in the middle of Time." And Neal's last message from Mexico—"I'm going to stay . . . until you get here . . . you've got to save me—"

As Allen in 1948 foresaw the pathos of Neal's life—"doomed never to rise out of time and illusion"—he nevertheless perceived the irrevocable nature of their friendship: "Perhaps you are a temptation rather than an angel. Yet you have a star in your forehead; that is why I long ago was happy to think with you that our lives were bound together."

Now words bound and done, dreams and memory one—"I woke up and thought him still at my side;" quoth Allen 1953 from Waley's Po Chu I—"I put my hand out; there was nothing there at all."

Barry Gifford

THE
FORTIES

*There are no letters from Allen in my collection in early 1947 be-
cause Neal didn't receive them when with me, or if so, didn't let
me see them and must have destroyed them. He wouldn't have
wanted me to know about his "deal" with Allen, which I didn't
until I read these letters of his to Allen.*

                                                              C.C.

                                                        [New York]
                                                      Jan. 17, 1947

Dear Allen;
    I really feel quite badly because of the many obligations I feel to-
ward you, however, I can only explain what has happened & hope
sincerily hope you can understand—by a sort of instinctive recog-
tition—of my complete (almost shame) humility for my imposition
on you, but to get to the point.
Lu Anne has failed me—for what reason I don't know—I can, of
course, make generalizations, but on the surface, at least, she has
left me. Therefore, all of your things are not in my possession—
they are at Mrs. Cohen's who lives at 91 W. 46th St. Bayonne,
N.J—at first I had thought of getting them—by mail—& sending
them to you, however, I find that impossible, so you must go out
there & get them yourself.
                                        I'm really quite sorry.
                                        Neal

P.S. Bob has a small brown cardboard like suitcase there, *please*
pick it up & give it to him. Thanks, N.
I almost forgot—your radio, stove & dishes are all there, but I have
with me—& need it badly—your suitcase & toilet articles. Thanks,
Sorry,
                                        Neal

Kansas City
March 6, 1947

Dear Allen;
   It has just occurred to me the thing I lack is the address, no, just
the names of the publishers, not only the New York ones, but, also,
Horizon in London & any other ones you know, while your at it,
please, send me the names of magazines such as "New Directions" etc. that I might Dig.
   However, the primary purpose of this missive is an urgent request that you go around the corner to where your tailor is & pro-
cure for me my only pair of trousers that are any good.
   Now, as for the address, send the publishers & magazines information *immeadiatly*, if you please, send that on to me addressed
thus;
                     Neal Cassady
                     c/o General Delivery,
                     Denver, Colo.
   As for the trousers, send them Parcel Post at the General Post
Office, 33rd & 8th Ave, to me at an address I shall send on to you
tomorrow, understand?
   I am only writing this to you now, here in Kansas City, because
of the sense of urgentcy & rush which I feel, rather than waiting
until I arrive in Denver.
   I'm quite sorry but the bus is leaving & I must rush, in fact, the
entire letter is written in rush.
   Don't fail me now, send the letter immeadiatly & get the pants
out, so you can send them tomorrow, when I send you my address.
   Sincerily now, I really mean this
                     Love & Kisses,
                     Neal,
P.S. I'll write tomorrow.

March 10, 47
Denver

Dear Allen;

Sorry I'm late in writing to you, however, I've been seeking a place to live & as yet have failed, therefore, you must send the trousers on in this fashion;

Bill Barnett
1156 Gaylord
Denver, Colo.

address them simply that way & I shall recieve them O.K. Thanks.

I trust you have recieved you shirt by now in the mail send my pants parcel post also if you will.

I have been unable to see Mannerly because my suit & over coat are in the cleaners. I intend to see him though when I get them out on tuesday.

Hal I will see tue. A.M. just before I speak to Mannerly.

I have seen Lu Anne & have been able to convince her of the need to, for the present, stay at her Mother's & work so as to save money to pay Haldon back & such.

I am seeking a room, then a job, then a typewriter, then some money, then to leave here in June.

Other than these things nothing else of intrest.

I find that due to not being settled yet I can't begin to write to you as I would desire to, so you see, I & you must wait until I'm settled to begin to speak of other things—understand?

Write only after I've sent you a permanent address for I don't wish our correspondence to fall into alien hands, but, do send on the trousers to the Bill Barnett address.

I shall write again in a few days.

How are you & Jack making out on the overcoats? I could sell 2 now if you could send them to me—both of them are my size—one fellow wants Brown & the other wants a blue one—

'till later,
Le Enfant,
N.L. Cassady

1073 Downing St.
Denver, Colorado
March 14, 1947.

Dear Allen;

As you can see I have procured a typewriter the only bad point is that it's only half mine. I feel certain you will excuse me using it to write personal letters to you, since you would have to decipher my juvinel scrawl otherwise.

I have found a wonderful place to live & it only costs $6.00 a week. My meals must still be taken in cafes however. I have not as yet went to work so I am really in debt.

Speaking of debt, sent on those overcoats as soon as possible to aleviate my deress.

I am honestly amazed & overwhelmed at the truly great mass of information you have sent on to me concerning the poem. I appreciate it very much. Needless to say, especially now that I have this typewriter, I shall copy the poem & sent it to you within the week.

To say that I got "great kicks" out of your recital of what happened at Vicki's after I left that night, would almost be an understatement. I find that the optimistic tone on which your missive ends is so heartening in it's implication that I fear I wouldn't be able to bring myself to really think that the "Peace" will last.

Incidentally, I have found no peace at all since arriving. You see, my basic problem has developed into seeking the proper relationship with Lu Anne. Due to our seperation she has fallen into a complete apathy toward life.

Her inability to meet even the most simple obligations is almost terrifying. Her life is a constant march of obsessions. Her attitude toward everyone is so defensive that it constitutes continual lying, yet she still has many fellows who adore her & is, therefore, always getting drunk & has become very slipshod. I, as yet, can't solve this delema, however, in due course I feel a solution will be found. My life is, at the moment, so cluttered up I have become incapable of relaxing long enough to even write a decent letter, really, I'm almost unable to think coherently. You must, then, not only forgive, but, find it within yourself to understand & in so doing develop a degree of patience until I am able to free myself enough to become truly close to you again.

On your part, you must know, that any letdown in your regard for me would upset me so much that, pschologically, I would be in a complete vacuum. At least for the immediate future I must request these things of you. so *please* don't fail me. I need you now more than ever, since I've noone else to turn to. I continually feel I am almost free enough to be a real help to you, but, my love can't flurish in my present postion & if I forced it now, both you & I would lose. By God, though, every day I miss you more & More.

Understanding these things I hope, nay, in fact, know you must pour out more affection now than ever, rather than reacting negatively & withering up so that all is loss, or would be, between us.

Let us then find true awareness by realizing that each of us is depending on the other for fulfillment. In that realization lies, I believe, the germ that may grow to the great heights of complete oneness.

I have not seen Haldon yet, just called him once. I saw Mannerly for 20 minutes & can say that I emerged the victor, however, I merely mentioned "a poem"* & let the suit talk for me. So, you see, each new time I converse with him my statute will grow.

I shall find a job tomorrow & perhaps by losing myself in work again I may become more rational & less upset & unnerved by the emotional shock of returning. Write soon I need you. I remain your other self.

                                                            Neal.

                                        1073 Downing St.
                                        Denver, Colorado
                                        March 20, 1947.

Dear Allen;

I have just finished copying the poem, since I am not a typist you will see in it several mistakes that are so glaring as to almost fill me with shame. I have, however, stuck exactly to your puncuation etc. Also, I have sent you the poem in carbon, now, if you need the prime copy or the original don't hesitate to let me know, and I

---

*The poem Neal talks about here is probably the same one he showed me to impress *me*. Written by Allen, but said "by Neal Cassady" on it and was apparently part of this campaign to make Mannerly impressed with Neal & his progress.—C.C.
Columbia U. 1947. *G. E. Woodbury Prize Poem*: "The Last Voyage".—A.G.

shall sent it on to you.

I almost feel guilty about harping on the coats, for I see in your letter that it has given you some concern. Please excuse the seemingly desperate tone that I had unconsiously taken in speaking of them, my only explaination is that I am so conditioned to dealing with people who must be driven on to doing something by my assuming an urgent tone that I fell into that mannerism with you. I will state that if its convient enough to be done without too much trouble you might sent on one or two that are my size.

One thing that is really important though, is my trousers. I am honestly in need of them.

Your speaking of Bill B. only makes me want to meet him more than ever. I trust that in June you will come west we shall see he and Joan at that time. Continue to keep me informed as to his tribulations etc. just as you did in this letter.

I place you in such high regard academically that I merely reacted normally to your amount of information concerning the literary scene. I presupposed that it had all come out of your head without effort, just as I without effort can speak of football, therefore, when I expressed amazement at the knowledge, it was artificial in that I was complimenting you simply as a means of showing appreciation. So you see I was not truly impressed, but, rather accepted it as further proof of your value. In fact, what you pointed out about it in this latest letter was understood, and understood so well that I find a lack in myself in not implying that, rather than using the false complementary style to show my thanks to you.

I have given much thought to what I am about to say. I must, I fear, become somewhat incoherant near the end of this paragraph, but, bear with me as I am consiously trying to formulate our, no, my feelings. First, realize I am not intellectualizing nor doing anything other than being governed by pure emotion (incidentally, I feel that is the key to whatever awareness you sensed in me) in my effort to state to you what my present position is. Now, I shall tell my fears, desires, feelings of all types, and then, if possible, attempt to analize them. Allen, this may sound strange, but, the thing that is uppermost in my mind at the moment is a fear. How can I state it? I believe it is almost paranoiac in its intensity, with each of your letters I feel it more. I have difficulty in putting my finger on it, but its a real fear of losing you. Its a combination of a knowledge of lack on my part, not only academically, but, in drive as well, also, a sense of outcast that makes me feel at times as if I were really imposing on you for me to try and become closer. I have become more defensive pschologically in direct ratio to my increasing degree of realization of need of you. The thing that is closest to the truth is the simple statement that you are too good for me. I am above feeling envy of you, and don't fall into a sort of loving admiration either, rather, I have a sort of confused sense of loss when I think of you. The whole thing is quite beyond me at present, yet, somehow this is different than previous times when I felt an inability to cope with our relationship. This time, although, its negative in its psychological aspect, I find true concern of our need so much that I, in reality, feel stronger than at any other time since I met you. I mean, stronger in desire and ability to struggle to handle our affair, rather, than healthy positive drive toward freedom for us. You can see I am now in a position for the first time of being a drain on you insofar as I have become aware of a nerotic negative almost compulsive need of you. I feel as if I were a woman about to lose her man, primarily because as you become more straight through me, or otherwise, you will need me less, and, also secondarily, because I know as that happens I shall need you more. This is as I say, the uppermost fear. Along side of that is a remnent of the old feeling I had in N.Y. of a need to free myself of Denver and all it implys before I can progress, at least, with you. Then there are other things which are bothering me, but, they are unimportant compared to the above.

Allen, forgive me, but I must break off now. I have been really busy these last few days and haven't had any rest, right now its 5 A.M. and I must rise at 9:30 A.M. I am completely beat, causing my fluctuations in thought I think.

Let me end on one line in your wonderful letter—"I will be prepared for you I think, when we meet, but on other terms than those which I'd formerly concieved and which I tried to force on you" I find that statement holds true for me as well as you Allen, whether for better or worse we must see, but, whichever way it goes, I know I can't help from profiting thereby and perhaps you can also (though, I fear you can't since I no longer have anything to offer, and, therein lies my lonlyness).

I leave you in complete weariness and apology.

But, By God, L'enfant or no, whether you think its mad or not, whether "its not as we feel or I want to feel" to quote you. I still love (what a weak word) you.

Bah! I'm tired.

Neal

P.S. Speaking of overcoats, don't try and sell them, we'll wait until this fall and get more out of them then, not only that, but, when we set up housekeeping then we'll make a record machine and really

get gone and yet be straighter than any 10 psychologists. Use the
record machine as an indication of all things fine and the other as a
statement of our disiplainaryism.
              I'm so tired I can't even type, let alone think.
                                            Please excuse.
                                            N.L.C.

*A letter to Jack Kerouac on March 27th explains Neal's troubles &
reveals some of his methods in dealing with people.*
                                            C.C.

                                            1073 Downing St.
                                            Denver, Colorado
                                            March 30, 1947

Dear Allen;
    I recieved the pants and just today got the Van Gough. I have
put the Van G. above my bed & it is just what I wanted, thanks a
million.
    I think you have the right idea about the coats & we shall try it.
    I had already presupposed that I would get a Ricehian analyisis,
but your news has made me even more aware of its advantages.
    I don't know how to say this, but you've hit the nail on the head.
No more sacrament, no more directing my efforts in the nervous,
stupid, neurosis you have outlined so well. I understand perfectly
Allen and by god, you're right! Man, from here on out it'll be a
breeze. Really, the formulation you gave is just what I needed. I'm
overwhelmed with joy, I feel a sense of relief, I almost know peace
again! All of this just thru understanding and agreeing with you.
    Its not that I didn't see the "rise I might get out of you" by my
last letter, or didn't know you might react by "sacramental sad-
ism" or "sacramental masochism", but I felt I must show my fidelity by that method, since I had little else to offer at the moment
and knew you needed a sense of security, however, all thats past
now. I had forgotten your insight, your mental straightness of
understanding, here, in your last missive you've made me aware

again and damn it all, its perfect! No kidding, this really affects me, you see thats just what I sensed, but couldn't formulate, not only that, but I felt perturbed, not through missing you as much as confused in how I *should* move with you in correspondence, therefore, I fell into a overblown "sacramentalism" toward you, . . Dig?

Theres nothing else I can say to you, you have put it all so well anything I could say would be artificial and unnecesssary. All I can here state is that I wish you had the letter you wrote so as to keep straight on its impications, you see, I have it and I suspect it will become a bible in that here you have the germ, at least, of what will become to me not only a foundation for our relationship, but almost a "system" in so far as I know this is what I really am. I too, have destroyed "sacramentalism" in almost everthing, but being constantly accused of "brutality"-"con-man" & all that have almost come to feel guilty & forced feeling in some instances.

What you say on "Play" is honestly what I've been doing, or striving for, all my life, therein lies our, or my, confused sense of closeness. Also, I fear, therein lies our strengh of tie to each other, I say I fear, for I *really don't* know how much I can be satisfied to love you, I mean bodily, you know I, somehow, dislike pricks & men & before you, had conciously forced myself to be homosexual, now, I'm not sure whether with you I was not just forceing myself unconciously, that is to say, any falsity on my part was all physical, in fact, any disturbance in our affair was because of this. You meant so much to me, I now feel I was forcing a desire for you bodily as a compansation to you for all you were giving me. This is a sad state and upsets me for I want to become nearer to you than any one & still I don't want to be unconciously insincere by passing over my non-queerness to please you. Allen, this is straight, what I truely want is to live with you from Sept. to June, have an apt., a girl, go to college, (just for French to sit in on classes etc.) see all and do all. Under this arrangement we would have each other, a girl, (this is quite similar to you, Joan & Bill) and become truly straight, (thru analyisis, awareness of "sacrament" and living together). This, of course, doesn't mean you wouldn't have perfect freedom, in fact, I feel you'd have more freedom that living by yourself, because of the pschological oneness we would obtain. If you grew tired of me, or the arrangement we could always not see each other, or move, or something. So *Please,* Allen give this a good deal of thought & even if your doubtful of its advantages, try & come to accept it, at least temporarily, in the next few months.

I've just reread a portion of your letter and it is really good, my, my, what freedom it gives me toward you. A lot of trash is almost automatically cleared away, I repeat, from here on out, I believe it will be a simple thing for us to come to a better knowledge of ourselves & each other.

Let me leave you with the idea that through this understanding lies our ability to progress together, rather than, slide into a sincerity that through "sacrament" will (and has, a bit) become shopworn and false in that, that part of us that is similar would be nullified by the other differances in our individual makeup.

Neal L.

1073 Downing St.
Denver, Colrado
April 1, 1947

Dear Allen;

Recieved your letter yesterday, I think its very funny. When I was done chuckling I began to try and figure out what to do. From what you say it appears that Mannerly has already made up his mind that I didn't write the poem. Be that as it may, I know that I'm going to be as indignent as hell with him, upon his return.

I presumed that Haldon had probably told J. that it was your work, rather than mine, for I had not even seen Hal since my return and, therefore, he didn't know what we were pulling on J. This was not the case, however, for I saw Hal today and found out he has not even seen J. for at least a month. So now we know that J. was just guessing, unless Ed White had, in answer to J.'s query as to whether I had written anything while in N.Y., said no I hadn't.

So although J. has inside his own mind decided that I didn't do the work, he has no actual proof. Now, if I really bear down on him when he comes back, i.e., show him all the stuff I have, explain every line, compare your C. Reveiw stuff with it, rave on for hours, be indignent, etc. I think I can be just capable, not of convincing him, but at least, make him indecisive and unable to reach the honest conviction that its not my work.

When I believe I've attained as much as I can toward making him truely unable to decide, I tell him to go to hell, reject him completely, demand *my* poem back and stalk away. Thereby freeing myself of the necessity of paying him the money I owe him also,

since, after all, he "doubted" me, wasn't deserving of me and all
that. Knowing him as I do, I'm certain this will have no effect on
him, at least outwardly, but, by going through this I, again outwardly, obtain a degree of freedom, respect, and if I pull it off
properly, save "face".

So that is what I'll do. If it fails its not important anyhow for in
reality he and I are so far apart it would all be false and artifical
even if it truly were my poem. Incidentally, in our very distance
from each other lies most of my strength of argument with him for,
in the final analyisis, I've not hardly talked to him for two years
he has no way of knowing if I've progressed that much or not. The
negative factor therein is that when I did see him I was very mono-
toneous and dull in talking and he has only that to go by, so no
wonder he doubts I did the poem, I shall twist this around to where
the reason I didn't show enlightenment with him is due to the fullness of my awareness of him and how unimportant, sterile, shallow, base, etc. he is and since I was weary and felt no stimulus
with him how could I shine?

Enough of this, as for you, I can't, just as you said, see anything
in your postscript. I feel sure the only reason this is so is because
I'm trying to read too much into it, so let's not be too concerned
since I know that I can only understand, obviously, as much as I
see and feel, however, in the p.s. of yours lies so really far gone
abstractions, though they're concrete, that I am placing importance on them only in the light of your last letter and its realities.
dig?

Thanks for showing such concern and insight about J. and the
poem, of course, I'm so tickled by the humor, just as you, that I can
place no objective importance on the whole thing, again, just as
you probably I must dash, I've an important date at 6 p.m. and I
want to get this letter off anyhow, so to compansate for the business air of this one, I'll really hit the ball next time, please understand.

Again I urge you, think long over what I spoke of in my last letter, concerning living to-gether.

Love,
Neal

P.S. If you've seen J. again before he left don't fail to tell me all
about it. Also, naturally, if you disagree with my plan as to him, or
think I should alter it in any way, send the info on right away, since

he will be here the 6th, and I should see him right away. I'm going
to hold off seeing him until I hear from you though.

                                                    Hows my boy?
                                                    Neal

                                                    1073 Downing St.
                                                    Denver, Colorado
                                                    April 10, 1947

Dear Allen;
    The main anxiety of yours concerning sexual play has, I believe,
caused you to presuppose some things, also, I find, there has been
a slight exaggeration of all the manifold angles of the entire business, due to this, you instinctively realize there is some lack to your
formalization of the problem. This lack comes not only from your
overconcern, but, your supposition that we are using the proper
method in dealing with this. I, almost unconciously, think of a picture in which everything is just slightly overdone, the lines are a
little thick, the paint is a little heavy, everything is distorted and
yet the distortion is so slight that one must really look to know that
it is exaggerated. This comparison of a picture and our affair does-
n't truly mean, or explain anything but it does show that I sense
that we have overdone and overused our concern for each other im-
properly. Due to this we both are not sure of *exactly* what is to be
done.
    But, this really, as you know, is not the point. Neither am I try-
ing to excuse or justify myself, for I know that somewhere I have
failed to state my feelings and because of this failure to properly
commune these "nonverbal" things, I don't feel too badly about
your misunderstanding. The thing that concerns me is how am I to
get my abstract realizations across to you, not only to prevent
things like this crisis to arise, but also to bring us down to a plane
where we can both move freely within a groove which includes
both of us and yet has no faults in concept. In your "sacrement"
letter you brought this out clearly and *that* is why I answered you
as I did, where I failed is in using such words as "conning", etc.
You may as well forget that you ever received that letter, I know
that, in reality, I did not mean what I said, I can't explain it, but
somehow, I was being honest with you in New York and yet, again

somehow, you were perfectly right in accusing me of artificiality in
your recent letter.

I believe, that instead of this being a complex thing it is rather a
simple lack of knowledge i.e.—you naturally, presume that when I
spoke of us living with a woman I meant that I select the woman,
whereas, in reality, I meant that *we* find the proper woman. Now,
this example shows a simple failure on my part to tell you these
things and I believe also gives the proper slant to an understanding of the whole business.

You suggest that I don't try to alter my emotions to fit yours, or
to appeal to yours, also you tell me not to say what I can't feel or
deliver. This is not, I fear, really thinking deeply enough, you see,
in this sense that is to say, from this approach, I honestly cannot
answer you, cannot "really know" what I feel or how I will act. You
yourself, realize this, for you said that we couldn't tell until we
were together again.

I suggest that instead of further, non-progressing, talk in this
vein we fall into a mutual groove in which, however false in logic
this may sound, we assume a responsibility toward each other
(family tie idea), entertain a certain erotic attraction (lover idea)
etc., until such time as we do see each other.

Now, as for Mannerly:

I shall do exactly as you suggested.

I have been struggling to obtain a job. The latest news is that I
will probbly drive a taxi here, this is really difficult to fall into and
in the process of getting the job I may go to jail on account of a past
episode, at any rate, if I talk fast enough I'm in clover, if I fail—I
suppose I can get a letter smuggled out to you from the bastille.

Don't fear that Hal and J. will get together about you, they see
each other only by chance (which is so slim that, as yet, they have-
n't seen each other) and even then would only exchange pleasan-
tries.

Tell me the latest info on tea, if not Norman's connection, then,
Bill B. and his raising it.

Have you seen Jack or Claude?

In reality, Allen, I'm a simple, straight guy, and in thinking of
what I want for the next year I know that without you I'd be lost. I
feel a normal brotherly need emotionally for you, just as with Jack
or Hal or my own brothers, in fact, my emotional needs are not too
strong, for example—I know Hal is the only one in Denver that
means anything to me, and yet, I don't even bother to see him. I
called him once, breifly, a week after arrived, and saw him once,
breifly, after getting your letter about J., and then, only to find out

if he'd told J. This lack of interest and drive toward projecting myself, or even simply seeing Hal, is not through feeling I would be
imposing on him, or that he doesn't particularly care to see me or
anything of that nature, quite the contrary, he's similar to Jack in
that he urges me to drop around etc. but, I just don't need Hal
emotionaly enough to do so, I've brought this out so you can see an
example of my lack of compulsive, emotional need for anyone.
Even women are the same, honestly, I'm pretty independant that
way, on one hand it bothers me to think I'm unable to be affected
emotionally as much as other people seem to be, on the other
hand, this objectivity of emotionality, has, in my life, enabled me
to move freely in each groove as it came, therefore, the prime difference of our respective personalities lies in this, and once fully
realized, will I hope, tend to weld us together, rather than be a
cause for conflict.

I'm on a spree tonight, I'll tell you exactly what *I* want, giving no
    Having gotten that out of the way, and knowing that the above
differance is our most extreme dissimilarity, I've come to see that,
other than that, there is every reason for us to live together next
term. I hear you cry "other than that! why, by God, thats all I'm
interested in him for!" I know, I know, but, look at me—I've already mentioned I be lost without you from Sept. to next June, as
you can see, I mean in *every* way except emotionally, thats why I
suggest a woman with us (not only that, you need her more than
I)——now, Allen, for christ sake, don't get in an uproar about
nothing, you know fucking well that when I say "emotional need"
I mean psychologically, I get my nuts off just as you, you rave on
about "objectivity" & "sacrament" I've got that, its only that I
felt unable to live and commune that way with you (or anyone) that
has motivated my seemingly false attitude toward you, I repeat, in
your "sacrament" letter I thought you saw and understood, my
fault laid in assuming this, and being sloppy in my reply, thereby
causeing this misunderstanding. Beyond that I'm guilty of nothing. So you see, we must understand and move on, if we cannot,—
bah! don't think of it.

    I'm on a spree tonight, I'll tell you exactly what *I* want, giving no
thought to you, or any respect or consideration to your feelings.
First, I want to stay here and drive a cab until July, second, go to
Texas and see Bill and Joan for a few weeks, third, (perhaps) dig
New Orleans with Jack, fourth, be in N.Y. by early Sept, find an
apt., go to college (as much as they'll let me) work on a parking lot
again, and live with a girl *and* you. Fifth, leave N.Y. in June '48
and go to Europe for the summer.

    I don't care what you think, that's what I want. If you are able to understand and can see your way clear to shepharding me around the big city for 9 months, then, perhaps, go to Europe with me next summer thats swell, great and wonderful, exactly what I want, if not——well, why not? Really, damn it, why not? You sense I'm not worthy of you? you think I wouldn't fit in? you presume I'd treat you as badly or worse? You feel I'm not bright enough? you know I'd be imposing, or demanding, or trying to suck you dry of all you have intellectually? Or is it just that you are, almost unconciously, aware of enough lack of interst in me, or indifferance to my plight and need of you, to believe that all the trouble of helping and living with me, would not be quite compensated for by being with me? I can't promise a darn thing, I know I'm bisexual, but prefer wo-men, there's a slimmer line than you think between my attitude to-ward love and yours, don't be so concerned, it'll fall into line. Be-yond that—who knows? Let's try it & see, huh?

I like your latest poem, in fact, I like most of your poems, through reading more poetry I've become a bit better able to judge and appreciate your work.

Relax, man, think about what I say and try to see youself moving toward me without any compulsive demands, due to lack of assur-ance that I love you, or because of lack of belief that I understand you etc. forget all that and in that forgetfulness see if there isn't more peace of mind and even more physical satisfaction than in your present subjective longing (whether for me, or Claude, or anybody) I know one cannot alter by this method, but come to me with all you've got, throw your demands in my face, (for I love them) and find a true closeness, not only because what emotional-ity I have is also distorted by lonliness, but also because I, logically or not, feel I want you more than anyone at this stage.

I'm really beat, off to bed, and a knowledge of relief, for I *know* you must understand and move with me in this, you better not fight against it or any other damn thing, so shut up, relax, find some patience and fit into my mellow plans.

Love & Kisses, my boy, opps!, excuse, I'm not Santa Claus am I? Well then, just—Love & Kisses,

Neal

P.S. I'll keep you informed as to the Mannerly business, and do my damndest to make you a full-fledged myth.

P.P.S. Say, it just occured to me from out of the blue, probably since I'm in the act of closing, that you meant it when you called me a "dirty, double crossing, faithless bitch" I've had your letter four days now and I just now suddenly saw that you meant it. In-stead mocking or admonishing you, I excuse you automatically, yet

seek a hurt reaction inside myself, failing in this, I realize truely
what an unsensitive bastard I really am, here the most important
guy in the world calls me that in all ernestness, is honestly hurt
and upset by me, and how do I react? do I feel guilty? do I beg forgiveness? hell no! I'm so emotionally shallow I can only worry
about my own lack of emotion in not reacting at all. That's my
paranoia. ha! ha!
Write soon.

                                                    N.

                                        1073 Downing St.
                                        Denver, Colorado
                                        April 15, 1947.

Dear Allen;
    The taxicab deal has almost fallen through, this has saved me
from jail, but is forcing me to get another job—I haven't worked
except for one day since arriving here and am really in debt. At any
rate, I shall work here until July first, then, go to Central City—35
miles away—on July 6th and work there six weeks as a bellhop in
the Teller House. In the middle of Augest you and I shall go to
Bill's, and go to N.Y. near the first of Sept. I feel I, too, can't
squeeze in New Orleans this summer.
    I will tell you all I know about J's ability to get you a job and all I
can of Central City: I have, naturally, no idea of what he had in
mind when he spoke to you about a job here for you, however,
since you mention Central City, I presume you'll work up there in
his hotel, either as a bellboy, usher in the opera house, keeper of
the books, laborer, bartender's helper, janitor or any other way
that he can fit you in. This, although it sounds terrible, need not
depress you; it is really unimportant what you do, for, really, all
anyone does there is drink, bang & fuck off in general, Now, you
can see your official capacity is immaterial except in the amount of
money you draw. As for Central itself, the festival starts about July
5th each year, last year it was July 6th, & lasts six weeks. The
people are usually in three catagories; the prominant, all-agog
over music, Denver & New York socialite backers, The arrangers,
directors & opera stars themselves (J. falls in this group)—that's
catagory number one. Number two is made up of all the many who

come for one reason or another—social, (400), true interest, heard about it, etc.—this group have two things in common: They are outsiders, they spend all the money. The third catagory is what we'll be in; college guys who fool around at something up there only to satisfy some personal desire—women to prey on, money to filch from someone, prestege to be gained etc., other than this, all other people there live there.

I have't seen J. yet, but will do so tomorrow, in school, and arrange some night this week in which to see him at home for the evening. I am putting off any statements until after this interview, then I shall unload in a torrent not only what went on in it, but also all I have to say regarding the whole thing in general, after that it can rest in peace.

Your springtime rebirth seems too much the product of external events to last, but rest assured that I'm with you even though I know that I don't see the reason for it. I fear that in playing with all this business, you have become overinfluenced by J. I don't mean he's changed your life by objective guidence i.e.—he can't teach you, but I sense, subjectively i.e.—due to your feeling of mastery over him & wanting to continue the egoistical show, he has seduced your basic lonliness into a false hope. To clarify: You've become excited about nothing, J. is not only holding our psychological fool's gold, but is also so far beneath you that I unconciously think of a stupid cowmaid luring a Balzac into the barn, of course, its O.K., but, somehow, I had felt you were able to cope with J's character & not reeled from the heady wine of victory & allow yourself to fall into this sort of juvanilia. I hope this last paragraph is all off the beam and you are just really looking forward to the west, without any high hopes or artificial thoughts of enthusiasm concerning anything other than a full summer of new experiances, not gain, or worldly profit.

You don't have to answer this if you don't have time, because I'll write again at the end of the week to tell you about J's actions & reactions etc.

Love, Neal L.

1242 Clarkson St.
[Denver, Colo.]
May 8, 1947

Dear Allen;
    Can you ever forgive me? I mean it, can you? really, I feel very
guilty about my failure to write, of course, I could rationalize myself indefinatly concerning all the lack of time I've had, troubles
etc., however, I shan't do that for I should have written anyhow.
The real reason I've failed to is, I think, due to my not knowing
what would happen next. As I recieved your last letter I was pack-
ing to go to Las Vegas & gamble. Quickly I dashed off a letter telling you so, & the reasons why, then, before I mailed it, I had a
minor brush with the police which, incidentily, caused me to move
to this address. This change in plans voided my unmailed letter, so
I started another, but just then I got a job, and I mean a *job*! honestly, I work ten hours a day and its so hard on me that even after
ten days at it, I can still hardly drag myself home to fall into bed. I
have not done anything, haven't seen J., (although I phoned him
two weeks ago and made a date) haven't seen Hal, haven't even
written to you, man, I've been beat into the ground by this hard
work. enough of these excuses, onward—
    Your last letter was a pip, truly the best you've written, insofar
as the groove we've been striving for its perfect. I feel as I reread it
that your right in there, now all we need is for me to fall into it properly. Of course, you've forgotten most of what you wrote but thats
not important. Your in!
    I must repeat the jobs I suggested as J's best are only what I
think, as far as I know he might make you vice-president, so try not
to feel any drag, and about all remember, He's fallen for you hook,
line and whatever else he has, I'm quite convinced that you are, by
far, the most important and best loved thing that has happened to
him in years, so during the summer really bear down on him and
where he'll now eat out of your hand, then he'll even feed you out
of his. If it means anything.
    I swear I'll see J. before the weeks out and then write to you on
the "whole thing in general" whatever I meant by that.

May 15, 1947.

Dear Allen;
    The letter I have enclosed dated May 8, is self-explainatory. The

reason I must start anew—and this is the fourth time I've begun a letter to you in the last month—is only that I really don't know what will happen next and have been putting off writing until I had something definite to say. Even now I'm indefinite as all hell about what I am to do.

                                                    May 17, 1947
Dear Allen;
   Great news! Here's our plan—please bear with me now. I leave here today to go to Trinidad, Colo. to work, I leave there about June 10th or so and dash right over to Bill and Joan's where I shall meet you and about June 30th or so we come to Denver to work at Central City from July 6 to about August 13th. This is the best and only way for us. After Central we'll be all set. I'll make enough the next three weeks at Trinidad to have a few bucks and we'll save the Central money we make (since I believe our room and board bill will be almost nil up there) to goto N.Y. on. Please Allen steer this course with me this summer.
   I know you'll excuse me for all my previous failures in writing the last month when you realize its only because I've been having trouble with the police, Lu Anne etc. You'll see when I arrive at New Waverly the middle of June. You must be there to meet me.
   You can write to me at 1242 Clarkson and they'll forward it to me. After you arrive at Bill's write quick and give me precise directions as to how to get there.
   Love, Love, Love—write soon, I'll see you in June. I a poet too.
                                        Love again,
                                        Neal L.

                                        Neal Cassady
                                    care: C. Robinson
                                        Box 1008
                                        Colburn Hotel
                                    980 Grant Street
                                    Denver, Colorado
                                        [June '47]

Dear Allen:
Bill Thompson told me he had just received a letter from you stat-

ing that you were now in Texas; he didn't show it to me as he has none of your letters to him——something dark going on——what have you been saying?——I'm kidding.

I haven't written for two reasons: one, I was indecisive whether I would come to Texas for a week or two to meet Bill and Joan or postpone that until the latter part of August and see them just before we went back to N.Y. two, I didn't think you'd be in Texas until June 15 or so according to a post script in the last letter I received, and I didn't want a dead letter hanging around Bill's house, because it would probably be invalid by the time you arrived due to all of my fluctuating. For example, I've lived with Lu-Anne a couple of weeks; lived with a couple of old family friends, nurses, a week or so, etc. My work life has been quite similar, so you can see things have been in a fix.

J. has been hedging, as usual, in fact, I am fearful that whatever commitments he has made to you about procuring you a job may not be fulfilled. The basis for this judgement rests only on my personal experience. Therefore, it's probably inaccurate, for you have impressed him enough to force him to go out of his way and find you some beneficial employment. You may suspect by now that he has not done the same for me. As it now stands I shan't be at Central City. I can't say that I'm too sorry for I have found a new interest. I sense Haldon was right in his summary of Central City as being "too gooey".

At any rate, you musn't remain hanging on a limb in Texas. Although, I can promise you nothing in the way of living quarters, work life, even social activity—I still insist that you hurry to Denver so that we can work something out. I am anxious to see you, also whatever you may bring with you; i.e. tea—may I repeat—tea.

When you arrive, contact me at 1830 Grant, Apartment 306; phone MA-4493 since I am living day by day and they will know where I am.

Haldon has drifted further away from us, due mostly to his mad preoccupation with his work, so you can't expect too much from him in the way of social contact.

I have met a wonderful girl.* Her chief quality, I suspect, lies in the same sort of awareness or intuitive sense of understanding which is ours, (your's and mine) chief forte. She is getting her Master's at D.U. For some strange reason she came to Denver last year, abandoning better places, because she could make money at

*Carolyn Robinson (Soon Cassady).

DU. But she's not really as vulgar as she sounds. Her lack of cyni-calism, artificial sophistication and sterility in her creative make-up will recommend her to you. She is just a bit too straight for my temperment; however, that is the challenge, just as that is the challenge in our affair. Her basic inhibitions are subtle psychologi-cal ones tied up indirectly with conventions, mannerisms and taste; whereas, mine with you are more internal, fearful and stronger. She knows all about the Theatre, draws a fine line, and is quite popular. Don't feel that I am overawed by her, though. I would have a justifiable right in being subjective to that. Some-how, my respect for her seems unimportant. I feel the only reason, reaallly, that she affects me so is the sense of peace which she pro-duces in me when we are together. Secretly, she is the reason I am postponing the trip to Texas until later in the season—wait till you meet her.

Remember now, I am really at sea here, so when you arrive, I shall almost be dependent on you, rather than vice versa as it should be. But don't let that drag you. We will hit the ball this summer, so barrel on——rush up—hurry to me!

Love,
Neal

The gap between June and these next letters was because Allen was in Denver with Neal. Both wrote a letter to Jack on August 22nd the day before they left for Texas. Allen shipped to Dakar on September 13th and Neal drove Bill to N.Y. Sept. 29th. There's a letter to Jack in which Neal explains what he did to Allen that caus-ed Allen to ship out.

C.C.

I arrived in N.Y. expecting to rendezvous with Neal—he'd return-ed to San Francisco maybe two days before to marry Carolyn, leaving me a brief note.

A.G.

New York
[Fall 1947]

Dear Neal:
I received your harsh note this morning. I can't understand it. I have always thought you were wise and would be infinitely wiser someday: Perhaps you are now. I have always loved you as much for your Pathos and fatality. And so, finally, your letter gave me Pleasure.
I suppose I must say goodbye then. I don't know how. I believe it is real, and that is why I linger so long.
Remember me well if you will remember me.

Yours, as always, with love,
Allen.

[San Francisco]
Robinson
561A 24th Ave.
Nov. 18, 1947

My dear, dear Allen;
My good and lovely boy, please, please, forgive and forget my terribly, terribly; badly done, trite, and illiterate trash, i.e. my last letter.
You show yourself to be your old wonderful self in your letter, your critisisms are delecious, simply great, many thanks.
The above must be the Kingsland influence in me—I wonder if you know how much love I have for him—my god! What am I doing?
I stop the above "inspired sterility" and come down to *you*, (only you)—You, (say I in a presumptious tone) my ahistorical soul-mate; are correct, you are so right, insofar as you gointo it and understand the exodus; you are the true genius, but I must accept my role also, and realllllly think I am doing it the way *I* must!! Damn it, you are almost insolent and overbearing to the point of absurdity in your attack on my overdone and stinking prose, and I think, delved into that unnecessarily long to the exclusion of the main point of our relationship i.e. my development to

maturity, to strengh, and grace; since you do have the understanding Allen, as evidenced by your wonderful, but still partial, knowledge of the reasons for my leave-taking, use that understanding to
trust me to my own self, and sense of destiny; seperate and entirly
apart from my straightness, or artistic self, this is a matter of
levels, as you know, and I can't allow you to chasten me by using
these weapons. Don't think of this duelisticly, my friend.

Canton Cheese by Cassady
The above interlude was neccesitated by my failure to put ' between n and t in Cant, *so* I made it Canton, then, of course; why
not do a take-off on Allen and his "interlude"—*so* I did, *so* I don't
like it, *so* I condemn it as not good prose style for its triteness in
using Lord Chesterfield, instead of, say, Pete Smith. *so* my interlude is not as good, *so* that still does't mean because the artist is no
good, neither is the art—look, my boy, see how I write on several
confused levels at once, *so* do I think, *so* do I live, *so* what, *so* let
me act out my part at the same time I'm straighting it out, *so*asto
reach an authentic destiny.

It *Can* Be Done——I'm doing it. What am I saying? I started this
letter in good faith and have somewhere gotten sidetracked onto
good fun. Let be, let be.

Having solved all this in my "Life with fater", "*Corn*el Blimp"
way, I now speak of more serious things, now you take taxation for
example, there *is* a problem, or, the degree of pressure at 10,000
ft. in the ocean, its amazin', says our natural philosophy prof. N.
Cass.——Am I mocking myself enough, am I here doing enough
penance to suit you for the time being? answer me, sweet Allen.
On the contrary, I mondify and say I strarted this letter, not on
good faith, but good tea, yep I met a niggar and bought some, as
soon as I got high I sat down to write this, have been at it three
hours, have had three thousand seperate and distinct thoughts,
have written less than three hundred words and, have lost my
thoughts, have said nothing, have no regrets, however, for I know,
(I repeat) Carolyn is but a step and so is—fuck it, I'm hitler. I
mean; I'M HIGH.

                                    [no signature]

This letter was written after Allen returned to N.Y. from Dakar—
(like it says)—after Neal dumped him there.
                                                C.C.

                                                New York
                                                [Fall 1947]

Dear Neal:
    This is a stanza from a poem I have been writing all today, this
one is after I saw your letter —
        "This was such grace, to think it is no more
            I cannot mock in dignity, but weep.
        And wherefore dignity? the heart is sore;
            True lovers have no dignity to keep,
        And till I make departure from this shore,
            My mind is sorrowful and will not sleep;
        and mockery is no good, nor mind is, nor
            Is meditation, sadness is so deep."
    This letter will be different from the last and maybe different
from any other, I hope for our sakes. I have protected myself,
armored, since I arrived, from grief or too much self pity and as a
result I saw my mind turn more than ever before, with some other
circumstance, into isolation and phony goodness—to the point of
retiring from the world, which I have not yet, to a furnished room
to write cold hot poems. I have no place to stay yet permanently
tho I have several comfortable temporary residences with others,
yet I want to be by myself now. So I have been touring the city,
seeing everyone I know and testing them and turned away from
most—except J. & B., & Kingsland. Even Jack bothers me and I
think I will see not even those when I settle.
    I had been writing all day a poem "The Creation of the world"
on benny for the first time since I left Africa and my spirit was
opened and near exhaustion when I saw your letter which slowly
has broken me down. To write what I am is hard because I tend to
slip into poetry or prose formalisms or even neatness of expression, or exaggeration or understatement. Even, in fact, to realistic
denial of my message. Yet I was in bed a few minutes ago—it is
4.30 morning now—and I was thinking restlessly of you, allowing
thought of you to penetrate deeply in me for the first time since I

have arrived. Not that I neglected or even feared thought—I had just simply protected my mind before, unconsciously, because the shock was too great to allow to breake in on me all at once. I think you know what is comming in this letter, it is serious; if you don't want to I won't ask you to read further or to reply for that matter.

You know or (at the moment) I am smarter than you & cleverer in ways and I don't want to be smart or clever at this point, even subtle. I must admit that I have known more or less consciously that all the "purity" of my love, its "generosity" and "honour" was, though on its own level true, not at all my deeper intention toward you, which was and is simply a direct lover's. If we were equal and I were as strong as you in the relationship "I could afford to be"—I would naturally flow into common generosity. But we are not, for all my purity and abnegation is a stall and a sell out, and all my "gifts" to transmit, if they were to be any use to you which I really thought they would be, were unimportant in my mind and subsidiary to my main beggary. I would have been capable of continuing it, before, even to the point of renouncing any sexual claim on you as I did in my last letter; but that I know and knew was possessiveness taking the palatable & generous form. I had no clear ideas in mind when I told you to come back, except to follow out my agreement to the letter, though perhaps not in spirit, and wait for you to pity me again and sleep with me.

I think that you must be further removed from me than I from you but I do not care at the moment, even though that may make this letter sound out of key and insane.

I do not know how I can hope for any love for you because my own love is one compounded of hostility & submission. I don't understand and can't, your own emotions, even when explained only because my drive is so blind that I cannot comprehend even intellectually the possible realism of your statements. And I can't well plead a case of love for you truly because at my most sweet or straight or goody-goody or sacrificing or demanding, I am always conscious below of stabbing you in the back while I lead you or deceive you. This is not so much conscious as merely known, by both of us, I suppose.

But in this exposition I am losing my purpose & emotion and I must send it to you if only as an expression of my hatred. It broke my mask before to read your letter, not the content but phrases— were you mocking me? I don't think so—like "My good & lovely boy", "Answer me, sweet Allen". And for the first time I thought of you for such phrases, and for promises I made you make and which were not kept, and so I went to bed, then half forgetful and I

lay half trembling, with recollected desire, breaking moment after
moment, till I cried, and freed myself to think freely almost without the armor of these last weeks. I don't know what I can do Neal
now. You know you are the only one who gave me love that I wanted and never had, as you have—this does not humiliate me any
more—a number of others, and I sometimes wonder about them.
What must I do for you to get you back? I will do anything. Any
indecencies any revelations any creation, any miseries, will they
please you. Or will they frighten you as this does? I mean to bend
my mind that knows it can destroy you to any base sordid level of
adoration and masochistic abnegation that you desire or taunt me
with. This has style, and it is now so much vomit. Or do you look on
it as such? I do not care what I think really, I hate & fear you so
much that I will do anything to win your protection again, and your
mercy.

I am lonely, Neal, alone, and always I am frightened. I need
someone to love me and kiss me & sleep with me; I am only a child
and have the mind of a child. I have been miserable without you
because I had depended on you to take care of me for love of me,
and now that you have altogether rejected me, what can I do, what
can I do?

All this above is still not sincere I cannot come down to the point
where I was when I rose from bed. Neal Neal I am weak now you
can inflict any punishment on me you want. I can't write except
with you in mind—I have two hundred beautiful lines from Dakar
and I don't care about it except to show to you & have you praise
me for them. I have sad lines, so sad I wept when I wrote them.
and if you had any heart would weep to see all the soft torment and
suffering that is in them, all the miserable torture that you made
me go through. I blame you yet I still ask for the whip.

I don't know what I am when I speak like this but it is near my
true speech. Don't think that I forget myself, it is only that I have
so much soul that I can rise above you not in mockery or mind but
spiritual genius, for all the suffering, at the moment when I most
beseech and cry. And it is my hatred for you that drives me in fear
of my obscure and not known power to supplicate and kneel, to
blow you and turn away unsatisfied when you are sated. What can
I say but that I am not worthy of you in a real world, and that you
have no cause or passion's cause to handle me and give me love,
and deal with me at all. I did not mean to challenge you, I am
frightened. I meant that I was impure and pure, too pure to be
drowned in vomit. Yet all I am is, as well, vomit, and I am drowned.

I have never asked you for a true favor, a gratuitous gift from you but small ones once or twice when I was driven to it by your love & purposeful or unconscious frustration of me. I have always been obedient & respectful, I have adjusted my plans to yours, my desires to your own pattern, and now I do ask—I pray—please neal, my neal, come back to me, don't waste me, don't leave me. I don't want to suffer any more, I have had my mind broken open over and over before, I have been isolate and loveless always. I have not slept with anyone since I saw you not because I was faithful but because I am afraid and I know no one. I will always be afraid I will always be worthless, I will always be alone till I die and I will be tormented long after you leave me. I can't give up now for this time the one chance I have of serving not being served, the last time, my only time. Already I am aging, I feel my life is sterile, I am unbloomed, unused, I have nothing I can have that I will ever want, only some love, only dearness & tenderness, to make me weep. I am moved now and sad and unhappy beyond cold unhappiness, beyond any inconvenience that will cause you by my affection. And I will pay you back, you will see, you have never touched my intellect, I can teach you, really, what you want to know now, I will give you money. You know, or will someday learn, that you have no existence outside of me and will never be free until I free you. You have not loved yet and you have not served, and if you can you must come to love & serve me by that love: not by service, by emotions by care and kindness that I need. I have genius, and I have had to pay for it with torment & horror; my every act is a trial of the soul, my guilt makes me mad; I have descended depths beyond depths into my own personality, even to the point of exhibition, of self-pity that is not self pity but knowledge of tragedy. Neal, how can I change, what can I do? Don't you see that I cannot be composed, I cannot reconcile myself, because there is no other reality but loneliness for me and before I am dragged back into isolation I will clasp and grasp and claw in fright even at you without consciousness—even I—and I am afraid that I cannot survive if I have to go on into myself. You do not care, you have all genius and fortune and worldly & spiritual power and you can be happy and take what you want. I have nothing and can give little of value and don't know how and am unsuccessful and awkward with people. Now I call you to save me I see and I have lost my reasons. Can you do it for a love of me, even not physical? Can you do it out of pity? It is pure pity that I beg now, now comradeship or love or sympathy, sheer driven blind powerful pity. Is not my state so wretched that you who once loved me cannot think of me without guilt. Or if it is guilt that will call you, then guilt, I am not so strong that I can afford to choose my weapons. Didn't you first come to me, seduce me—don't you remember how you made me stop trembling in shame and drew me to you? Do you know what I felt then, as if you were a saint, inhuman, to have touched me so, and comforted me, even deceived me a moment in my naieveté to think I was loved. I remember that night, and it is so sad now in my mind, to think that it did happen, if once, that I think of death and only death afterwards. Do you think I am lying again? I don't mean Death as suicide, I mean the unknown, the unforseen, the horrible.

I would go on and on but in my eye I am afraid that all my emotions will only bore you and that you will turn from me with every pleading phrase, I am afraid that you could and this leaves me now as I end, speaking to you, sitting here, waiting in silence, speaking to you no more o god neal please Come back don't be harsh on me I can't help this I can only apologise and beg and beg and beg.

Allen Ginsberg

New York
[Fall 1947]

Dear Neal
    At the moment, on bennys I am sad that you haven't been moved to write me? What is the matter? The tone of my last letters perhaps, so presumptuous & chilled & so usual for me, adjuring you to truth? of course in a way you rejected that fantasy of "truth" in me so it is—in a way—natural that you feel a drag to write, even, perhaps thinking you might gladly do so. Well dont, sensing that it is all untruth, but it is as usual partly my fault, or even better (I don't really care about my fault or yours) the unreality of the situation. Do you know a week or so ago—before I sent off my last letter—I had sat down in Paterson, after thinking very melancholily and patheticaly of you, and wrote you a long pitiful appealing letter. It came out of me, a true part as well as the equally true part in the tone of the one I did send. But when I wrote it (the first) I thought I would send it, yet didnt, first, because in the most "vomitlike" manner of mine, all the sincerest childlike guilty hurtedness was, though, emerging purely once in a while, hinted at mainly with unconscious deception, mockery, or false prideful self-

aggrandizement. Yet there was something in the letter I wanted you to know, which you perhaps do know anyway, that I could not in part of mind or on one complete level, accept the rupture. And yet I do so really, but this is just going on & on. I didn't finally send it not because of "prideful" or self-centered shame for my thoughts or for myself, but because, in a way, I saw no use in exhausting that one level & pouring it upon you masqueraded as the whole response of my mind—which in the letter was apparent, that I was all confused & severally intended toward the situation. Yet a fault was, that I exhausted or presented as the whole response, the equanimity & balance that I also have, to see you go your way. (That way, things are too convenient, as they are opposites, too inconvenient on the first supplementary level.) That balance, which I have sustained mostly, has made the problem, except at moments of "penetrating grief of an impulsive mourning" to quote a poeme, pretty much faded in my mind as an *actuality* a real still existant choice for us. That is I see the situation really as over as far as final meaning for me or masques for you. & that is why I am so curious & so *interested* (have psychic interest) in your attitude now, for it shows, now you have stripped yourself of the compulsive or false response as you saw it, it shows I continue, how much of a real interest in me or mine you have. Once the stripping or break has been done by either of us, we see where we are in a limited way or maybe a full way. So then why your reticence or silence, do you sense that you have nothing real ever to feel or say to me when our relation has been put on this basis? Please see that I think I am willing to know your mind, and "care not" how it blows, in the sense that our communion is so removed by absence of parts & communication that it no longer matters if I, or my interpretations, are repudiated & disproved. I even think I would bear with equanimity from you a final letter to the point, that, after all, we are so different, you have so much your own life & problems, so unmatched or untouched by mine, you have your personality that meets mine only in false relation, so there is no more possibility of meeting of minds between us. I once often told you that *that* was a guilty sense I had which I oft [counsuled] or complained of, and asked you, poetically, to disprove; yet if it proves true it will not hurt me more than anything else has to know it. So as in my last letter I more humbly ask you to explain what you think is the situation between us, or, perhaps better, the situation between you (or me) & other people, the world.

I once insisted that I was an "exception" in your cosmos, which, if it were true, were true, so I made believe & acted as if it were

true, with your "blessings" almost on the project. But what's the
cosmic score now in your mind? This seemed chahotic expression,
but I reread what I have writ so far and it seems to present what's
on my mind comprehensively—please write (I wonder as I get to
this point, because it had not entered my head that if you did not
immediately reply, last time, I would push myself, or be moved, or
"care anymore" to save my vanity or the situation by writing
another letter. I did not think it were called for then, and it was
even more vanity that made me think I was "enraged" or strong or
"cool" enough not to be interested enough to write again, before I
heard from you. My ethics on this score are similiar to your courtesy of sexual self-respect: that you demand of women no action, at
least superficially or physically, *no* service to your body, that you
are unwilling to render unto them. And if I knew, in that sense,
you had too little interest to absorb your mind on me still from time
to time, that you were really indifferent, I suspect that though I'd
be hurt (though not so much as, after all, I have been, by more
subtle if more sweet disappointments) by this realization of the
extent of my self-deception, the truth of our mutual (or your) dis-
respect, I would not, still, suffer too much and would be too composed to "pursue" what is not mine. The amount of "suffering" I
have now has to do vanity over my "insecurity", real as well as
self-imagined, about the present state of our relation; also, about
my compulsive continuance of mutual self-inquisition. "Give my
heart ease" then, and write me a loving and true letter. And if you
are not loving & true, but merely respectful, or even, secretly con-
temptuous in a fine deep way, write me so I shall know. I would
want to think (as in a line from Dakar doldrums) that you are.
        "Most near, now nearest where I fly from thee"
    Yet it will do neither of us good, not me, not you, if I want that as
a mere foolishness. I think, I guess, probably, surely, I have
enough "nonsexual" human rapport, or love, with you for us still
to address & communicate, if not, as I hope, with "straightness of
will", at least with sincerest impulses of mutual respect. Love as
ever and even better also, Allen.
P.S. Read *Nightwood.* I could be Dr. O'Connor as well as almost
    everyone else there. Read The *Idiot.* I did this month. Read
    Henry James "Wings of the Dove". Do you want me to send you
    a Journal-book, like mine, for Xmas?

Walton,
561A 24th Ave.
[San Francisco]
December 30, 1947

Dear Allen;

The new year is upon us, and with it starts a new season for me. I'm to live by myself from now until spring when I return to Denver. At that time I'll get my sister and my father and we shall live together all summer in Denver, at the finish of this business I'm off to N.Y.

On December 1st LuAnne came to town and since then has been a constant thorn; she is with an old beau and a girl friend and together they all live in a downtown hotel. Since she doesn't work (although both of the other two do) and does nothing, even read, she has much time to come by my service station in his car, call on me in the mornings while Carolyn is away and before I go to work; in short, my efforts toward an annulment have been little rewarded, however, now that I've at last, (during several emotional scenes) made it plain to her that all is finished she has again promised to have her mother gain our legal seperation. If this fails this time, when I get to Denver I'll spend the necessary money to get the damn thing.

Helen has gotten married and went to Mexico for the honeymoon, Ruth is all alone and is apparently in need of some companionship so, when you write to 1830 Grant St. apt. 306 be loving.

I am stumbling thru a daily journal and try as I might am having trouble with the recollections of my early life. This first writing task will be all the more difficult in that I do it daily (everyday thought) and also, in the novel form (my life) just to get started.

I am moving by myself again because Carolyn has practically gotten married to me in the eyes of her family and unless I break quickly things may become drastic, I also can live much more cheaply that way and, needless to say money has become quite important since I must have some saved by May for Shirley.

I hope to see you next fall, if not, I'll suffer. goodnight, started Dickens again.

I love you,
Neal L,

New York
[April] 1948

Dear Neal
  I spent 30 hours at Jacks—we talked, drank bottles of beer,
showed each other the latest manuscripts, and mooned about
you—The great event was your letter—we had assumed you were
in jail or something—I of course had fantasised you dead, more or
less, and even suspected suicide some months back. Myself. This
spring has been one of madness, much like yours. Frenzy, frenzy,
creation that is worthless, drinking, school, etc. I've been working
part time and so I had about an event stint of money, and bought a
lot of records. What finally pulled me out—to name an external
cause since they are the signs by which we mark seasons—was
Jack's novel.* It is very great, beyond my wildest expectations. I
never knew.
  But I will let him tell you himself, and then fill in another time, I
want to talk to you myself.
  Now, I suppose I should congratulate you on your marriage. So
O.K. Pops everything you do is great. The idea of you with a child
and a settled center of affection—shit, I don't like to write prose
because you have to say something simple & direct. My mind isn't
made up into anything but complete amused enthusiasm for your
latest building.
  I wish I had your letter here, but it is just as well. I have an
image in my mind of the vast realistic vision you spoke of and am
struck with a joy at the thought of your possibilities—moving toward realization, toward expression.
  When (by implication of ideas or directly) I criticise you, you
know and I know I do it out of tension and self justification on obvious levels obvious ways, and it is hatred showing; so take it as that
and if I seem unaware, and you are offended, point it out to me, so
there will be no mistake.
  However I am slowly comming back or (going forward) to where
I can accept you for yourself (whatever that is) without hassels &
tension & competition for power; and would be done with my
''wrath'' toward you and I believe by next season in N.Y. we will
be closer than last and I less retiring and arbitrary. Is this not great

---

*The Town and the City, then in manuscript.

gentility? Sweet fate.

Allen

P.S. I seem to have thrown out Jim Holmes's letters.

160 Alpine Terrace
San Franco. Calif.
[May 1948]

Dearest Allen;

You and I are now further apart than ever. Only with effort can I recall you. The last half-year has left an indelible print of an utterly different one. (these are comma's—the tail doesn't show. poor ribbon) than that which you are a part of—in fact. to be presumptous. I honestly doubt if you could feel my sadness. —so. let's skip it.

Since I've not let you see myself of late. you are. of necessity. way. way. way off base in much of your letter. Let's look at it. "now. I suppose I should congratulate you on your marriage. so. O.K. pops. everything you do is great. The idea of you with a child and a settled center of affection—shit. I don't like to write prose because you have to say something simple and direct. my mind; isn't made up into anything but complete amused enthusiasm for your latest building."

You should congratulate me—as you would congratulate me on. say. buying a car. or some such impersonal object. Everything I do is not great. I've never done anything great. I see no greatness in myself—I even have no conception of what is greatness. I'M a simple-minded. child-like. insipid sort of moronic and kind of awkward-feeling adolesent. My mind doesn't function properly The child and Carolyn are removed from my conciousness and are on a somehow, secondary plane. or. i.e. not what I think of. or dwell on. or am concerned about. except in a secondary way. If you do have complete amused enthusiasm for this latest building. your being enthused about the wrong thing. at best. the secondary thing.

What I'M trying to say: if you wish to share my intellectual life. or know and deal with what I'm aware of. or concerned about— your wasting your time and love. Since december I've cared for nothing. of late. as I returned. I came to see only one thing. women

—primarily. whores. So. how can we talk of bitches? do you feel
your belly writhe when you pass a women? can you see every infin-
tesimal particle of their soul at a glance? at a sick loathing glance?
—fuck it.

"I have an image in my mind of the vast realistic vision you
spoke of and am struck with a joy at the thought of your possibilities—moving toward realization, toward expression."

Oh bullshit. dear Allen. bullshit. I spoke of no vast realistic.
"vision" What possibilities? I'm ill man. why. why. do you speak
of realization. expression? I wrote for a month straight—what
came out? terrible. awful. stupid. stupid trash—it grew worse each
day. Don't tell me it takes years. If I can't write one good sentence
in a month of continuous effort—then. obviously. I can't realize. or
express.

Three pages of good convincing "art is real" talk. why all this?
I've never disputed that other than the obvious about sterile art.
You see. I'm so degenerated I can't even discuss the better parts
of your exposition on art. Kerouac. Cézanne. Shakespeare—beyond me.

From what I can understand of them your doldrums are fine. All
I can see is the long. continous doldrum I'm in.

Any amateur psychologist will look at this and pronounce dog-
matically: "This young man. Allen. is writing a pronounced defensive letter to you. undoubtedly due to his heavy sense of guilt toward you and his reactionary statements can be attributed to this
guilt." see. if you can. thru my defensiveness. the need for a new
psychology.

I am aware of one half-possible way out for me—music. Music
sends me I love music I live music I become truly unaware of all
bullshit of life only when I dig it. I must realize all all all.—of
music.

No shit. now allen I can understand more than you can.—hah?
Not a foolish. sacraficial understanding of the sadness or such
vapid——I hate words. they are too much.

Let us stop corresponding—I'm not the N C. you knew I'm not
N.C. anymore. I more closely resemble Baudelaire.
                                                    Cassady

New York
May 1948

Dear Neal:

I don't want to cut off communication with you, though I cannot say that it would be good or bad that we write to each other. I love you, and always have, with changing love. I understand your letter as much as I understand anything, which is very little. Please forgive me for my pride or weakness as I forgive you, and love me for what I am and not what I am not.

As for communication, please understand me through the eyes of your new psychology; if you have no understanding yet complete, it will come, perhaps. I do not yet understand, but I have no more desire to understand in my old ways. perhaps I will never break through, permanantly, yet I am trying to achieve a centrality and fixity on the hope. I have done this in the past without being aware of it. The light broke* for me several times in the past weeks, partly owing to your letter. I cannot explain any more than you, I however, do hope that we are both still on the same road. It is useless then to write. Perhaps I will see you someday soon, and be able to help you; I hope that you will be able to help me. I think that inwardly I cherish you well. I had thought you did the same.

Nevertheless as you say, we are confused; or I am, yet I have known my way, or perhaps am moving in my way. I think we may be talking about the same things; perhaps always have. I have always thought you were nearer. No more, but love, Allen.

[160 Alpine Terrace
San Francisco]
August 3, 1948

Dear Allen;

The strangely weird peace of utter perfection is surely brewing in my awakened soul's being. I taste the touch of life and pray my mind to preserve it's good name. Gone, with cheerful eye, is youth; now I neither fondly preen, nor have restless dream. It seems as though no thing can ever again disturb my breathless

*Refers to a vision of Wm. Blake.—A.G.

beam, the sun a welding torch has fused, at last, a wholesome one.
Yes, now past is the peak of pulsated paste, yet, long till the
sadness of evening's fate. Not green, not moulding; wise grace of
life my hand is holding.

I am a blithe idiot. in the spirit of a prodigal, sickened son who
has wronged his father into a disgusted renunciation, do I write.
No foolish pleaded forgiveness, no unfaithful redhead's "I'll never
do it again, I love you; honest, I'm sorry" as she twirls her daddy's
hair with her finger—no ambiguous lover placating her man—until
next time. My guilt, somehow, is not as personalized as it once
was; perhaps, Allen, it's because you are the *Semi*-personification
of *truth* to me. I've long ago escaped admiration—as such—however, you stimulate whatever degree of hero-worship I've left. But,
beyond all this, you stand head and shoulders above any one man
I've ever known—that, in itself, is love—calls for love. Again, look
at yourself as Prince Mischkine—the idiot—you manifest more of
the mystic, the Dostoievskian religious, the loving Christ, than
does anyone else. Or, even, as young Faust, you show more of
these supposedly virile, masculine, enigma problems than does,
say, Haldon; or . . . even, especially, Jack. (much as I love him).
However, off the intellectual now, you are not an abstract symbol
to me; nor quite a personal love which I must combat, fear—or
flee. Rather, (at last I reach the point) I have a new vision to add to
our collection—you are my father. I ask not to begin anew, I ask
not to be again to you what I once was. I ask not to have my suffering be offered as compensation to yours. I do ask, as one mature
man on this side of the continent speaking to another mature man
on the other side, by my father, as Jack is my brother, as Carolyn
is my wife. Can you, will you, if not,—

The above paragraph is a beginning of sincerity, and the vision
of the father—a good *partial* one—degenterated in the last few
lines into a juvenile and overblown triteness which twisted it's
meaning, left a flat taste, and finally petered out completely into a
vague, unreal request. Disregard this silliness—let's start again at
the line above "I am a blithe idiot".

Of course, we've all been long familiar with Dost.'s work "the
Idiot". Personally, I first read it in 1943 in a reform school on the
pacific coast; at that time I had never heard of Dost. and that paru-
sal of the Idiot was my first introduction to him. The supply of
books, and other reading matter, at the institution—Preston is it's
name—was not too limited in quantity, but, woefully lacking in
quality. I can't recall too clearly exactly why I choose the book, I do
recall a sense of rush, since the officials allowed the inmates only

10 minutes after lunch once a week to select one book. I recall the title rather repelled me, and I guess I finally choose it, in the last rush of attempt at reaching a decision, because I wondered what kind of stupidities the author would probably state—in describing an idiot. Also, I felt a heightened anxiety because if it were not good I'd be stuck for a week with a poor book—as had happened before. At any rate, (to escape this verbosity)

Aug. 4th

Allen, Oh Allen!

I had left this letter unfinished and had gone on a freight train run which took 17 hours, got back this A.M., completely fagged, Carolyn was not here (at the doctor's) and just as I was to fall into bed, I saw your letter perched on top of this sheet in the typewriter.

My eyes were red with fatigue and lack of sleep, my legs ached from pumping my bike home up hill from the depot, my breath came short, I sweated. With hands black from my bicycle's handlebar grips, I opened your letter. It is difficult to describe a tired mind's reaction; a weary emotion's response; a prostrated soul's answer to your sombre note.

Wait, I try to speak simpler; you know I've been wallowing in dark profundities; blackened meanings of things have plagued me, different shades of darkness than I have ever been liable tobefore. The resultant resolvement entailed much; much thought, much insight, much strength, much love, much wisdom—in a word: much growth. From ennuied hysteria to vibrant sanity in seven months is an experiance capable of causing many changes in many ways. Two weeks ago, if one can place a time on such things, I came out of the cauldron cleansed. I'm stronger; better in every way. I enumerate: Looking first at outward manifestations of my activities and interests; I work with zest, function perfectly at it, am not prone to bitching, etc. I get things done, matters of everyday I handle better than ever, no Mannerly-like fixation on it, but, simple accomplishment. I utilize time more fully, having only 8-12 hours at home every 24-36 hours I, yet, am more creative than previously. I see all shows worthy, (for example, 6 months ago I didn't deem even theatre worth a block's walk) art museums, concerts, etc. also, (this is most important) I can, once again, walk into a hip joint, smell hip things, touch hip minds—without crying. As for self-improvement: I'm starting music lessons soon; I'm all set, if necessary, to get psychoanalysis, (got introduction, cut-rate price, at Mt. Sinai; supposedly good) but, perhaps, more interesting to you—I am writing daily; poorly done, poorly executed, woefully

weak ice words I string together for what I try to say, maybe, only
one paragraph, maybe differant subjects each day, maybe, crazy
to try (for I seem to get only further embroiled in style) but, I am
trying.

I must interrupt here, I just reread the last paragraph—it sounds
exactly like Vicki, or Norman, or a resolved Hunki, or any tea-head
who is swearing he's cured. Marajuana and psychology seem not
to mix well in most cases, the neurosis is first heightened, then
fought; any solution becomes intellectual, invalid, and fluxuates
for the period of time that each individual's make-up allows in-
volvement. Some never stop, or, perhaps, reach partial alleviation,
and then, let things ride. Conversely, marajuana and psychology
are necessary if one is to become awakened, i.e.—eating your own
bitter fruit of knowledge of life: yourself. It follows, therefore, that
why most tea-heads fail, is lack of strength with which to temper
their insight into their own soul. A Ginsberg soul with a Kerouac
spirit is needed. This paragraph is somewhat jumbled and sounds
mostly intellectual, or as if I were thinking intellectually; that is not
true, I just can't make a point of anything without falling into this
style, which is, I believe, a carry-over from the intellectualations
and prose style of my youth (you see, I'm just starting to write
again, and I'm beginning where I left off 4 years ago).

I am more concerned with factual problems at present (how to
learn music technique, writing technique, and, in general, a return
to many of the factual interests—history of clothes; knowledge of
flowers, trees, earth; learning to dance (dancing, a peculiar thing
I've never told you, is a real inhibition of mine) becoming more
learned in art, design etc., reawakened political and economical
problems, etc. etc,) than am I concerned with such non-factual
things as we usually deal with. Let me try to elucidate; allow me,
please, to try and make myself more clear about this; listen, if you
will, as I try to clarify:

In my early years—7-14—I amassed a huge, unassorted storehouse of facts. Related, or unrelated, if it was a fact, I knew it.
Important, or unimportant; whether the amount of coffee grown in
Brazil last year, or the weight of Trotsky's brain, I dealt with facts.
(psychicly, I used this fact-knowledge to impress—I can recall in
the third grade skipping a half-year because all thru that semester
I'd run to the front of the room to ask the teacher if this fact or that
fact was not so, return to my seat in triumph as she assured me it
was, and, thereby impressed her enough to have her recommend I
be promoted more quickly) When I was 15 years old I discovered
Philosophy and a complete flip-flop occured. By this time I had im-

pressed about as far as one can go and not be too obvious; I had retained my ability to make older people believe me brilliant (witness one sargeant Thompson who ran the prophylactic [. . .]

I'd erase the triteness on the latter half of page 2, but, I leave it purposely to show you how my mind wanders shallowly about trying to fix itself on something of worth.

I have periods of semi-consciousness, similar to dozing off or just waking, which are not dreams, nor guilt nightmares, but, are great impressions of things. Often, as I sit on the sand-box of the huge locomotives, I am lulled into a stupor by the drive-wheels rhythm, and this phenomenon occurs. This is not a new thing to me—I first had dreams of such vividness years ago—but, now they are not as they were then. For example: after a year in jail, I'd awaken in a tremble, reliving all the terror, seeing it all again with ten-fold intensity, remembering for days afterwards. Gradually the gratefulness I'd feel at waking each time to find myself free and not in a cell passed into a less intense form of emotional dream and I started a more intellectual type of dream—like this; I stand before crowds, oratory flowing from my lips, moving them to compassion with my tales of prison life, then, having them feeling the tragedy of it all, I'd expound my theories of penal reform, advocate psychiatrists at each city jail with extensive apparatus for immediate and thorough examination of all persons picked up, months—if necessary— of analysis to place them properly, in the gallows, in a whore-house, in a nut-house, etc. etc. I'd have other types like this; seducing women, confounding senators with my wisdom, etc. etc. I'd also have great, horrid guilt and inferiority dreams—real loathing of myself would result from these: I'd be depressed for days, rationalize myself into humility, or rage, etc. However, todays dreams are not yesterdays, in fact, they are not exactly dreams, the best I can describe them is a sort of coma, or dozing stupor. at any rate, they go something like this: —no, I can't (wont) tell. suffice to say this, from the material of these visions *alone* I'm writing a play. It's a tragedy; it's close to Shakespeare, close to symbolic modern dance, (Martha Graham?) close to opera. I'm writing it like James Joyce would perhaps have done. I describe the costume, setting, action, dialouge, thoughts, emotions. I have the third act perfectly set up; am only having difficulty with handling it. i.e.—I've got the plot, scenes, characters (even to facial expression) perfect, yet, I'm having terrible trouble with making the dialouge good. I get over-long, or condense too much—makes it choppy and stilted. Damn, why is style so hard?

This, I'm sure, is the strangest, poorest, fucking letter I've writ-

ten in a long time, perhaps it's so poor and weak because of that
very fact; I just havn't written a letter in a long time, I don't know.

I must give up this letter, Allen. But for knowing I'd have more
difficulty if I started another, I would throw this away and try
again. I'm sure, however, you know how I feel; contrite, humble,
but, mostly, gratful and thankful for your extreme kindness in
offering, once again, your hand to me; no masochistic love is left in
me; I'll never bite off your fingers again. It's not as simple as all
this, I know, but, if you (or, perhaps I) must wreack your love ven-
geance on me, do be tender. I stand now in need of much help,
but, it would be taunting your love to ask foolishly for technical
writing aid, when I came not to your aid, showed no sympathy,
flaunted you, like a baby I—you see? You may be thinking "I need
his heart, want his love, his soul, yet, what does he want or need of
me? does he express a desire for my understanding? does he say
he needs and loves me? NO!. ha, he says, oh, so sweetly," "I'm so
sorry, Allen, for 10 months (Almost 2 years) I hurt you, now, in one
letter I expect forgiveness, and say, let's start where we left off—
oh, yes, by the by Dear Boy, now that you've forgiven and all that
and everythings O.K. now, ahem, ahem, would you be so kind as
to aid me in furthering my ability in showing off my nice, sweet,
tender little soul—so that people will want to have my autograph,
touch my skirt's hemline, gaze at my cute profile and remark hush-
edly "Neal L. is great"/?" "Well. fuck him, tohell with Neal L.
the sterile prick is worthy of nothing. I writhe in agony, I offer myself again and again to him, does he show anything? even one iota
of love? NO! the fool, the damn fool that he is, he says, thank you,
Allen I knew I could count on you, then, blithely goes on sucking
me out of all I can give to satisfy his own selfish self". I love,
Allen, but, it may take long years to show you how, can you forgive
that. please help me to be worthy to be with you. Write soon,
                                                        N.

                                                 New York
                                                 [Aug. 48]

Dear Neal:
    You want to stay by me; I want to stay by you, is this so? If so,
then let it be so with no more such questioning and abrupt breaks

as has led us to now into misunderstanding. The constant quality, the X, of our mutual knowledge I will vouch for for my part, as far as I am able to vouch for anthing in *Time*. In eternity, I am not able to say anything, but that my intuition has before shadowed to me the truth, so I can give you as much assurance of mental fidelity as I can give myself. Let this be so for you, too: I mean, I take it that it is so. If not, I don't know what we are talking about.

I am glad you at last recognise in me the elements of Myshkin; it has taken me this long to recognise them and to be able to affirm them myself, at least the true elements. My intuition before led me into presumption of love, where then was no true love (of world) but nonetheless, these phantasies were shadows of the truth that is within me and which will one day emerge in all its power and intensity. I cannot be your father: you are putting yourself in a false situation, perhaps, apropos Jack & Caroline; but that is none of my affair except as your fellow human & your lover. As to young Faust and the "enigma problems" that you speak of, that is perhaps also true, that I contain or show, rather more than they. However I cannot speak of their souls, nor yours, for I do not know them as well as I do my own. How I am learning to know my soul in relation to itself, not to others; and to know it in relation to "god". This at another time might enable me to compare, but not now, except in wasteful phantasy. The empire itself—the enigma as I have come to understand it is a simple actual and universal thing— I have understood; and I have been growing in it these five years, thinking about it in a pale way; but now I love *in* it. I wonder, thinking back, whether what you now see in Myshkin is what I saw last summer, which was both true and false: true in that such thoughts are symptomatic of the inner mind, truly seeking for truth; false, in that such thoughts are only stages on the way, and "lies". At any rate I am superficially pleased that you see a dignity in what I have been trying to do, although I can only see it in dignity only in retrospect in the light of true *seeking*. You spoke of my note being sombre; I hope that the elements of sombreness will disappear, or appear in another light, even more sombre, and more joyful at once, depending on your own progress and achievements spiritually.

I meant to answer your letter but I can say more by myself. Have the patience to listen. Perhaps what I say will come as a surprise to you: perhaps you already assumed that I knew more than I did, as much, if not more, than I now know. Perhaps you have no inkling of what I have in mind. My life heretofore has been a way of narrowing circles—at least in the last five years. I tried by reason as I

knew it to reconstruct the universe, society, and self—all, incidentally, in a slipshod, ignorant, and "barbaric" freshman way.
Because I possessed soul, my efforts were saved from "structur-
ed" or "relative" error, but not from Death and Sterility. That is I
had the ideas without the feelings. In the last year—if you will
follow the course of thought & emotion of the Doldrums up to the
Poem "Denver Doldrums & Later Dolors" and particularly the
long Dakar Doldrums, you will see how without realizing it I have
been forced—almost as a man clinging by his fingers to the edge of
a tower—to let go of my grip on my mind. In the last six months
after separating from you my life was a kind of uncomplete waste. I
had moved at the beginning of summer into East Harlem, where I
live & wrote and cooked by myself, and threw big parties every so
often. Finally I stopped thinking: I had long ago stopped the enormous mental machinery that produced the beginning of a novel &
the Notebook that you will remember from Denver. The machine
slowed down, I stopped myself whenever it started to rationalize,
work through. It was almost a betrayal of my earlier attempts at
universal explanation; at the same time it was a logical outgrowth
of the natural failure of the mind to comprehend by pale ideas what
it refused to comprehend in all its senses: i.e., the Nightingale,
life, To Be, God, etc. Finally in a few moments of dispassion &
self forgetfulness I experienced the first warming flashes of the
transcendence which I had so long been seeking. They were in
many ways reminiscent of weed experiences (as a full mirror is to
many broken mirrors) and the vague sensations of reality that I
had on Benny, or on the road to Texas in the old ford in the rain in
Oklahoma—which, you remember, we commented on, I with surprise, you with recognition; and also on the road between New
Waverly & Huntsville, where I finally got across to you my idea of
mutual knowledge—and evil. ("Vomit.") But all these, and later
experiences in Africa & New York & Aboard ship, have been
incomplete presages of the full light that has been given to me in
the last month. I have had moments of *absolute, valid, literal*
knowledge: I have *seen* the Nightingale at last. All that in my wildest and most self consciously stylized idealizations of Love that I
had celebrated & prophecied have "descended" as from heaven. I
say as from heaven because I have done nothing yet to merit them
and posess them eternally. It will require from me in the near
future one single act of *will*, of self generation, to *be*, or transcend
in spirit and body into life. Tho I suspected that you in your own
disordered way were in some way or other already there. Also the
pathos of your life, which I long ago spoke of, that you were doom-

ed never to rise out of time and illusion, but only to percieve that there might be a higher and juster order in life than your sense of narrow self. This is why I assented when you call for silence; silence is proper. I long more to go to God than to you, and perhaps you are a temptation rather than an angel. Yet you have a star in your forehead; that is why I long ago was happy to think with you that our lives were bound together. Whether this is so or not I no longer care; I love god in you. I love you for yourself, not for what you are not. And my love at this point is not a matter even appropriately related to your burlesque. That is, I do not need your heart and want your love and soul. I do not wish any longer to be hurt, and I am not capable of being hurt. My one thought is of this transcendence, all else dies. Your proposal for me to help you with love is just and proper still. I am getting fouled up in rhetoric again. I mean, I love you, but not as before. And, also, lest you be apprehensive or misunderstand, I love you *not as you and I have understood love ever before.* I had changed before; but such changes were slices of the same. It is not now so. This is boring.

Action: at the moment I can't give you any advice on writing. I myself stopped all literary creation with the few imperfect poems that I enclose. I mean to take it up again, but not till I know what I am doing. Ask me specific questions. My knowledge in *Time* is limited (that is, out of eternity.) I don't know much technique. I have always suspected reality in the masters, so I have imitated them. I have no style of my own actually. All I know is that *form* or *style*, where it is not clearly the product of *absolute* inner knowledge, can be *imitated* and *shadowed* in phantasy. Our phantasies are in many ways reflections of true light, are shadows. They have powers of tragedy and pathos from that, seen from above, as well as seen from below. So that it is well, before the final centralization and break with phantasy, to go on with *imitated* or *hallucinated* or quasi-visionary schemes, fixations, and ideas. If you have an idea, embody it in related images. Find a central image to express all. Explore the image, narrow it down, and then, later break thru the image to reality. That is what I have done; my poetry has not been my own, but it has been good poetry, as poetry goes, because it was sincere. It will be my own in the future. I have no idea as I say what you are up to, where you are. I can't tell it from your letters, I'm not wise enough. Now, the process of centralizing the image is this, (at one point)—as I write a sonnet, I fix my mind as closely as I can on the *sensation* (Cezanne) or *motif.* I try to eliminate all irresponsible thoughts, all subjective etc. I try to write as closely as possible to a single ideal. I bind together all related thoughts, but I must make sure that all which is suggested is *resolved* in own terms, *clarified,* or *related.* This is the idea of artistic unity. Why unity at all? This goes back to the original ideas which I have been expressing. It is a circle of reason, but within the husk or shell there is truth. This is why Lyric poetry is perhaps so easy to write: & also so difficult. I do know for sure how to write prose, except on the same principle. The work of art is an equation for the enigma.

But these perhaps are not problems that are disturbing you; they are my own. This is why I have not expressed them clearly. I think henceforth (and I thought, perhaps, for this letter to try, but had no patience & wanted to get in touch with you over-hastily) that we had better *compose* letters, rather than beat around the bush. But as I say, this composition is an artificial way for me to centralize my mind & narrow it down to the still point of thought where I can hold it in my mind, destroy it, and live anew. & if you are further advanced than I please send me instruction if you deem that instruction possible. I suppose it is not, but a matter for each.

Yours,
Allen

P.S. Tell me what you please about your visions. I would also like to see whatever you have written, good or bad—can see thru the bad to the good. From what you say I think that your first ideas (of coma-stories) are natural acts of genius. God bless you.

P.S. I have been reading *Blake*'s Songs of Experience & ideas of good & Evil, *Yeats*'s last poem & symbolic plays, *Eliot*'s 4 Quartets, St. John of the Cross (a mystic), and others who have been helpful; also Cezanne. The clearest expression of what I have in mind is in Blake & Eliot. Look for Miracle. Look for the Impossible —in me & in yourself.

[San Francisco]
'48 August 20

Dear Allen—
All my previous offspring have been boys, but all of Carolyn's family have had girls first;—at the beginning I presupposed I'd be content with only a male, however, after a degree of thought, I would be as pleased with a girl. If it is a boy I shall name it: Allen Jack Cassady. I anticipate him always signing his name thus: Allen J. Cassady. Gradually the rather strange sound of Allen Jack will

be modified & the middle name, Jack, fall into the oblivion most middle names do fall into & become simply "J."—now thats alright—Allen J. Cassady. All this is external—as for me—I shall (as my brother used to do to me in tender moments) always thruout his life call him: "Jocko" "now, come here Jocko and I'll share thrills with you of tales of wonder & awe etc. etc." or; "climb the tree & get the football Jocko etc." Jacques will also be his nickname, a sweeter, all-pure name of real import, Jacques will be used by me to call him to my side to tell of tender things, of life's meaning, of the soul etc.

So, there you have it—Allen Jack Cassady—Allen J. Cassady he will become—but, to me, he's always Jacques, Jocko, ("Jackie me lad" in an Irish brogue) & at times of anger "John".

If my child is a female I have decided to name her: Cathleen Jo Anne Cassady. This decision required much effort—but, listen on a while yet. I couldnot call her Jackquline—& there's no good feminine name of Allen—turning them to the child's (perhaps) wishes I thought that altho Cathleen Cassady is too stock as an Irish type (she would find it difficult to look Irish anyhow with her father only 1/2 & her mother 1/10 Irish) it would please her vanity in her romantic stage & earlier in life as a young tom-boy (& later in college) she'd be known as simply "Jo".

Among her working friends & about the house others would call her: Cathy. She will sign her name: Cathleen J. Cassady.

As for me (partially since I've always had a hankering to be named Joe)—I'll always call her "Jo". Just as (& for similar reasons) I'll call the boy Jack, I'll also call the girl Joe.

So, again, the girl has many choices: Cathleen Jo Anne Cassady, Cathy Jo Cassady, Cathy Cassady, Cathy Anne (at times) Jo Anne (as an alias perhaps) Cathleen J. Cassady, C.J. Cassady, C. Jo Anne Cassady. C.J.A.C. (at her initial-happy stage) & finally simply, Jo.

C.C. is her mother's initials & C.C. is her initials. Both the Boy & the girl will have J. as a middle initial. & I'll have names starting with a J. for them.—Enuf.

Too wise to know humility I laid weakly wallowing in fitful fallacies of sickened sadnesses. My tortured tantalized taste was heightened by my body's enfeebled flickered faithlessness. Misread was my minds diseased sight into my shallow soul's dimmed light.

So I wavered, indecisive on all issue. I considered choices. Fooling myself again.

Love was beyond me—my pretty face denied me its usual right.

—How trite.

Above is another of the coma-state thoughts—on the caboose as it comes down the hill into San Jose, Calif. I have a thought in a flash, as I doze, & dash it down—just as it stands—trite style & all.

Your right—your not my father. I have none. I felt the need for one lately & artifically picked you. In fact, had a recent moment of insight (vision?) & saw what might have been had I had a great Mannerly (or I'd not grown beyond him)—but, I fear I've forgotten fathers & can't find one—so, we'll forget it, O.K.?

How & where is dear, sweet, fine cat Herbert Hunkie? Let me have news of that fine friend—(5 times closer to him am I than he would dare believe.)

The acceptance of me—"for what I am & not for what I am not" —is indeed the essence of your love—beautiful, but, heavy with ponderous knowledge. I feel the same great part of olden sorrow of deep darkness of K N O W I N G . The quiet sweetness of life, flower is it?, is in myself I know.

Does the penninsula of past I traverse daily in toil—have me? nor can the leveled desert of sanden hills claim me as soil, for I fear

Aug. 22 (2 days later)

Dear Allen -

I'll never get this off to you—I can't say anything, is it because there is little to say?—now.

Oh well, I do have moments with you—as perhaps, a semi-symbol; or Your sunken soul? Bah—

(This is First Letter, pick up on Sept. 7, one)

Love you, Allen, my Mate.

my balls object for today (I fear)

oh, well, I insist I've dreamed of you, my boy, of you—me, too. (any how)

[160 Alpine Terrace]
San Francisco
Sept. 7, 1948

Dear Allen;

Last night I took Carolyn to the S.F. Hospital to give birth, at 12:49 this A.M., to a female. Both are well.—7 lbs. 3 ozs.

Life is fine, I awakening again, so sure, so pure.

Like Rimbaud I've gained, at last, the wisdom of renouncing the literary "sacrament".

I have seen your awareness of my flaw. Thank you.

The hunger hasn't abated, but, my tongue is cloven to my mouths roof. I can't speak, my thought is sacred now—private knowledge has gone too far. Literature can't answer for me, I must look to my music.

aprapo—I've found my niggar Mannerly—name is Leroy "Baby Roy" Johnson—Leather goods, short poem writer & pianist. He was great gone hipster on piano from 17 to 27—then, exhausted; contracted T.B.—spent 2 yrs in a sanitarium. Came of this-conversion; yes, like southern Baptist negro he got religion on his reaction. So, now, renouncing all the hep life he writes spirituals—arranges & plays music for his church.—Finding this refuge because he's no brain—he, nonetheless, is disatisfied but, can't admit his guilt at knowing religion is not enough to save him.—He condemns himself for not believing enough—no faith, but, enough of his intellectual dealings with his psychic soul.—He's great otherwise. Teaches me piano, & tells me what to do to improve my "mechanics" reading music etc. etc.—fine man.

Carolyn is going to Hollywood the second week in october to try out as a beginner at Western Costume Co. She is thrilled at this chance she's tried so hard to get to crash Hollywood—She begins at $1.11 an hr.—then $1.34 an hr. & if she makes good as a costume designer—$500-$1,000 a week. So, my dear boy—*if* several things break right for me—I.E.—1) if the full crew law is retained in the Nov. Elections. 2) Carolyn makes Hollywood money. Then, you are my guest—forever. See the possibility—1)garaunteed life job—at good pay— on R.R. for me—2)—Carolyn making lots of money.—*if* this comes to pass—You are to live *entirely* on my money. You can come to the west, or, if you prefer, stay in the east.—(as I would if I could; the west, particularly Calif., has such a Bastardized society) either place you like is O.K. with me in the west, or with yourself in the east. THE MONEY TO LIVE ON & allow you to not work is yours. (IF THIS COMES THRU) I had been working on the Brakemans extra board, liable to call for any train from Sacrament to Wat Jct.—Local Freight, passenger service, thru freight etc. but, now 've been assigned a regular run; #201— thru freight between San Francisco & Watsonville Junction 100 miles southward, down the penninsula. So for 2½ months I'll go back & forth from here to there & everything's fine in the way of worklife, except—in the november elections the people are to favor or disfavor amendment #3, which is the railroad full-crew law. The roads have tried for years to break this law—which states that for every 25 frieght cars in a train their must be 1 brakeman—obviously, if the people vote "yes" & the law is broken—I'll lose my job—so, pray they vote "no".

Yesterday, sunday, I got high on tea & dug the DeYoung Museum in the Golden Gate park, Great collection there—I thought of you & I at the N.Y. Metro. museum that sunday long ago.

Bloom was Jewish, Dedalus was irish, you are not Leopold, nor am I Stephen; but much is told of us by Joyce.

Allen, Dear Allen, the *only* reason you & I can't see (without seeing one another & speak to each other any more nowadays is because in the last year you & I have both grown into different levels of outward comprehension, & our private terms have changed—so, since we think on unlike levels now, our incomplete letters to each other have not been strong enough to fight (or love) our way thru into changing terms (as our minds have changed) so—disatistfaction—for both of us;—you are my souls lighter (not light as my soul's light) but, rather—you are my soul's light-*er*. You illuminate my soul—. (God, I'm a lazy little "punk"—look at me Allen, as if I were a "punk" (as a true queer, likened to Wild's or Gide's boys—(in literary terms)—I'm a lazy "punk" at that—to allow my love for you to be stagnated by a use of intelectual masks to allow my elusive cherry to escape from you.—enuf of "punkness," (can't take it, perhaps?)

I, reinterate—its music—I know (or do I?)—any way, music I'm going to try a while—I need you, my boy for direction of my taste—and love.

Only a soul I give you—la, la etc. I love skinny women & strong-chinned (queer's ideal) men.—as of this writing, at any rate.

I love all—sex—yes all; all, sex. anyway I can get it I need it, want it shall *have* it—now. I wanta fuck—In despair I cry "Allen, Allen will you let me splatter my come at you?
                                        N. Ect. No, I mean Etc.

Dear Neal:

I will try for a change to write a letter where I have no axe to grind—not even metaphysical.

Life continues in New York. It continues! God knows how, there are so many events and crises, each more cataclysmic and definitive than the last. Also people come & go, but I seem to stay here for good.

All of one group of people that I knew from Columbia—Walter Adams, whom you met, for one,—have departed for Europe. I have been giving parties (4 this summer of size) and each brings with it a fresh blow of wind from Europe. There is now an American Colony in Paris of some size—a great many people, too, whom I like or suspect of having secrets, great & small. I would very vaguely like to run away but N.Y. is my fate and I am maintaining for the moment an ignorance of Europe.

Did I tell you that I have an apartment? I have been living in Paterson—now am back in N.Y. looking for a job. Things are not going too well, due to my weakness at life and lack of decision, and also my lethargy and spiritual incompletion. Thank you for an offer of a life stipend. If fate goes against me I will accept it greatfully and look on you as an angel from the Cosmos. But I think that I must be my own angel if I am ever going to bring messages from heaven myself, and I will conquor or—Conquest at the moment is a matter of steeling myself to adjust to society—It seems anyway that I am wrong in everything I think so I might as well believe everybody and be a saint and make money in television. I have been gathering connections. (My magical reputation at school—it is magical since I see not so much magic in myself as I do see dishonest magiclike motions) Anyway 2 professors, one Barzun & one Van Doren, both big wheels, gave me letters of introduction to a big wheel in Radio named Gilbert Seldes, who I am to visit & consult on my problems of employment. Also, I have been invited to collaborate by 2 people on radio scripts—with which I could make a professional name.

One idea is for a Children's show based on a series of books about Dr. Dolittle. I don't know if you are familiar with these child's phantasies but I read all the Dolittle series when I was a kid and I still read them, and like them enough to want to work with them. The doctor is a pudding-like victorian Englishman who talks

to animals, and is a world reknowned vetranarian. I myself see in
the whole idea more than cuteness—in fact it has St. Francislike
overtones, but all simply written for children.

The second is for a Jewish program called the "Eternal Light".
I am getting near enough to religion to like the idea of writing for
them, and I expect to work on a script about a man named Samuel
Greenberg, who was an uneducated N.Y. Jew, who looked like me,
wrote mystical poetry—very crude, like you, but inspired—& died
at 24 in a N.Y. poor hospital in the Bay of N.Y.—of T.B.—back in
the 1920's. Hart Crane read his poems & stole & learned from
them—They were recently published. If I can do them scripts (if I
can get myself out of this bog of inaction) I will be well on my way
toward one type of social freedom. Also I think that steady Creative labor will solve a lot of my problems—that is the decision &
will & will involved is the same decision & will which will lift me
out of this *inexistence*—it is a will to be. But there *are* even greater
problems.

I want to go into television finally and produce blank verse short
plays. Plays like poems. The poetry should be a literal statement,
in common and not classic language, of unspeakable mysteries.
These things (the mysteries) will have to become not mysterious
but spiritual *facts* to me before I can do. I think in my recent
visions I also was given the key to dramatic form, which, with labor
& pains, I can embody in popular plays. A rennaisance! Imagine
being able to talk and illustrate Time & Eternity right in every
body's living room. My desire to do so now might be merely snoop-
iness, but in time I will be making love to everybody in amerca
right in their own homes.

The only thing for *me* to do is to stick to facts until I see the facts
which are beyond reason. Not to think. Above all not to talk. I keep
talking to everybody—I accost perfect strangers in bars to talk
about Eternity.

Axes. If I can't have axes, I get flighty.

You asked about music. I have listened to classical music a long
time, but not "scientifically" or "scholarly". There is a difference. I don't really know much about it now—or really appreciate
it. do know of several striking pieces of music that you might like.
I put it so vaguely & flatly but I do feel that in these pieces are
expressed consiously emotions & messages that are the summa-
tion of knowledge. Etc. I mean they are gone.

If you want to hear someone calling you—*calling*, out of heaven,
listen to Bach's passicaglia & fugue in C. Minor (Later Stokowski
recordings) His Goldberg Variations (for Harpsichord, Wanda

Landowska) are beautiful & formal. He is clear and pure and severe (to you or to me) in a series of what are called sonatas and partitas for unaccompanied cello.

Know the Beethoven chamber works? Start with a quartet opus 132 and listen to them, especially the 3rd movement, until you like it. They may sound like scraping for a while but they are near to pure intellegence and/or emotion in music. For that matter here is a list of chamber music that I once made that you might be able to use—I used it, but never completed listening to it all. Everything I heard I liked. The likings I am speaking of are not the likings of fancy of the moment but of general long range imagination.

I looked but I can't find it at the moment and I am not sure that's what you wanted. If you do I'll make an effort or make another one up.

You talk of Tea. I'm off drugs. Send me Dr. Cassady's Plea for Marijuana. Write up a pamphlet and send it along. Anyway, I mean I want to see a sample of your Apologia that you mentioned to Jack a long while ago in the subject.

"Dear fine cat" Herbert is still the same. He stole about $200 worth of goods from me while he was living here, and is now on Times Square. I'll take him in again perhaps when it gets good & cold & he comes crawling to my door. I showed him your note and he said "Does he really mean that", so I said I thought so. I'll write you a little more detailed info some other time. Pardon the offhand manner of some of this letter but I am feeling generally offhand and not in touch with anybody but myself & some of the world.

Fuck you, N.C. Next time you write send me some come so that I'll know you're sincere. Congratulations on your little child. How does it feel to be a father? (I mean it even if it sounds simple.) It certainly feels fine to be a grandfather. If you send me some details surrounding the psychic atmosphere of his birth I'll write you a triumphal ode like the one for W.S.B. I've put little Cathy in my will—I'm seeing my lawyers tomorrow. She will inherit zillions of dollars when I die. Love,

Allen

P.S. Blessings on my daughter in law, for a change, and on you too, son.

*Neal left S.F. Dec. 15th or so to go to N.Y. and returned the first of
Feb. 1949.*   *C.C.*

[Liberty St.
San Francisco]
Feb. 3, 1949

Dear Allen;
    I've arrived and have a good job, but since all I sell is on a commission basis I'm not sure of any money, in fact, I've made no money yet just laid out almost 10 dollars to get started.
    I *must* have the car registration slips at once. The new plates etc. are now due and the letter I got from Carolyn had my car slips enclosed for me to use to prevent losing the car. I forgot this letter at your place and you'll find it in your desk somewhere I believe. Tear the place up if need be, but, please find it for I not only know that I can't get any new ones but——you know, it must must be done.
                               Neal

Note from Kerouac added, ends "Excuse these Crassities."
                                 —*A.G.*

[Liberty St,
San Francisco]
March 15, 49

Dear Allen;
    The Ides of March and your punk, puny Ceasar Cassady, is at another of his phoney Rubicon's. Let no die be cast, I am purple paste without will or way to cast it; I broke my hand. I'm a southpaw so I hit LuAnne with a left thumb to the forehead, caused an incomplete fracture of four bones about the base of the thumb.

This particular "Bennets Fracture" took three different settings, plus x-rays etc. which included an awful total of 21 hours on hard benches over a 3 day period. I ended up with an operation wherein the stupid slavic doctor shoved a steel pin thru my thumb under the nail and thereby created enough traction so that, with the aid of a large wire extending over the cast, the bones could be strech- ed sufficiently to allow it to heal without deformity. This happened a month ago, so the cast will come off next week, let us hope it leaves no stiffness for I fear with the already enlarged fingers and joints I have by nature this further bullshit of the thumb will inter- fere even more with any sax playing I may attain.

Your pleasent little note came at an oppertune time, you see I am now formulating plans for the current year and your poiegnent offer of refuge to me was touching. My gratitude is much height- ened by the lonly manner of my present existence. I'm lonely and restless in that the conviction of action seems not to stay with me. Action in the sense of continuity of purpose is now quite imposs- ible. I lead a shallow simpleton life, little agreements of mind and emotion escape my endevors. Long or involved speech, coherence of logic, literate leadership of conversation; all quite beyond me. I'm listless without reason, I sit as would Rodin's statue were his left arm dangling, (The Thinker's brow is false) I sigh with looking out the window over the city—to the east—and north, horizons, clouds, the streets below me. I'm as far west as one can go; at a sloppy ebb-tide.

Joan is brittle, blasé brittleness is her forte. With sharpened laughs and dainty oblique statements she fashions the topic at hand. You know these things I need not elaborate. But, you ask for an angle, well Julie's hair is matted with dirt I am told; oh fuck it, normal disentergration of continued habit patterns (child raising here) has Joan laboring in a bastardized world wherein the supply of benzedrine completely conditions her reactions to everyday life. ETC. I love her.

MARCH 17, 49

Dear Allen;

St. Patrick's day; I drive my snakes out, let it be a present peace or no: I like it.

I'm free of Lu Anne, my friends are my friends; but, I have a child. My life's blood she is, lovely and perfect—she wakes at this very moment, I stop to kiss her. SO. I live in the child for as long as is possible, thats my stand; after that: the world, you, saxophones, and harden struggle to suceed. You see, its all very clear to me: I

will take care of Cathy as long as Carolyn will allow me, which may
be, I hope, forever; where she servers relations I will lead other
lives, until that time—Cathleen Jo Anne is my charge.

[no signature]

New York
May 1949

Dear Neal:
   Are you too occupied to write, or dont you want to for some
reason concerning your relationship with us in N.Y. No reason
occurs to me, that seems important, despite the usual fantasies of
hassel.
   The golden day has arrived for Jack and he has sold his book.
[The Town and the City]. He has a % promise, on sales, 85% on
movie rights (which I believe will materialize as a matter of course
after considering the nature of his work; but this has been my
opinion for a long time; it now seems to be more generally accepted, and so may be true) and most important for the actual money,
$1,000.00 (a thousand) cash advance, which has been in his
possession for several weeks. He is not mad at you; as matter of
fact 5 out of the 15 sandwiches he denied you in Frisco went bad
before he could eat them.
   Bill Burroughs has been arrested and faces a jail term in LA. for
posession of Narcotics and guns, etc. There is now no telling what
will happen but he may get out of it without jail. Joan wrote, and
he wrote the next day having got out on bail quickly. If he is to be
jailed I expect to invite Joan NY to stay with me with children at
my apt. If he gets out, he will have to leave Texas and LA. as it is
hot there for him; perhaps to Chicago, or Yucatan; doubtful of
N.Y. as his family objects to this city, and much will depend on
them financially, I think.
   Claude is writing stories and being psychoanalysed. These are
radical developements which I, at least, have hoped for and I believe it is the beginning of his regeneration and the assumption of
an ideal power and humanity for him. He broke with Barbara this
month. As long as I have thought of us as artists, it has been
Claude who I thought of as central to any active inter-inspiring
school or community of creation, and him to whom I have looked

for the strength to assume responsibility for the truest aesthetic knowledge and generosity; it appears, somehow, that the unseen magnet has begun to draw him at last. And so a kind of potential millenieum, that I dreamed of years ago with juvenile and romantic prophetic power, is being actualized in its truest forms, and in the only necessary and inevitable way. I talked with him all last night, heard him outline the method, plot, and technique (to give his ideas categories) and it sounded, what he had to say, essential, accurate, and so unexpected as to be inspired to my mind; and yet proceeding logically from his whole past position; but surpassing it. Anyway, another myth come true. His concern is with action and facts and things happening; but he seems (I say but because though that is the concern of all writers, ostentatiously, except crackbrained alchemists like myself, he seems succesfully concerned with facts and their harmony and relationships, and all suggestion of what I would look for as the metaphysical or divine seem to rise from his stories as they do from life, and more so, because of the objectivity and sympathy and seemingly self enclosed structure of his tales; so that there is nothing extraneous or purposeless in his work; he says everything he says because he intends to. This self evident principle I discovered for my own poetry (everything must have a point and not be rhetoric) last summer consciously; but I have not been able to perfect many poems to clear realization because of my own abstract and vaporous tendencies; but I see it successfully applied in Claude potentially more than Jack. When Claudes imagination becomes freed of fear he will be a great man. I dwell so much on this because now Claude is again in the fold, the great RAM of the fold much improved from before; once again we are involved in the same work of truth and art all together. Maybe I am making too much of a good thing, however so let it pass.

I am again in a doldrums, a weak link in a chain, only surpassed in weakness by yourself perhaps. Herbert has been with me draining my money and vitality for months; now Vicki and a man named Little jack have joined us, and are operating out various schemes successfully. Money is beginning to come in; I am to sublet my apt to join Joan and Bill: they will pay my way (Little jack, etc. in return for apt for summer and now. But Bill's arrest casts a shade on that and I do not know what I will do. I would like to leave the city for the summer (June July, August) if possible to stay with Joan and Bill. I am not writin much or well, but I have always been dissatisfied with what and how I have written; now however my artistic impotence now seems more real and radical and I will have

to act someday, not only writing more, but on large scale, commer-
cially usable (poetic dramas for television as I dream) etc. However
my theoretical and visionary preoccupations—fixation, based on
experience which was gifted, as it seemed, from a higher intelligence of conscious Being of the universe, or hallucination, as the
doctor dismissed it when I went to arrange for therapy beginning
Sept., has left me confused and impotent in action and thought and
a prey to all suggestions, winds of abstract thought, and lassitudes
and sense of unworthiness and inferiority that rise continually
before my now dulling eyes, and a prey to all suspicions, my own
and others, that come forth. The household set up which I both
hate and desire, that I have, is an example of my uncertainty of
path and dividedness. It seems that the road to heaven or back to
sanity requires me to deal in realities of time and circumstance
which I have never done, and to learn new things, which I'm unused to. But I seem to have like Joan passed some point in my brain
which I cannot go back from, and for the moment forward either
except by some violent effort I have been incapable of since I can
rem·mber. But perhaps therapy will help me. Any way, I am making preparations to teach in Cooper Union College this fall, and so
have some financial security more than now at A.P. Then I will
be by myself and try to think, unless something unexpected
happens from the outside to change me or my relations with
others. Next year this all amounts to saying, I will try again; now I
am caught up in weariness and defeat and sterility and circumstances which have no end or meaning. Perhaps by leaving town I
will activate and escape this inertia. Perhaps if you thought well of
it I will come to California. At the moment however, I am not in any
active suffering, and my mind is active and comparatively clear. It
is long inaction and too much introspection and lack of practical
ambition that weighs me down. However my pad is hot, and I
expect a visit from the narcotics people since they seized several of
my letters to Bill in the course of his fall. If I were able to keep
clean that would be OK, but with Vick and others pursuing their
busy rounds there is always something for the law to object to. I
can't seem to put my foot down, or make up my mind to mostly
because that is why they are using my pad in the first place, to
operate out of, and my end is to get enough to travel off their work.
Perhaps I shall find that I have been self destructively greedy on
this score. But when I see the treasures rolling in I find it a powerful argument against any cautionary impulses, of mine. And
maybe nothing will happen. That about summarizes what goes on
on York Ave. General intimidation. Herbert was beat, and now

just begins to prosper, so I can't well put a stop to it all. Or not
easily anyway. I guess this sounds cowardly; or maybe its only a
baloon I blow. Claude and Jack dont seem to approve, and that is
why I am concerned at all. Or what brings the concern to my mind,
anyway.

What are you doing? When will your heart weary of its own
indignity and despotism and lack of creation? Why are you not in
N.Y.? Can you do anything away from us? Can you feel anybody as
you can feel us, even though in N.Y. you did your worst to sur-
round yourself with a sensate fog of blind activity? Or are you
learning something new wherever you are now? If you wonder the
motive for these questions dont undercut it with suspicion of
sexual motives of mine; I have none now and was not dominated by
them when you were last in N.Y.

I am writing a set of Psalms; they begin

Ah, still Lord, ah, sweet Divinity,
Incarnate in this grave and holy substance
Circumscribing the hexed endless world
of time. . . . .

I see a number of people; some you haven't met. Next weekend I
am going out to Anson's. The drugstore in his town, incidentally,
saw me take the ice cream, and made him pay for it next time he
went in. They didn't want to embarras him at the time. I guess
they make allowances for Anson in his neighborhood.

Jethro Robinson (sonnet poet, remember?) was in town. I visited
him, and he talked to me through my masks and broke me down
and told me to get out. It was a frightening experience. The ways
of truth are hard. Dick Wietzner is now talking beyond my comprehension, about something to do with Blake's Jerusalem having
become, and Jews, and alienation, and Greek rhythms of speech
as a secret key to universal Mind. He is gentle and not crazy,
unless I am too. Hollander tells me to publish a book, and so (he
being the wizard on the path) I will clean out my poems this
summer, and try to publish a book, though before I was too proud
to do so before I could speak with prophetic authority; but I can no
longer depend on some future vision which is probably the shadow
of a past hallucination. So I must enter time, "like a man".

I wrote a poem which I thought at the time was accurate, but like
all things is blurred now:

Go back to Egypt and The greeks
Where the Wizards understood
The spectre haunted where man seeks,
And spoke to ghosts that stood in blood;

Go back, go back to the old legend;
The soul—forgotten, the most true
In all things most and least imagined;
No other, there is nothing new.

The giant Phantom has ascended
Toward its coronation, gowned
With all glad dreams begun and ended;
Follow the flower to the ground.

I dont know what this communicates. I first called it the Myth of
the Rainy Night. Jack and I have had long dawn conversations
about this book,* of that name, and of the horses of rembrant,
spectral machines, and of a hooded stranger that appears to us in
our sleep, from year to year, and probably appears in yours too.
The occasion was his appearance in the form of a fat man in a black
bowler to a dying invalid in the first scene of a dostoivski movie we
saw high in the Apollo with Herbert called 'The Eternal Husband.'
A dying hysterical invalid, who screamed at the doctor in exasper-
ation because the doctor didn't believe that he (the invalid) was
being constantly followed by the stranger. The doctor calms him
down, and everything is cool again, till the man goes absent
mindedly to the window, after everyone has left, and sees the man
in the hat staring up at him. Then he closes the curtains nervously
and goes to the door, listens at the keyhole, and suddenly opens it,
and the stranger walks in. The two of them begin to wrangle, and it
goes on all through the picture, nobody knowing just what is at
stake, hints, vague accusations etc. But you must see the picture to
see how it all goes and ends; or read the story. But the important
thing is that everybody has someone with deep socketed eyes and,
or a green glassy visage, staring at him, in a crowd in a dream, of
following him unseen in a desert, or seeking through the window-
pane.

Love, Allen

Doctor Sax by Jack Kerouac.

May 20, 1949
New York

Dear Neal:
Letters between you and me is like conversation between to equally beat bums, either we are garrulous and complaining or short-writ and enigmatic; but I dont think we make sense. Take this as garrulity. If I thought writing you a 1000 page letter would answer enigmas, either mine or yours, I would sit down with quill & scroll and furiously scribble. A week ago I reread all of my Denver & texas notebook, long ramblings of subjective worry, and was absolutely amazed at how cracked it sounded; rewoke in me memory and breath of how totally unified, my soul was in love rapture; but read it; so long winded and frustrating it seemed I could'nt finish—not boredome, but oppression.
The and and . . and style of my last letter was like Ezra Pound. And I received a letter from him in same mail as yours, in answer to letter to him asking questions about meter. He wrote A. Ginsberg & address in wavering infantile scrawl allover the envelope front, and covered a whole page of blank paper with the notes:

S. Liz. (—this means St. Elizabeths
Bughouse Wash.
A.G.

Dear Ag
None of yu
peopl hv least concept
of FATIGUE.
I hv/
sd it all in print.
i.e. all answers to yrs.

———

Cantos no use to people
writing shorts.
E.P.

Dont know Hope's poem; this is Lawrence Hope? Never read. Please copy out or direct me to it; and will do imitations? That what you meant?
And Jack said two nites ago, the cryptic line, is a quote of Jack on YOU not himself. How accurate is he?
I dont see Van Meter much; been taking out Dusty myself; not in yet; him neither at all.

Bill's Letter to me:

"I guess Hal when he gets to the states, will be telling everybody how I tried to get in his pants and got sore when he turned me
down." And goes on to say "But he has to give me the brush in the
nastiest way he can devise, in front of a third party. I guess he
could only (bitchyiest) scrape up one wittmess on short notice."
That sounds like a mad scene. I did'nt know Bill & Chase were on
sociable terms there at all let alone familiar enough situation for
Bill to be getting ideas. Give me details (Bill did'nt & wont I
guess); or ask Hinckle to write me giving detailed gossip of bill &
Chase which interests me very much. I cant imagine what C. is like
now, what he's interested in generally by life.

Strange, unusual relaxed hair down tone in your letter I never
saw in you before—almost humorous. Appreciate the communication.

I read & got great kick out of mad novel by mystic P.D.
Ouspensky, short, almost like bill in condensation and single-
trackness. Called the Strange Life of Ivan Osokin. I will mail it to
you as you may find it useful. Reading it gets you on mystic high,
almost physical. But mail it back.

Your discription of writing block I followed as carefully as I
could; found some things similar to myself (who dont write seriously at all now.) Tonite for instance I had to write a job letter and
needed to get it done, but could'nt get through second paragraph
wording, wound up wasting hours, blowing my top screaming in a
pillow (seriously—just so frustrated), beating head with fists,
cursing self, dreaming about heaven, hating world. Much less try
to write a poem. It's all EMOTIONAL. That is, has nothing to do
with your talent, your literary merite, your equipment, even train-
ing, etc. it all has to do with UNCONSCIOUS conflict. You either
have to drive through at heavy cost in sweat woe and dispair, but
continue; or underestand what's at the bottom of the frustration—
which is not mechanical choice of words or method—that last
reflects unconscious conflicts. You should perhaps still make
attempts to get analyst, because what it all boils down to is the
facts that someone outside of ourselves, not tied up in our worries
& selfhoods etc. & habits, can see and get clear what is in our unconscious, because he is looking from the outside watching while
we unconsciously reveal our trouble. But it has to be done by
someone objective with no emotional ties or even love of any kind
for us. We love ourselves enough for two. That's why we failed
yrs. ago. (between us at the same effort—as I meant it then).

This process still continues with me (analysis) and is getting along to more deep understanding; but so far it has left me as you see now, empty and uninspired. However I do have some hope of coming out of it. At this point however everything about life is rotten. Partly because some peace hope ahead, but it means efforts (work & emotional independence) which I am afraid still to accept & put out, preferring to rot in passivity.

As far as unconscious goes, I mean I was'nt really aware before how differint I was from other people: in that I lived in pleasurable but unreal fantasies—some one will love me because I'm a poet, I'll get a book published and win the Pulitzer prize, I am romantic when I dream about suicide, etc. And on the other hand how little attention I have paid to solving real problems of money, housing, travel, etc.

At this point incidentally I have 10 cents to my name and no job and not sure what next step is, but dread humiliation of asking father for money to go look (as I have for months already) Monday for Job in N.Y.

If you were around to ask I would ask you, but it would be the same old Allen looking for some one bigger to cherish me and protect me from life.

I dream how that someday I'll come and save you. Which I guess is just as much bs. Nevertheless old man; as one beggar mumbling to himself in the alley, said to himself, If I had a lot of money I sure would know how to invest it. Well, shit on me.

Claude is maybe getting slightly degenerately drunkerdly. Seems lonelyer than ever. Think he intends to live alone for while and stare at his navel for the first time since he got out. Always he's been on some outward activity—work, drink, women, etc; but now his job is all mechanical; Lizz is going to Europe in month; and drink hurts him more & more afterward.

I cant write anymore because I feel too crazy. Everything seems so much like the end—blank end. Apparently the blank end is really the paralysis of joy; and not reality. So lets not worry.

Joy, boy.
Allen

Fuck getting you tea, I havent the energy or the cash. Yes we'll go to Mexico someday, baby.

You and I are very much alike, dispite obvious differences.

Seriously: You should attempt then something you think I may take & others take for granted: an outline of your emotions of loss of love, a long confession of your secret feelings; not only the frenzy and perceptions and activity, but the deep single real personal

unstated suffering you feel and felt. By take for granted I mean
you never avail yourself of human ears to confess to, you always
confess your crimes, but I know little of your feelings as a boy and
man—even in Joan letter. Certainly I never understood how much
you wanted Luanne. Did she? You have felt more unhappiness
than almost anybody, but seldom do you allow it to be shared—as
Jack knows: he remembers your crying in the eatery now as the
center of his book. God, Neal, I wish I could see you, (in a timeless
world in the sunlight)—I suppose you know all this.

Even that fool Bill, in his last letter, told me all about himself
and then ends his paragraphs "I hope I'm not boring you with all
this." Heaven, heaven, things Ive been waiting and wondering
about for years.

Any questions you have about me I'll answer: I am in new confessional season. We are all mysteries, as usual.

You came to N.Y. as last thrill before oncoming blankness?
Reread the Tempest maybe. Again, Don Quixote, modern library
ed., deathbed confession P. 931:-932: "My judgement is returned
etc."

P.S. I will write you a long letter sometime this year before summer maybe)—Ripeness approaches.

Earlier today I had sat down at typewriter and wrote one classic
sentence which, though I was not high, knocked me out: "I want to
die and am afraid of suicide." How many times I have read &
thought that, too.

THE
FIFTIES

Dear Neal:

Am I doomed to this incompletion . . . must I stay like this forever waiting for the moment to descend when I will fully understand—not understand myself in the same old way as before—but understand outward things? I mean that I see now, as I never have seen before except in fantasies, that their is something bigger than myself—myself that I knew. I will not care here nor there what I will be then. I will be. I look at the surface of this paper and see that anyone may read without understanding what I and the rest of the world—am up against, and as if I didn't know what I am talking about. Well, I dont, but that is not to change the subject, but to bring it clearer—to a negative statement of what is bothering me. I can say at least what it is not, although the moment (as now) when I become too affirmative in my negatives, it comes into doubt. Clearer as I say, because it seems to call for some discription. Why, I don't know, perhaps it does'nt. I am in Paterson, and I have been here for several weeks, reading and writing a few preliminary essays—essays on Cezanne and Dante trying to *fix* my mind—but to no avail; I worked intellectually, and that did not work. No, Neal supposes that I will find it in action of some sort. I think that poetry is an action, perhaps, but as tonight, when I tried to write, I found that my "inspiration" if I may call it that, has dried up. Not for ever, I hope. That is, I hope to learn all over how to write. I notice now things in poesy that I had never seen before while I am writing mostly is that sense possibilities of clarity. I can construct in my mind ideas that are not reflections of good, but as it were crystals that have the light passing through them. To many of my thoughts and words are *black* mirrors,—that shut out light. But even now—as for several weeks—I can see through to what is the final goal; I can see through to eternity the paper that I write on. Even this accident on the paper falls into a motivated clarity of being. I am writing you—I started to try to write poetry, but I was overwhelmed by—blank. I said my inspiration is run dry, so it is—I can't leave out of my mind the fact that I am notwhere my image is. I mean that I sit here, trying to write a poem about a few minutes I had on time square a few days ago, when I saw the City as it was, a City in the sea. The people looking in the window at bickfords were looking all at each other, aware. The only reason

that it seems that everybody is a zombie most of the time is that
they refuse to admit that they are in love with everybody and when
we, or I, also refuse to admit that I am in love with everybody, I
too become a zombie and walk around as if dead, full of empty
thoughts. But as I tried to write I found that I was trying not
"writing"—I refuse to use Benny* any more—and that I was sitting here, not in time square, so I could not think about my image.
I was'nt sure what the image was anyway. Me sitting here trying
to write times square, or times square, or the image of eternity
that floats about 6 feet above my head like an invisible cloud ready
to become visible as soon as I turn my head. My words were also
not very colorful in the few lines I wrote, so I immediately got to
worry whether or not I was a true poet. I think that there are such
things as true poets, for the art, or Art—is I see now an exact and
laborious & specific thing. A watchmaker has to fix a watch a poet
works with material sensations, material relations, God is material, not with frenzied ideas. Speaking of material sensations, I
wonder if you still want to learn from me about life or art or whatever it was—I sometimes do feel not like a real father, but that all
men are fathers to each other (the wiser to the weaker) or sons, or
brothers, and that they must look to one another, without thought,
for love is knowledge or contact. No, none of these things, exactly,
except contact, Love and knowledge as I know things are false—
except *true* knowledge, which is either thing—That is where men
meet. That is not love or any other thing we thought of, but just
meet. Meeting on Earth. I always thought of the forest of Arden
but now I think of it without the image, and i often live in it for
moments. I remember Claude once said—"ah, Aristophanes! how
true was thy half-jest!" A famous line by now. I live in the forest
that I, because I am aware that it truly is a forest, no matter how
stricken with Adam's curse of false knowledge I am. The Ceiling
however has descended, so that it is no longer in the stars but
hangs over me about 6 feet or so, I guess. Sometimes it comes
down to the ground and i walk about in a spell, where the trees
bend down over to one like living creatures. If there were birds
around I could talk to them, like St. Francis. I had a rude conversation with a dragon fly the other day and I thought he actually heard
me, but he flew away; if I believed enough he would have settled
on my hand—I don't think I would have been afraid. But the sky,
the clouds are one, in a procession—*everything comes alive*—
everything is always alive around us all. The old saying God is

*Amphetamine (Benzadrine).—A.G.

Love—and Dante talks about being "rolled with the love that loves the sun and the other stars." That is literally true, I discovered. What is this love? How can you see it? It can be approached intellectually by its motion that forms a pattern on memory—That is why we love music & poetry. They are actually eternalization. Or say better, that being—love—makes etc. Everything is actually one thing and that is what men called God. I used to be an athiest but I can say I suppose that I still am, since I see so few people that believe in God are aware of him or it. Do you remember the road through Oklahoma? That was God showing itself.

I have been conjecturing on form. If you want to write, *see* first. See the moment as it is in its harmony. That is the motif. (The clearer motif I don't know yet.) I mean that all poems are about Being, and that the moment we see being (if we see it only in flashes) is to be described: this way we have something to talk about—the things we see. Thus we see men prowling around each other; we talk about them doing that in relation to their love. I have not worked this out so I don't write.

Why don't you write me? don't you believe me anymore? There may be something more, but I have learned to believe in everyone. That is the secret—belief in people. You always knew this. Belief like myshkin, but he is somehow an unreal character. He is in literature. By believe, I mean, if you see through to the bottom of their souls, to them as beings in god, then there is no more argument. If you believe them completely (closing the circle completely) then they believe you. And it is true, that disbelief brings no sure knowledge, no knowledge at all.

How are you? are you still entangled in fright. Actions such as yours seems to me to be a fright, all those things to do, responsibilities that you have and really want but are using for something else? or no? Are you happy?

I can't say that I am happy, but I try to be. Unfortunately I have things to do that prevent me from being happy, and I mean to throw those off one by one till I am completely free to choose some work that I will love—and someone that I will love too. I feel the need for love, but I am not ready for it myself yet; but I see the necessity for a woman. Not however that I fully want one. I did want a girl a few months ago but she turned out to be a spiteful and nasty creature, so that there was no way that I could make her understand that all the self righteous and self directed preoccupations that she had were keeping her. I was at the time too brutal and finally her cold spite got into my bones and I had to become indifferent. She really upset me. So much to work against, so much to break through, so much insult to take, so much wasted time. it did'nt accomplish anything and it made me miserable so that there was nothing else to do.

Huncke stole my typewriter and a lot of books & clothes. How can we live with one another without spite & deceit? The worst deceit is frustrated love coming out in spite; I have seen enough of this in myself, so that I know a little about it. Love is always self-frustrated, there's no other trouble.

Everything is very quiet. I saw jack the other nite & talked and showed him my essay on Cezanne, which I think he began to understand, and he found it good, but too intellectual, which it was. I also finally got to bed with Claude. Strange after all these years. I was impotent. That's even stranger and more true.

Allen

Paterson, N.J.
Tuesday Oct 31, 50

Dear Neal:

Though months have passed without a letter be sure I do not forget you. I was hoping that you'd write me first, as you are the one that is travelling, and, therefore, doing new things. I thought first I would wait to hear what kind of echo you had, but as no sounds came towards me from you, I did'nt know what harbor to send my falcon to. (I avoid the word dove for the moment.)

Speaking blind, therefore, again, I refer to that darkness which is a subject of common interest between us, before I relax. Though I have heard it said that "See? Nothing really bad ever happens!", something has happened which might be thought of as "bad." I think Jack has been writing you, so perhaps you know that Bill Cannastra was killed under positively shocking circumstances in the subway a few weeks ago. I had been seeing him a lot during the summer and after, and I closed the San Remo with him after a 5 hour talk with him about death a few nights before, so I felt the Presence of fate near by for a while when I heard about his end, though that as you can see has become watered down somewhat by conversation thought and activity of my own since. I enclose a newspaper clipping for you. (Please return it. You know what a mania I have for collecting dead things.) Everybody was all hung up and changed somewhat, even, interestingly, Claude, who was at this time living next door to Cannastra on 21 St. with a girl who, incidentally, I fixed him up with in Provincetown. But everybody—Carl, Howard Moss, Ansen, Holmes, Stringham, everybody who knew him—so many—as well as those we don't know from the past—got all big theories and weeklong drunks, everybody's pride was beaten for a week. As in greek tragedy, the purging of pity and terror.

The great question on everybody's soul, was, was it an accident or did he do it on purpose? I met Ann Adams, who was with him, and she gave me a minute account of details. The party was leaving her house after a night of sticking and wandering, and on way to Claude's, Claude & Cannastra had become friendly and got drunk, pawing each other, recently. Subway to Claude's to get money, a touch O'the dawn. When they talked about the Bleeker Tavern (negress Winnie's hangout) Bill lurched out of the window as a joke. He stuck his head and shoulder out, but apparently had misjudged his lurch and found himself half hanging unbalanced out of the window. The others rushed to pull him back, and hung on to him, as the subway roared through the tunnel. His coat ripped, and they could'nt get a grip on him by his shoulders as he was too far out. When he saw what was happening he began screaming to be pulled back. He ducked, trying to avoid the pillars in the tunnel, and hunched his head, but suddenly there was a thud and he was knocked out of the window to the tracks, out of their hands. When the train stopped, she went to the last car where his body was dragged and saw that his head was broken and brains showing out of the temple.

Now, these are my generalizations:

1. tragedy depends on chance. this is in context of our conversation in harlem. Where there is a continued invitation to lesser and major woes, even as Carl spoke of Cannastra's "an invitation wrapped in a joke", or a defiance, or apathy, or knowingness of personal sort, etc., it is sooner or later to turn into a fact; i.e. shadow changes into bone.

2. Those who invite a shadow bone are those who possibly do not realize the seriousness of life and death, the depth of bone, the finality, the fact that you can't play around with nonexistance and ambiguity.

3. there is no life after death, which makes the preservation of clarity and ease in life of final importance. I mean I do not think Cannastra knew, when he was issuing invitations, cutting himself up, lurching toward windows, what it really meant to die, and that

it was really possible for him to die (early and unnaturally) and that "bad" things, unprepared for and unforseen, happen, and must happen in the long run where confused will works towards it.

4. every tragedy is preceeded with intuitive warnings, where situation is result of personal style and direction. The point is to heed intuition or conscience, which is consciousness of logical chain of probabilities and inevitabilities even: control fate as much as possible by learning to will not death but pleasure; eliminate that way the wide range of unpleasant probabilities, eliminate the unwanted intrusion of chance as much as possible. But this is only sense of commonness of life, to avoid needless danger. Life is like a machine, which if you know how it runs, you can cut down the ills and hazards. You don't cut down chance, since chance is all, but you can eliminate bad chance caused from within, and leave it to the outside world to produce whatever bad chance you run across; that's cruel enough.

Well, enough of this. My temptation is to think of it as a sermon to you, but actually it's only my own preoccupations with bones and ill chance that I'm writing about.

I had incidentally quoted Cannastra a poem about him and Huncke, in the Remo, that I started while you were in N.Y., I think. It was'nt finished, but there were the lines:

In Judgement*

He cast off all his golden robes
And lay down sleeping in the night,
And in a dream he saw three fated
At a machine in a shroud of light.

He said, "I wait the end of Time,
Buried and bound in ravenous wrath.
But there is a lantern in my grave.
Who hath that lantern all light hath."

And now the prophet of this dream
Is sunken in the dumbing clime.
Much is finished, much forgotten
In the wrack and wild love of time.

Who talks of Death and Angel now,
Great Angel fallen out of Grace?
O Lord why has Thou taken him
There was such beauty in his face.

*See *Empty Mirror* (Corinth Books, 1961).

It's death that makes man's life a dream
And Heaven's splendor but a wave:
Light that falls into the sea
Fails within its ancient cave

Where all the crystals of the skull
and skeleton are cooled in shade,
in an eternal shadowless night
Where shroud must rot and memory fade.

Where the man of the apocalypse
Shall wait upon a silent bed
Until the sexless womb bear love
And the grave be weary of the dead,

Tragical master broken down
Out of a self embodied tomb,
Blinded by the sight of death
And woven in the darkened loom.

He quoted me, in turn, a poem he liked by Moss that had the lines Plants cannot travel,/ water cannot speak,/ the green lead is rooted,/ The blue lake is mute,/ but if love is a miracle/ and I may marvel/ last night when I woke,/ plants knew distance/ and the water spoke.

Kind of a nice rhyme, what?

As for me, Oh I am horrible this month. I lost my job at the labor newspaper* for being what you know of me in relation to the factual world of knacks and carpentry, incompetent. Really a terrible blow to my pride, to be a flop even as a pissyassed reporter. So I hung around thinking awhile at home, and decided to get a job with my hands, at a machine. So I got a $1.25 per hour soft touch in a ribbon factory, but I was so stiff and bumbling, I got fired from there today. Truly the real world is my downfall, or as Helen Parker's oldest son said one night to the younger as she drove them off, half drunk, to bed, "Don't worry Brucie, it's only reality." I ran into a couple of nasty cunts at work who fouled me up by putting the freeze on me when they were supposed to teach me the workings, and as a result I got so self conscious and anxiety stricken, my eyes unfocussed, I would daydream, I lost track of how to do the simplest things, and wandered around embarrasedly trying to fit in. What a terror, for 2 and half weeks it lasted. It's kind of a bug I have—that's why I never learned to drive. If I did,

---

*New Jersey Labor Herald, Newark, N.J. (official AFL)—A.G.

you know, I would get myself in an accident within a month. That's me, all over, as the fly said to the flyswatter. Well I don't know what next, for work, but I don't seem to be able to hold on to any kind of job I've had, and not through fucking off, but through some kind of inattention and diffidence, that is almost out of control, and wrecks things. I suppose I will have to persever and stumble till I get over this unmanly weakness of character, but, to tell the truth, it's very upsetting and full of drag and anxiety and feelings of inferiority, great glimpses of being out of contact, shudderings of selfhood, and humiliating servility to fellow workers, all out of keyedness and shame. I would avoid it if I could, but Time and Fate seem to have presented this as the logic of things and I have to accept it, am forced to, but circumstantial needs as well as "higher necessity." I always kept telling you to find some area of life where you would be tongue tied and humiliated like an inno-cent kid, but I was only dreaming aloud about my own fate, in fear of it. I really don't believe I know what I'm talking about when I come on Bleakly to you, so forgive the intrusions I make if you can find charaty to forgive the motives, which are god knows what, and who knows how snide. I would no more be a holier than thou. What a come down. After all, it all boils down, in my case, to sheer nerve and ignorance, very spoiled young self romanticiser. Hope you don't find the sword 2 edged, though I suppose it is as usual.

Well, and lots of things happened—women, including Rayanna, Provincetown trips, more paterson. I also started writing a huncke novel, but that's gooked up so far and not very promising. Mainly I've been trying to find a steady girl to live with. This letter is so long I have'nt gossip for the time for you, except a choice tid bit, where I call jack up to tell him come over and meet this here girl, and he says I only fuck girls and learn from men, so why should I come up? So I starts writing him poison pen postcards (anony-mous) saying that's why your so dumb.

Heard little from Diana, she seems worried about future, etc., as well she might. So you're back with Carolyn, eh? Well, you old scapegrace you, hope you're both having a fine time, though I worry about you. Why don't you all get married a la mohammedan customs. Jesus, what the hell are you all after in each other?

Write me a nice chatty letter full of woe and I'll send you another poem. I heard from Jim Holmes lately. Is he high. oops!

As evaire,
Allen

After the first "road" trip (Dec. 15, '49 - Feb. 1, '50) Neal took
care of Cathy, shaved his head, nursed his thumb & saw LuAnne
while I got a job—telling him ours was a strictly business arrange-
ment—to be over when I could afford to separate.
                                                    C.C.

                                              29 Russell Street
                                               San Francisco
                                                Nov. 15, 50

Dear Allen;
    I would have written much sooner, but I've been in San Luis
Obispo for some weeks and had no facilities.
    There is not much that I can say, altho there are more things in
my mind than ever. Since I can't think of any particulars that are
simple enough for me to make clear, I'll just ramble.
    When I left NY, so long ago, I got on a streamliner of the Pennsy
that was crowded as hell. I didn't want to get hungup looking for
my car so asked a young semi-hipster who seemed in the same
difficulty. We joined forces informally and managed to get settled
side by side in a car that was going thru to St. Louis. I went to the
head and blasted after going under the Hudson. I came back to my
seat in that peculiar way that I've developed whenever I've got to
traverse a distance under the eyes of others. The heightened sensibility that one experiences after a good bomber is so delightful that
it is absolutely imperative for one to really take it slow. The actual
process of placing the feet, swinging the arms and otherwise maintaining balance so as to float thru a crowded RR car was my
concern. I slid into my seat without the usual sign of recognizion to
this sharpie beside me. Its not only a flying mind thats the charact-
eristic of fine t, the whole body responds without restraint if given
the command, however, if one "goes", the big exertion—eventually—eliminaties that type of kick. again too, the oppertunity to
"go" seldom presents itself often in the manner one wishes; fuck
and blow. So, one takes advantage of available kicks and makes
the most of them—without regret. I decided, after a short 10 minutes of musing on what I was leaving and the trip and future, to
allow myself to dig this guy. He had been straining at the bit anyhow, a young blood without relaxation; one who had never heard of

tensions. By God tho, he sure had plenty of other points of interest
about which to have opinions. Never, in recent years, had I so consciously drawn out and controlled a piece of talk. Not that this poor
fool was not unbridled, that was just the flaw; how he could spout
horeshit. Worse, his catologue of trash was encyclopedic. Now
being hi, this huge dose of stupidity was doubly obnoxious; but, I
had vowed patience. The length of the trip was designed to be the
nemisis of any such firm resolve and defeated my tolerance. Of
course, at once I was sorry I'd opened the gates for such a flow.
One doesn't mind anything another says, no matter how poorly put
together, if the words imply that "tick" that all of us are tuned
to—Dig that colored cat in Fitzgeralds Poughkeepsie; the one with
the gospel. It all began casually enuf, murders he's seen, taken
part in; cops he'd helped waylay; toughies (brooklyn style—it all
took place there, under the shadow of the great bridges) he'd
known; gangfights etc. From this collection of James Cagney (he
even looked like him) ideas, we passed on, with me still able to get
in an agreeing word or two, to the broader fields. To him, this was
Science. We all know about that (I have happened to further
rehashed this field and am in possesion of all the facts, any specific
you might worry over, consult me) but, I was more than generous
in giving full allowance for his youth (20, I guess) and mind and
was prepared to hear everything I'd heard many times and not
cringe or puke and just dig all the world thru him and the rest of
the car as I listened to the drone. The possibilities of imagry when
one has decided to open up the mind completely are without number. I have perfected this technique to the point of art. The one
thing I've accomplished these last years. Naturally, crushed to the
plush of a RR car, surrounded by the Fellaheen, I surrender with
more grace, wit and pure self-knowledge; I had blasted again by
now. From his fasinating thesis on the great wonders of science
and his wholehearted support of its value, He carried over into our
next subject the self-confident enthusiasm this one had kindled.
Yessir, by golly, no stopping him now. While he's been shooting
off his mouth about the way things are to him, the student of holy
science, so loudly the rest of the car had fallen into embarassed
silence & even old women without a grain of brain had sensed foolish statements (he knew no facts, not the simplist second-hand
"popular Mechanic" or Public School texts) I had been evolving a
little plan which I liked the more as I mulled it over. It was in self-
defence; every man for himself now, and I needed sleep. Carefully, to prevent any premature oration too far afield, I mentioned
books. This warmed his ego like nothing else I could have brought

up would. He was about to reach out and hug me he was so happy. His eyes sparkled, one could feel his brain pulsating orgasms of ecstacy, I had hit his subject. He caught his breath, literally restraining a torrent of babble. He switched to the casual. Why yes, he knew books, literature was his real interest. "In fact", he leaned close to confide, "I've done a couple of little things my-self—pretty good too, in their way of course." And here he popped out with the one thing *I* could have wished; that which made the initial plan crystal clear and its fulfillment so easy that I couldn't resist the first ego gloat I've had for some time. (there are many gloats; the one I must needs use constantly to keep within every-thing without flagging and to retain a grip on the rock in the belly of the mind is the gloat of knowledge: looking out anxiously on the whole of all thats before me each moment as tho I was about to die every minute and therefore straining all ways to *feel* the experi-ence fully and hunger to store it all and save everything in the mind so that when I feel any similar emotion it will recall the scene and conversely, when I see any object or hear any sound that has the aspects of an object or sound that was seen or heard in one of the moments when I gathered in a strong emotion, I can then, whenever its necessary, release some of the hoarded memory to think of it and when I do the resultent emotion becomes one of gloat; a gloat of knowledge, self-knowledge to be sure, but one that bolsters with a poignantcy that renders me truly inarticulate and the flood of sure truth saturates my brain and I reel under the meaning of life and I wonder that it is there and the sheer beautiful bliss of being allowed one more precious minute of conciousness, so as to feel these things, overcomes me and I thank God unreserv-edly) So, this young fool said he'd done a few little pieces, but, the best thing he'd written was: "an objective, clinical scientific study" called, "The confessions of a dope Addict". I think you'll agree my ego gloat was justified. I slowed my pace even more and it was my turn to have considerable difficulty in restraining a pop of the gut. My happiness was offset by concern that I wouldn't be able to pull this off properly and to flub, or even booble, such a perfect chance to squelch this overextended slicker; show even blind and cocksure him what a bumpkin and dupe he actually was. In a sudden flash I saw I could throw a pure scare into him both ways; awaken his shallow mind to fear for itself—if only a transa-tory fright—and make his yellowbelly flip over enough that he'll be afraid to peep and I can get some sleep. Weeellll, I asked for a little description of the noble work. A vague general statement, a couple of "youknow's" and after that, blank. I pressed him harder, in ratio to my insistence did his silence grow. I wasn't overbearing at all, just simple little questions "How does one begin to go about finding out what a dope addict feels, thinks, or would want to confess, objectively?—i.e. how does his clinical scientific method peer into the addicts being? How can one begin to know, let alone write about, the convictions that preceed any confession; how they came about, what they mean inwardly, to the mind and soul of the addict? Then I began to get hot. "What!" I yelled, "you mean you didn't even preface the work with any clue, statement or otherwise, as to specifically what type of Dope he was addicted too?" Then, naturally, I raved a bit about the differant types and their different affects. I also pointed out that in the end each man speaks for himself and even if one shared every iota of dope exactly with a fellow one could never know exactly what was up with the guy. Worse, indeed truly impossible, if one attempted to *deduce* by scientific method of objective external measurement such an essentially mystical thing as a confession of a dope addict would be—unless, of course, the confession was a catologue of incidents leading up to, or while in, addiction. Even an intelligent man, carefully attempting to accurately confess to the lay world the kernal of something the addiction produced that changed him from what he was before as well as what makes him different from them now, would only be able to come up with an abstraction, further modified by writing, of the "it". So howin hell can the labratory, with or without the addicts aid, help to bring a single grand logic out of any confession, etc. Now, about this time I felt I'd better put a good cap on the whole business while I had him floundering in, "I'd not meant that", "Oh, I didn't intend to write it that way", "I didn't want to get close to the addict, I just wanted an objective clinical study, I wasn't concerned with the soul." So, I suggested we adjourn to the club car to quench our thirst and I could there get him really alone to nail him thoroughly; he bucked and squirmed to get away, but, had no reason at hand, so accompanied me. In the luxurious surroundings I held his eye and said, "You know I'm an addict". He had been expecting it, but, when I said it he still wasn't prepared enough and there came a big slack in his jaw which was instantly covered with a blustering, "I knew it all the time, why I even knew it *before* you got on the train, in penn. station I looked at you and said to myself; now there is an addict thats under the influence right now." I told him I'd not been hi getting on the train and asked him to guess what I was on. He surmised I had been smoking opium "or something" and in his ignorance wanted to know if I knew where I was, what I was doing or if I would pass out. I had him scared alright and decided to pour it on because he really was malicious as well as dumb and truly deserved it. I talked quietly but, practiced a seething-seeming self-control which I easily made to seem just under the surface and about to bust loose at any moment. I told him how the powerful Marajuana I was feeling caused a murderous surge of hatred for anyone who crossed me, how strong the stuff made one,—bending a heavy silver spoon quickly—and how hard it was to control myself whenever I thought of anyones neck; I got hungup on the neck, I elaborated fully on the urge to throttle all necks, especially feminine and skinny ones, I explained I wanted to squeeze until I was exhausted, press my palms together with a neck between, until the exertion made for collapse. I boasted about what I could do to a neck; oh, I really warmed up to the subject, began to image new things as I progressed, what heaven to posess a neck, etc. I had his old adams apple twitching by golly; he didn't finish his beer, got up in the middle of one of my words and left the dining car. Oops, damnit, I've done it now, I went too far; he'll tell the conductor, call the cops, or just plain blab the whole thing to all the train in general and our car in particular. I sat there stunned for a few minutes, deciding never to fuck with squares again since theres never any real pleasure anyhow, then went back to my car to face them. There was no trouble, he was sitting mute as I slid pass him to my seat next to the window. We never spoke again, he was afraid to and perhaps ashamed; I put him out of my mind in a few minutes and soon was digging the pennsylvania countryside until I fell asleep. As I dozed thruout the night I occasionally came to and noticed everyone in the car was asleep except him. I observed him closely from lowered lids, he was sitting there like a ramrod, refusing to sleep and eyeing me now and again with tense worry in his expression. I farted and returned to sleep. The next A.M. the car thinned out and he took another seat. That P.M. as we approached St. Louis I saw he'd hooked up with a dimwit soldier just like himself; more so, even louder. They began pacing the train, leering at girls, giving out with where they'd been, what they'd done, what everything in the U.S.A. and the rest of the world was about, particularily pertaining to War. I noticed they finally settled in a standing position in the vestibule near my end of the car, some 3 seats away. They began looking at me and whispering, I knew the fool had told all with relish and distortion; I was happy. The journey was over and these boys were wondering and clucking to themselves. For any provication there might be violence but I knew they would start nothing themselves. Altogether, I came off so well that when I found in the St. Louis station my pass was all fucked up, I had the old drive and dashed downtown to the Wabash offices, got the RR pass to Denver and further got it fixed to be good on a train just leaving and not usually free for Brakies and was on the train and gone again in less than one hour and still found time for two innings of All-star Major league baseball. So, the end of the ''scientific clinical objective'' story.

Since I'm returning Canastra without delay I presume to ask for Jim Holmes scribbled (I'm sure) letter to you; I would like to see the old boys Hi. Thank you. Hows Carl, Claude, your girl etc. I got a nice PC from John Holmes, I shall write him. I think we all know intuitively what you generalize about tragedy and chance and death, I, for one, have always felt that way. I will be in NY in Jan. March or May, if not then maybe sooner, later or never. I've had several fairly exciting RR wrecks, two that I might have gotten fired for, one that tied up the RR for about 16 hours, 3 or 4 that stopped first class streamliners and the first trip I made when I got back was just finished and I was coming home with a few other guys when Myself, my conductor and Stiengasser stepped between moving trains, when it was over the conductor was pale as hell, I was nervous and gulping and Stiengasser is still in the hospital with smashed skull and paralized limbs. I had a fine little note I wrote to you which was the beginnings of a letter, I wrote in longhand with pencil but leaving SLO I forgot it so this is all I can come up with. I have finished (tentatively) the prologue in 3 parts, begun the book only in that I've created my opening page of the manuscript. The tape recorder I have helps not one whit, don't ever think you can write by using a recorder of any kind; a fantasy for sure. I'm broke as hell, this fucking RR hasn't got it like the parking lot had, however, I'm never going to work at anything but RRing again, not that I like it, or that its easy, but its the closest to eliminating the job hangup and the way conditions are I shall have to ''Boom'' across the country every year to get work and so shall get to travel. Of course, even after 20 years one can get fired at any time, so I can lose SP job but still work on other roads—unless they find out I'm color blind; a test of each RRs physical is a color test and luck has to be with me to fool them. Every new thing I discover or come to believe I keep like a secret, so am getting my mind back and having convictions after so long without them.

Love
N.

Paterson, NJ.
Nov. 18 1950

Dear Neal:

I got home today from Jack's wedding to a girl named Joan Haverty, which took place last night at 6 followed by a big party at Cannastra's pad which she leased and Jack is now master of—a big quiet party which began around 7, with the arrival of the wedding party from the Judge's apartment, several blocks away, where the cerimonies took place. Claude and I stood as best men, fumbled around in our waistcoats for the ring, kissed the bride, who's a tall dumb darkhaired girl just made for Jack. Not dumb, really, since she's "sensitive", and troubled (trying to be on own from family in big city at age 20), and has had men (Cannastra, once for a short season), but full of a kind of self-effacing naivete, makes dresses as vocation; but I dont know her well, but in my opinion (strictly between you and me as I am on hands off policy as regards interference with process of other's free cherce) she can't compare with Jack in largeness of spirit and so I don't know what she can give him except stability of sex life, housekeeping, and silent, probably sympathetic company while he's sitting around, and children.

He has been strangely out of town the last several months, in retirement and brooding on T alone, and when he rejoined N.Y. society he seemed to me to be more settled in reality, more sober. He talked in a more disillusioned way—not making a fetish of it as I do,—but like a post 20's survivor, F. Scott Fitzgerald after the party of ego was over. Wondering what to do in the real world of men and women who were also alive and facing same problems and just as deserving of grace from above as he, tho there is no grace accorded anyone special. So, he seemed come down more than ever.

Meanwhile he's seeing this Rayanna chick (who I had my hands on till I stepped out for Jack as she is too old for me) (but who I intend to see again unless I get attached before which I doubt), and she's sharpe, a real N.Y. "on the town" pro type, but all of a sudden appears on the horn this Joan, in C.'s pad, making a vulturish shrine of it (on the pretext that they had been great lovers though he thought she was an insufferable prig), next door to Claude's on 21 st.

So, with Claude's encouragement, and prodding, I start moving in on her leaving notes at her door, making meets, etc., in the hope of sleeping with her and ultimately taking over pad with her, also under impression she has money, which she has'nt. But when time comes, fuck up by being out of self control, overbearing, and impatient with her sentimentalized version of self, not wanting anything but "friendship" with menfolk, wanting to be alone and keep shrine and have big parties. Anyway, I never figure her or myself out in relation to her, and retire from field depressed. Next thing I know Jack ran into her, two weeks ago, slept, and stayed on, decided to marry, and did yesterday. This is a very sketchy account, not even an outline, but I am just jotting down distorted recollections.

The main things I see is this increased wariness and caution in life of Jack, and this mad marriage, they hardly know each other. But maybe it will all work out for the rest of his life. I think he hopes for permanence. Or maybe they know each other on levels which, tho I am aware of them, neglect and don't take seriously for real, so my opinion is out of the picture. Anyway I say fuck it, but we all should have beautiful intelligent wise women for wives who will know us and vice versa as well as we know ourselves (one another). I say let the home be the center of emotional and spiritual life.

And let several families gather together, menfolk and womenfolk, childfolk following, for society. Thus my ideal is everybody married living in the same area of city near enough for short walk, with telephones in each house. But maybe I want to hold together the old vain grouping of us exclusively. O dull Time. Perhaps I shall seek refuge myself someday in sull wife and exclusion of all other important society, though I do not want it now. How sullen can you get?

Be that as it may we had a big party, Seymour (and I sat on roof and blasted and talked about women); Bill Frankel (know him? fat, eyeglasses, very straight, smart, literarey); the Bowmens, Hollander and little jewish girlfriend, Claude and Lizzie, Holmes, Lindens, Harrington, Lenrow, lots of other unknown women, Solomon, and Ansen, Winnie, others from village and elsewhere. I wandered around distracted, getting into conversations and breaking them off impatiently till at three A.M. Claude, Jack and I put our heads together and kissed and sang Eli Eli and held loving symbolical conversation. But anyway, I did not feel passionate or exultant that night but dead, as did Claude and I think Jack, as we were all too old and wearie to exult over anything but was new and outwidening into unknown joys beyond control, and this was not exactly like that, but anyway it did seem a big event, so that all

that day Claude & I sang Them wedding bells is breaking apart
that old gang of mine, but without real sadness, since we knew
that anyway we could break into each others apartment still in the
middle of the night.

When I get n arried I want everybody I know to be there and
watch including all regiments of family, in synagogue, where will
be great groaning choirs of weepers, sacraments, everybody in
flowers and dress clothes, slightly awed by the presence of eternal
vows, chastened by tradition and individuality of marriage. Then I
can go home to mad pad and have real crazy party with people
jumping out of windows, after. And womenfolk and menfolk separated for last goodbyes and vows of eternal fidelity too.

I got your letter today when I came home. I know you love me
because you wrote such a long letter. Boo hoo I guess I'll always
love you too.

Distrust my dove and vulture but trust me.

I read a letter you wrote to Jack discribing (at one point) meeting
early girlfriend at drugstore counter etc., and remembrance of
other times meetings. I noticed then what was partly unsaid, the
machinery of consciousness of place and time, memory, at work in
astonishing solidity of grasp, and so was prepard for and interested in—recognising what I found implied earlier,—your explanation to me of gloat of knowledge of moment. Rock in the belly of
the mind is great phrase.

I wish we could talk for several days and come to understanding
of memory and phenomenology. I find my phases and interests are
somewhat confused, and I am out of touch, impatient, or inatten-
tive to yours, because my preoccupations are sometimes so different and in different directions. I feel now however that it is time for
me to look around again at moment kicks of mind. Before, they
lead to centralization of thought and madness now they might be
real objective practices for me. You see, much of your train incident is "Paranoia", desire to control world through your central
perceptions. I (ahem) used to try that myself, though I did'nt
always succeed, which led me to believe that by this method, I
could myself be the victim of control (thru you, for instance) so I
have been trying to achieve a less competitive not ego tack, thru
Freud discipline. My doctor is an inferior intelligence who because
I have seen him so long and I have allowed him to, can follow my
deepest hints more strictly and objectively and ruthlessly than I
can myself. And so he tries to hold me to account for them. This is
in preliminary stage of process, though at this point the main
things he has done is broken me of schizoid paranoid beliefs (meta-

physical ecstasy in place of real world of dragging necessity) and
queerness.

Now I am faced with dealing with world of dragging necessity. But about you. Assuming the kid was talking out of hat,
dumb, it may also be that you, too were crazy in pushing him to
wall—what if, for instance, in process of pushing him to come
down of horror, you actually choked him, woke up, found yourself
in court, and had to give a reasonable explanation of why youd
killed? And Jack, who never knew you, was the Judge you had to
explain to? And you had not built up with him already the history
of thought? So we are in relation to world of men, all different, on
different kicks. But now I'm wandering.

Be that as it may the account you gave was remarkably inte-
grated. The only possible objection to it as a short story is that the
(I wander again) author's whole view of life is, in this story,
centered around the contention, in this ambiguous world, that he
is more gone and expierienced than his victim. Well, nobody
would deny that from the beginning.

The right plane of action in art is to remove the self from the plot
and point of the story and write an account of what happens to
other or imaginary people based on knowledge of their attempt to
make themselves the center of universe. As it is you only beat this
boy at his own braggart's game, not at the game of impersonal
Indian wisdom. But this is my own theory of myself,
really, as I say. I am explaining perhaps on what terms, with what
weapons I chose to battle you.

But as you say in the last page of your letter, which I understood
most, "I think we all know intuitively what you generalize about
tragedy and chance and death." Yes, you do know.

Enclosed find Holmes notes, but dont show him. Also, please
don't show letters to anyone (my letters) but yourself, as I find I
have not written as hotly as I'd like for fear that less forgiving eyes
than yours would see. That goes for all your wives. O.K.? Jack is
an exception, he can see them, if you see him. Secrets. Lets begin
to keep secrets from the world. The beginning of impersonal
wisdom.

Too much to say this moment, but to summarize, 1. my romance
with Mrs. P. is over with disgust as she is a veritable Huncke of
selfishness and deadbeat hassels. I dont want a whore, I want a
finished product of self education who has turned to Stillness. She
was in N.Y. last week but things were so tense in the end I was
glad to see her go. No immediate female prospects.

2. I will *not* after all I said in last letter, get factory job. I'm sick

of trying to be a hero of misfortune. So next I must figure out first steps in publishing career, or something.

3. I write very little and may start taking lessons from Anson in Greek or meter of poesy, technique. Study again. Novel dead again.

4. I have 4¢ to my name and am a dead beat on my family. Doctor fortunately has come up fine and is treating me free finally. So you see he's not so bad, at least sympathetic to the cause.

5. I hope to get a job and move to N.Y. in next few months, perhaps by time you get to N.Y., So society will flourish—but please, cool kicks. We will talk over life without smirking. Hot kicks only for the war.

What courage you have.

Love,
allen

[San Francisco]
Nov. 25, 50

Dear Allen;

It is not an easy task to write to you, or anyone; in fact I can't bring myself to write at all. In regard to this vacuum wherein I can find nothing to say to anyone, Diana has the worst of it. Accordingly, if you see her at any time please tell her I just can't write or do anything else and thats the end of it. I have many beautiful instances of my inability to function at hand, and could recite them for you, but need not since I really haven't the strength. I can't overemphasize too strongly how ugly my life has become, simply because of this "do nothingness", and how low I've gotten by realizing emotionally *every* damn moment what a really disgusting fish I am. Honestly its awful, not only am I unable to do the ordinary things necessary (brush teeth, see doctors, do important RR things, sleep) but also, can't do absolutely imperative things. i.e. my cars broke down, needs easy to fix spark plugs, do you think I'm able to walk two blocks to get them and take ten minutes to fix it, no, no, I've been riding streetcar to work for weeks, etc. etc. things even worse, but suffice to say I just eat every 12 hours, sleep every 20 hours, masturbate every 8 hours and otherwise just sit on the train and stare ahead without a thought in it. One thing I

do is think every 5 seconds of the things I have to do, I keep recit-
ing them over and over in my mind?, "fix car, fix feet, fix teeth,
fix eyes, fix nose, fix thumbs, fix bronchial tubes, fix asshole, get
new RR lantern, get RR pass for trip back here in March for
Hairy Jack and Haressed Diana, (if they want it) get started on
book, get lined up for RR jobs on way east, get dog (I got thorobred
cocker for Cathy) rabies shot, get backyard fixed for Cathy to play
in, get this read and that written etc." The net result of all this is
my belly is sick all the time, its loose, I eat and I feel sick after, I
smoke and get mad for not stopping, etc. etc. I wish I had a toad
stool to crawl under and die.

To attempt to get an exact fix on the ever-mysterious soul is
futile. But nowadays one must needs have abstract thinking and it
forces the physicist of the inner world to elucidate a fictitious world
for oneself by fictions piled on fictions, notions on more notions.
He transmutes the non-extended into the extended, builds up a
system of cause for something that is only manifested physiog-
nomically, and comes to believe that in this system he has the
structure of the soul before his eyes. But the very words that he
selects, to notify to others the results of his intellectual labors,
betray him. The word as utterance, as poetic element, may estab-
lish a link, but the word as notion, as element of scientific prose,
never. Easier to break up a theme of Beethoven with a knife than
break up the soul by methods of abstract thought. Images—like-
nesses, are the only way for spiritual intercourse yet discovered.
Rembrandt can reveal something of his soul, to those who are in
inward kinship with him, by way of a self-portrait or landscape.
Certain ineffable stirrings of soul can be imparted by one man to
the sensibility of another man through a look, two bars of melody;
an almost imperceptible movement. That is the real language of
souls—it remains incomprehensible to the outsider.

"Soul" for the man who has advanced from mere living and
feeling to the alert and observant state, is an image derived from
quite primary experiences of life and death. It is as old as thought,
i.e., the articulate separation of thinking (thinking-over) from
seeing. We see the world around us, and since every free-moving
being must, for its own safety, understand the world, the accumu-
lating daily detail of technical and empirical experience becomes a
stock of permanent date which man, as soon as he is proficient in
speech, collects into an *image* of what *he understands*. This is
world of nature; what is not environment we do not see, but we do
divine "its" presence in ourselves and in others, and by virtue of
"its" physiognomic impressive power it invokes in us the anxiety

and desire to know; thus arises the meditated or pondered image of a counterworld which is our mode of visualizing that which remains eternally alien to the physical eye. The image of the soul is mythic and remains objective in the field of spiritual religion. Scientific psychology has worked out for itself a complete system of images, in which it moves with entire conviction. The individual pronouncements of every individual psychologist proves on examination to be merely a variation of this system conformable to the style of their world science of the day. At any particular time, therefore, the current image of the soul is a function of the current language and its inner symbolism. Scientific psychology and the psychology of the same kind that we all unconsciosly practise when we try to figure to ourselves the stirrings of our own or other's souls is unable to discover or even approach the essence of the soul. Like everything else that is no longer becoming but become, it has put a mechanism in the place of an organism. Everything our present day psychologist has to tell us relates to the present condition of the western soul; not to the human soul at large.

The imaginary soul-body is never anything but the exact mirror-image of the form in which the matured culture-man looks on his outerworld. A soul-image is never anything but the image of *one* quite definate soul. No observer can ever step outside the conditions and the limitation of his time and circle, whatever it may be that he "knows" in itself involves in all cases choice, direction and inner form; is therefore an expression of his proper soul. And the soul remains what it was, something that can neither be thought or represented; *the* Secret, *the* ever-becoming, *the* pure experience. When one convinces oneself that one knows the soul of an alien culture, or man, from its, or his, workings in actuality, the soul-image underlying the knowledge is really one's own soul-image. In this wise experiences are readily assimilated into the system that's already there, and it is not surprising that in the end one comes to believe that one has discovered forms of eternal validity.

Since you are being the victim of a big fucked out of your Spengler,* because Carolyn refuses to part with it until I buy her another, I'll give you these quotes until I buy you a copy to replace my pricky theft.

There is not one, not one, thought in my head I've sat here 20 minutes trying to come up with an idea and there is none. Anyway,

---

*Bill Burroughs gave Jack a one Vol. Spengler. Jack probably promised it to me next but left it with Neal, or Neal borrowed my 2 Vol. set.—A.G.

I'll give out with some bullshit; just anything to get on with this nonsense—

The particular mexican t that Jack and I have been blasting (I ran out almost a month ago and if you lovely boys would take pity and just send me any small amount available I'd surely swoon) was different than any other t because I've noticed that anyone who uses it has a tendency to think the same strange things as do others who have it. I know t has similar effects on all of us, but this stuff was moreso; even Al Hinkle entered completely into the same pattern of kicks once he's blasted. In the light of this, and letteres Jack has written me, I suspect the brooding alone on Richmond Hill for what it was; a final and most disheartening realization of himself. This is not to say he was not happy, it was that itself which showed him the truth of the matter. Under its (t) influence he was really stoned consistently for long periods; and alone. When one is alone on this stuff the sheer exstacy of utterly realizing each moment makes it more clear to one than ever how impossibly far one is from the others. Not different from them or intolerant; one is more close than ever to people and the world, but, in the end alone for noone can ever follow the complexities that make up the mind that is so t conditioned. One, then, cannot make ones self clear to others; the difficulties of yourself tracing the trail of inner feeling and conviction are so insurmountable that not only in writing, but even speech and action, one is completely misunderstood—because all that comes out of one is a caricature of what one is thinking & that is so distorted from the actual thought that people pick up on this caricature as your action or thought about the matter at hand, whereas really one *had meant* it for a caricature (realizing inwardly the incapability of even begining to speak or show action about what one is experiencing) and once beginning this trait is unable to stop and so, actually, becomes artificial. A horrible fate to be artificial, no genuine feeling left; all is bemused thought that means nothing to anyone else but ones self. This artificiality is not too readily obseoved if there is noone at hand to point it out to one. The mind, when alone, is usually hungup playing with one theme and then another; hop, skip and jump. Trying to make pleasure one discovers tricks, then forgets them. When hi one is stunned at the fullness of the perception experienced, they mean so much one feels there'll never be doubt (of comprehension) again. And so it goes. (too obtuse to continue) At anyrate, Jack has had this and dispite saying he's writing the greatest stuff ever; he knows he is not. This may not be so in Jacks mind, theres no telling that; but, the reasons behind the marriage can be

attested to this t; so much so that I say without the t and its effects
Jack would not now be married. This can lead to trouble because
its just so much horseshit, but, you know I had to come up with
sumpin! Then, of course, theres my poor dead mothers chinese
wedding dress, if it had only been hung properly the tail might not
have ended so flat. In truth, tho, as you well show in your letter,
noone can say the reason for the marriage. There are no reasons
for so many actions of this type, in fact, I have perhaps more insight into this matter than any of the rest of us, you see, I can
clearly recall all my three marriages and the emotions and reasons
that led into them. Knowing Jack and suspecting his recent life
while remembering how he's stated for so long that he'd marry I
can put the memory of my past and my feeling about Jack together
and sense there is as little inner as there is outer reason for the
marriage. All this means nothing; reasons *for* marriage mean less
than you believe, Allen, you I think are so firmly pursuant of
making marriage *last* that you can't feel properly the mere whims
that led to marriage. That is to say, realizing permanence so well
you do not sufficiently give credit to those whims inside yourself
to justify action on them. A marriage such as I am inclined to
believe Jacks is, and know mine were, is a combination of willful
blindness, a perverted sense of wanting to help the girl and just
plain what the hell. Besides there are no good reasons why two
people shouldn't be together, excepting children, no matter what
the distance between. As for children, what can one say?, it all
depends on the attitude of each partner toward the other as that
attitude has been conditioned by the various actions and ideas that
have influenced each persons particular personality. The many
compromises, even tho intellectually not begrudged, push the
limits of love and soon each person affects a static comprehension
of the other and there is no changing this viewpoint. If one is convinced of the others integrity all is usually OK, but, if this is gone
there no hope. Then it becomes a matter of remaining together for
the children, if this too cannot be achieved because of emotional
(true) dislike, one can only hope the best one for raising them gets
the kids. I could go on indefinately from experience. There are
always things in a marriage no outsider sees, this can't help from
being so, also there are many things in a marriage outsiders see
and the married one cannot, but, this is a moot point and matters
not to the person involved. All in all each marriage is only what the
partners make of it and what becomes of it depends solely on what
they want it to be. The conflicting ideas of same are the crux which
combined with the emotional habits of each make for the strain

that, once ruptured, needs an external responsibility to save the marriage—church, family, pride, children or some such absolute. My god! I sound like the ladies home journal or worse and never having done this before give that excuse. I stop altho I haven't even warmed to the subject yet, or gotten halfway to the place where I could begin to make my points about Jack and his wife. It does not matter anyway, Jack will cater to her minds shollowness, in return for her bodys fullness, until such time as he breaks under the complete awareness of one females demands and his inability to meet them, besides which he'll tire of staying on her level, she would, but can't, get on his, so mutual frustration—which they'll (jack will) combat by vague retreats from understanding. This is a pretty good system and works almost as well as any I can now think of; whenever a point that looks as tho it might matter comes up one just quickly and magnanimosly agrees, forgets, or says it does matter anyhow since everyone is different, so as to hide the whole business more readily and slip into another backwash of thought less dangerous. It all depends on how much she'll leave Jack alone, I fear she wont be bright enough to see this, or strong enough to do it, when he wants (needs, as habit) it, this sure can become a big sore point if she'll inclined to goad. Then, also, there is her whole unknown world of emotion (from what you say of making Vulgar Canastra shrine, I'll wager she at least has a big, foolish and feminine one) which cannot help but be a pleasure for Jack to discover, *if,* he can find peace from other things to be able to indulge in that greatest of all gone kicks of finding out a woman from the soul (soles) up. As time passes he'll loose the strength to be consistent in this (as he knows more) and will hanker elsewhere even if there is great love and they are welded solid, for the actual task of rising to the game is too difficult, unbeknown to us all, and, unless by that time there are other things, Jack will fall prey to this inherant weakness (no hardon) and fuck big only in imagination. But, thats another problem. So where do we stand? nowhere, yet; I haven't said anything valid about Jack's marriage. Where does one begin? I prefer China since its furthest away, but, being practical, Ha, how about starting with looking at Jack objectively, Ha, Ha. More shit; I'm dashing it off now—

The intense drives that affect Jacks actions are extremely varied and strong; this is of prime importance and I must continually orient to one and then another of these multitudious forces to excape oversimplification, and so will seem quite contridictory—as he himself if. Ah! but to properly etch in the exact shades of his personality, so that the degrees of conflict can be approximated and

his whole upright self stand firmly, sharp and clear. A deliniena-
tion of his mind seems in order, but, his emotions are so pronounced! Ach, bah, anyway—But, by god, Allen, what a man he is, just
stop and think of it. Certain traits stand out so as to make him a
true peasant, as he says, "like a potato" and, again, what wisdom
he can flash! He lets people bully him, intellectually & otherwise,
he shows always a shy diffidence, a gentle nature; witness, tho, his
claws as he rants for pages on end and sometimes, at parties,
raises up in anger at wrongs (usually social) he imagines inwardly
or witnesses; yet, he'll be the first to wither under any real hint of
sweetness on the part of the other person. He has a morbid dread
of hassles (he will attempt mightily to escape even the suggestion
of one in his marriage) but when it comes down to it wont knuckle
under. He has consideration, but a manly selfishness, boyishness,
but a certain poise. etc. etc. Damn it, I don't want to, and can't be
presumptious enough to, give you any of this simple trash. You
know him a hellofalot better than I do, longer than I have probably
probably love him the more. You see, when I began this I was just
struck by the thought of the actual difference between you and
Jack. (what if you had married and I was writing Jack your traits?)
I realized you have only a few definate drives. Several instincts so
strong as to be ineffaceable, your mold is as that of cast-iron; stiff
and so set with its properties that there is no bending allowed, you
came from the forge doomed to splinter, you must crack under the
blows of the hammer of life, but, aha!, as long as there are any
remains of you, no matter the number or size of the clevages that
rend you thruout, the stuff of which you are made remains the
same; their is no altering your shape, always recognizable you are,
never any distortions of the kind possible with the pliable nature of
Jacks chemical; tempered Steel. I, of course, retain exclusive
rights to the granduer of the black mold; ingredients of the rose-
scent, the apple-blossom, all the pastures products and finely-
spun old lace combined with green lumps of eyeballs, louse-
infected chicken liver, purple pastes of puke, grey miles of intes-
tine, red-ringed assholes and brown bunches of bullshit which
created the chemical of my soul; low-grade slag, destined for the
pits of Hades, where I will quickly be found unburnable and so
tossed on His slagpits to wallow forever.

But the Springtime is gone, it has passed in character, with rush
and upheavel. The Summer, too, in heat and humid longing, has
fled I fear. Far into the shortness of Indian Summer am I, but
before me still lies the plump Autumn; season of understanding! I
trust the winter, cold passionless rage are its most powerful

storms; no heat involved. The present Indian Summer provokes the memory storehouse into Proust-like recollection wherein the egg-seeds generated by the past are carefully gathered in the brains basket so as to hibernate until nursed into bloom at au-tumntime. Etc., old boy.

Being as how you nasty easterners think This western fart can care for himself, I done went out last night and with beautiful struggles that could make a better story than any "Pennsy RR", I managed to fall into the most wonderful joint of t that it has been my pleasure to come across in months. Not only that, with my last few bucks, come monday, I'll pick up an oz of same. How do you like them apples, huh? Great, great shit I tell you—Carolyn was so hi, (stoned mind you, as I was on just this one stick between us) she actual'v fell on her ass when she attempted to walk across the floor; her equalibrium was so poor the floor just wasn't there when she stepped.

Love to everyone of you silly jerks who spent half their life suffering the cold, snow, wind and attendent hazards of the ad-verse NY weather; fools.

[no signature]

Still Paterson
[Feb. or March] 1951

Dear Neal:

Bishop (Henry?) Percy in the (17-18) century collected the remaining fragments of Poesy dear to his heart, from older ages, before the page should rot further, calling them Reliques. Percy's Relics, as its now called, and a few other such books, like the Para-dise of Dainty Devises of Shakespearian times, are great for sourcebooks for T studies of antique kicks, scholarly and other-wise. For instance, the above paragraph contains almost all I know on the subject, whereas Anson, for instance, has probably read them thru and knows the history of the verses contained therin, etc.

The present state of the Song of the Shrouded Stranger is:

| Bare skin is my wrinkled | Now, you have seen all this |
| sack (back) | before, but I sent it on |

When summer sun creeps up
  my crack,
When winter rocks me in
  these rags
I lock my lap with burlap bags.
My flesh is cinder, my face is
  snow
I walk the Railroad to and fro.
When city streets are black
  and dead
The railroad embankment is
  my beat.

I suck my soup from old tin
  cans
And take my sweets from
  little hands;
Where tigers in the alley wail
I steal away from the garbage
  pail.
In darkest night where none
  can see
I lurk in the bowels of the
  factory;
I sneak barefoot upon stone:
Come and hear the old man
  groan.

I hide and wait like a naked
  child,
Under the bridge my heart
  goes wild.
Shadow and bone are shreik
  and shiver,
Flesh starts dancing by the
  river:
I dream that I have burning
  hair,
Arms raised bloody in the
  glare,
The torso of an iron king,
And on my back a broken
  wing.

again (with its few lines
changed,) because it is the
only thing of which I'm proud,
and so harp on.

It seems that in England in the
17th century, the two mad-
houses were Bethlehem (for
Men) and Magdeline (for
Women), and when these got
too crowded, they sent the
Bedlamites and Maudlinites,
as they were called (Tom
O'Bedlam and Maud) out of
the House to beg on the
streets if they were cracked
but not deadly. As part of their
begging routine they would
sing songs, and I discover in
Percy's Relics (sent by John
Holmes yesterday) several of
these type songs, which I read
up on today in library; also
other books.

The Shroudy Stranger who re-
appeared to me in a dream
these last years is the same
man who shrieked on the
heath with King Lear, the Fool
(this I gathered in memory a
long while back) and also Old
Tom the Lunatic of late Yeats:

Who'll go out whoring into the
   night
Where I rage on the road in a
   lonely rite?
Dame or maid or athlete proud
May wanton with me in the
   shroud.
Who'll come lay down in the
   dark with me,
Belly to belly and knee to
   knee?
Who'll look into my hooded
   eye?
Who'll lay down under my
   darkened thighs?

Come let me sing into your
   ear
Those dancing days are
   gone,
And all that silk and satin
   gear:
Crouch upon a stone
Wrapping that foul body up
In as foul a rag:
I carry the sun in a golden
   cup
And the moon in a silver
   bag.

That also I knew before I wrote my own (out of lines the Stranger
wrote for me in a dream): but now, I find the 17th Cent. songs are
even crazier and also parallel in many ways my own, the essential
sexual yearning theme plus pull my daisy language so similare
that I feel as if I have reincarnated the old Tom in a new setting:
the differnce between mine and the elder being in images of the
times, now old Tom wandering on the RR. and by docks. In the
above poem, of mine, I paralled the refrain of one before I read it,
and have changed the line "Mother maid or athlete proud" to
Dame or maid, as this is the sequence given, and as my own line
was not right somehow. And now let me unfold for you a few of the
maddened stanzas of the ancient songs, which you must *dig*. They
are in a slightly different meter: The beginning 2 lines are much
like my own first 4:

And the song goes on:

From the hag and hungry
   goblin
That into rags would rend ye,
And the spirit that stands
By the naked man
In the book of moons defend
   ye,
That of your five sound senses
You never be forsaken,
Nor wander from
Yourselves with Tom
Abroad to beg your bacon.

The refrain goes:
While I do sing, "Any food,
   any feeding
Feeding or drink or
   clothing?
Come, dame or maid
Be not afraid,
Poor Tom will injure
   nothing."

When I short have shorn my
   sow's face   (shaved my piglike face)
And swigged my horny barrel   (he wore a drinking-horn)

In an oaken inn
I pound my skin   (pound means pawn, or pass)
As a suit of gilt apparel
The moon's my constant
   mistress,
The lonely owl my morrow;   (morrow means mate)
The flaming drake
And the night-crow make
Me music to my sorrow.

And:
Of thirty bare years have I
Twice twenty been enraged,
   And of fourty been
   Three times fifteen
In durance soundly caged   (Durance means prisonment)
In the lordly lofts of Bedlam

But I will find Maud, Mad
   merry Maud
I'll find what'er betides her
   And I will love
   Beneath or above
The dirty earth that hides her.   (If she's dead)

The gypsy Snap, and Pedro
Are none of Tom's Comradoes
   The punk I scorn
   And the cutpurse sworn
And the roaring boys bra-
   vadoes.

The meek, the white, the   (When abegging: great lines)
   gentle
Me handle, touch and spare
   not,
   But those that cross
   Tom Rhinceross
Do what the Panther dare not.   (Note I have in book says in

Greek PAN all THER beast, or
With a heart of furious fancie   God.)
Wherof I am commander,
And a burning spear
And a horse of air,
To the wilderness I wander;
By aknight of ghosts &
     shadows
I am summoned to a tourney
     Ten leagues beyond
     The wide world's end—
Methinks it is no journey.

There are other stanzas I dont have around, about him looking up
and seeing
               one night when I was sleeping
                    the starres at warre
                    For Phoebus' car
          And the wounded welkin weeping. (welkin. vault of
                                                            heav'n
and other stanzas about the gods (Venus turns to mars) fucking
and cuckolding each other: also, ballads about Maud looking for
her Poor mad Tom, as she (crazier than he) calls him:
               and so Maud goes
               with dirty toes
          and looks the whole world over.

     Well so much for that, I thought you'd like it, and would'nt be
likely to run across it as it is'nt too well spread in anthologies, etc.
     Now, any plot ideas, contributions of lines, images or hustlings
you have for the Vision of The Shrouded Stranger as a long poem I
would like to hear. Right now I am beginning at last to get im-
mersed in a real study of metrical possibilities. It seems the greeks
wrote not by accents.

bare skin is my wrinkled sack   /   I lock my lap in burlap bags
          or   /   or
dum dum de de dum de dum /   dedumde dumdedumdedum

The above is accents. four beats to the line, plus 4 or more or less
off beats (dum, a beat, and de, an off beat)
You can vary this amazingly: though the base rythem which you
blow on is
               de dum de dum de dum de dum
                         or

<pre>
                      my *name* is *cassady* the *great*
you can jazz it to
                  dum   de de dum de de dum de dum
                               or
                  Belly to belly and knee to knee
            etc to Who'll lay down under my darkened thigh
                               or
                  dum de de   dum de de dum de dum
                               or
              dum dum   dum   de de   de dum de dum
</pre>

this last is either 4 dums or 5 dums whichever way you read it, but it can swing and pass as 4.

Now all this I know about hazily, that interesting verse is rhythem, beat, and jazz variation/ as it were. More, it can be measured not by accents but, as the Greeks, by length of time it takes for syllables—like the I of IT is short, the I of SIGHT is long. I have not learned how to build lines on that kind of a measure. But if you imagine music as 1. the Bar (a cut of time according to the metronome) 2. the notes, or pitch, inside the bar 3. the length of time given to each note 4. the accent or intensity given to each note, you will see that in verse there are 4 elements too (of physical sound).

    2   By dum de dum we cover accent or intensity
    4   By shit and sight we cover duration of sound
     3 By "money mellowed in the bowel", alliteration, etc.
       we cover melody, or pitch, or notes.

BUT the problem seems to be no. 1, that of finding a bar or space of time to measure no. 4 (duration of sounds) by.

That is to say, shit is half note, sight is full note, but how many half notes plus full notes make up a bar, and how many bars a convenient line? Nobody knows or decided yet.

This is what a bar looks like:

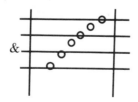

The bar is measured by vertical lines. The above statement of the problem is not really quite to the point, as I'm not sure whether a bar is a measure of TIME (metronome) or how its done according to beats.

March 15 Thurs Aft.

Nor do I know whether the whole parallel applies—further what is ¾ time, etc. Will investigate.

I found the rest of the songs of Tom and Maud: what I left out t'other day was:

I slept not since the conquest,
Till then I never waked
Till the roguish boy
Of love where I lay
Me found and stripped me
    naked.

(the fool in lear also says "This prophecy Merlin shall make: for I live before his time". Norman Conquest, sometime like 1066 AD. Merlin, 5th century AD.)
        (roguish boy is Erod I guess)

        Great stanza
I know more than Apollo,
For oft, when he lies
    sleeping,
    I see the stars
    At bloody wars
And the wounded welkin
    weeping,
The moon embrace her shep-
    herd
And the queen of love her
    warrior,
    While the first does horn
    (cukold)
    The star of the morn
And the next the heavenly
    farrier.

(God of Sun, and Wisdom)
(Phoebus or Apollo)
(sun set and night)

Myth of Diana loving Endymion, moral shepherd, but married to Apollo; Venus, love, making Mars (war), but married to farrier or iron craftsmen.
Vulcan (artificer, art)

And the Mad Maud songs:
    To find my Tom o Bedlam
    Ten thousand towns Ill
    travel.
    Mad maudlin goes
    On dirty toes
To save her shoes from
    gravel.
My griefs make satyrs civil,
The nymphs forgo their horn-
    ing
    The fairies no more
    Mislead me sore
All the night till morning.

(horning as above is cuckold-ing and lechery.)

Last of all Stanzas is:
O come, O come where Death
    lies,

Chorus:
Yet I will sing bonny mad
    boys
Bedlam boys are bonny,
    They still go bare
    And live on air
And want no drink or money.

so:
The night birds take the dark-
    ness
And hoarsely rail and weep;
    Juno, Silenus,
    Vulcan, Venus
Pair off in drunken sleep.
By ways most foul, by newt
    and owl,
With meteor to guide me
    I nightly haste
    To keep me chaste
From those that would
    bestride me.

In fiery fairy meadow
And moonlight-maddened
    hollow
    My Tom and I
    In mud shall lie
And melt the moon to tallow.

And tom:
Broad backed is she, and
    wistful
At beast with backs the
    dearest;
    But those who burn
    For Maud wait turn,
For Maud adores the dearest.
Apollo found I poaching,
Where my Maud lay
    a-sleeping.
    I owned him brave
    That he should crave
such a Raven in his
    keeping.

To feast and bout unending;
    Boor and blade
    And whore and maid
There find alike befriending.
Thru   red   hung   chambers
    passed I
To where Death sat
    a-sleeping:
    Here, fool, he said
    Is flagon and bed,
And an end to all they weep-
    ing.

In Percy's reliques I also
found these interesting lines:

Pluto laughs & Proserpine is
    glad
To see poor naked Tom
    O Bedlam, mad
        and
Last night I heard the dog
    star bark.
Mars met Venus in the dark.
        and
Forthe from mie sad and
    darksome cell,
Or from the deepe abysse of
    Hell.
MAD TOM IS COME INTO
    THE WORLDE AGAINE,
To see if he can cure his dis-
    tempered brain.

    The heavy line I'll use on
P.2 all alone of the Vision. (I
found holmes used it as refrain of poem last year)

    The man who knew all these and wrote great ballads on same
theme was Wb.Yeats—Using Old Tom the Lunatic and Crazy Jane

for his couple.—till, as Yeats said (after crazy Jane's)
      A woman may be proud and stiff
      When on love intent
      But love has pitched his mansion in
      The place of excrement) in his 70th year or so.
   I had to "shut her mouth when her language became too foul.)"
   Also very interestingly, the stanza form that Jack and I concoct-
ed for pull my daisy, without knowing the Bedlam ballads, was
almost exactly the same:
      This token mug I tup
      Runneth over broken
         Pull my daisy
         Tip my cup
      All my doors are open   equals one half the
ten line Bedlam stanzas (the 5 line fragments I quoted I took out of
otherwise dull stanzas.)
Now: Next (I am purposely putting off what I have to say about
      your Tale of Joan which I read this week)
   Jack took his mama down to N. Carolina this week; so Joan his
wife threw a "hen party" last nite for Liz, marian holmes, etc.
   Mardine and I have broke up mostly. Aint seen Dustbin since
she came back from 3 week trip home west.
   Saw Peter Van Meter a few times, not longer than 5 min at a
time in new bar off Sheridan Sq., Louis', which is NEW hangout
san remo having recently (suddenly without explanation) died a
kings death: long live the king. Also run across larry rivers a
few times, but no spark as yet.
   You knew bill sent up his novel; now he sent up some revisions.
I have 65 $$ from back taxes coming in few months and intend to
go to Mexico at last for a month this summer, with Claude and Liz
in car: also Jack says he thinks he and Joan will join party, moving
there permanently, if there's enuf money; probably by Aug or
Sept.—depending on when Claude gets car.
   I saw Diana 3 times for lunch and she is quite upset, since all is
in confusion, not so much amatorily (I think she's cured) but finan-
cially. She consulted my brother, but nothing yet has been done, I
think. She's ready to do something, as she feels you ran out on
bargain.
   Claude wrote a short story which was not so inspired in writing
in prose, but had shakespearian base; about old man (Fields,
except real aristocrat) and grandson showing him clubhouse, and
old man dying from exertion of fence-climbing to see. Shakespear-
ian base was images of yellow spring tips of green trees and
oldman's bedstead of polished aged walnut; jungle spring choking
winter.
   Holmes finished his book and I notice an improvement in his
soul, seems older and freer.

Carl left for Mexico with wife and has'nt been heard from yet.

I am still working at Empire state on and off and now looking again for jobbe.

I spent a lot of time with seymour, may move in with him for a month and half till he goes to England. He's played me a lot of fantastic modern music, which I am beginning to really hear now, just beginning, and aroused my interest in studying theory of music for purpose of mastering prosody (meter). Also said Seymour, one night discussing inevitable development of Bop— "Jazz has killed itself", as if from choice like Dosty or Cannastra character, the end of an age. Startling to hear from Seymour; but said with love, as if he killed ꓬlong with it his inner jazz, for a high inexorable and unfathomable jazzed up purpose.

Or Richard, opening up the door, unwillingly, was but Death.

I finally sent Mannerly his $10, and got a letter from him. I also sent him Dancingmaster Death poem, telling him it was writ at his desk. I got a longer than usual letter in return, about 10$, thanking me "It represented something that was'nt there in cash at all." Sez Chase is back in Denver.

I finally got your long letter of Dec. 17, the story by stealing it from Jack's desk when he was out. He was afraid I'd lose it.

He said to me, when he read it, "Neal is a colossus risen to Destroy Denver!"

I read it with great wonder, stopping and laughing out loud every few paragraphs, so much clarity and grace and vigor seemed to shine in the writing. I had thought, several weeks ago, in a mood of passion walking by the 5th ave streets that we passed when you were hear, that I should write you a long letter saying that your all-salvation and joy lay in recreating the universe in a novel that you were writing, but never did, because for some reason I find it hard to write you at length now, except on flat fact matters (like last few pages); and even now, it's hard to say (or feel, at the type-writer) how much I am impressed and astonished at the magnitude of the work you have done in the Joan Story, which seems to me an almost pure masterpiece. It's easier to speak of the flaws, which I will do.

Mainly, since it was a rambling letter, the subplots and flash-backs were a little in the way but could be easily edited to fit right in, but since you stopped short of the ending, made more chaos. Finish the story then, either to me (I'd be flattered) or Jack (also I was hung up with personal interest while reading, not tutorial as now, I was humbler then) and I'm sure you can sell it for money with practically hardly any changes as it stands now. Only

changes, it does'nt need the parenthasized apologies for misspell-
ings or word uses, certain ununiversal personal asides.

It read with speed and rush, without halt, all unified, one molten
flow; no boring moments, everything significant and interesting,
sometimes breathtaking in speed and brilliance—particularly serious philosophic asides like "To have seen a spectre is nothing,
etc." at hospital.

Echoes of Celine apparent, but graceful; wish you'd echo your
own gravity-dispair lunges instead.

Jack I believe has some idea of doing something with mss.
and it would be pleasure to take it to Trilling or Van Doren for
Magazine, *Short Story contest* set up, maybe even novelette. But
it ought to be finished first, in no different way than written.

I remember you telling me story in John at Psych and Anthro
bldg. columbia 1946. Were we looking for Chase? We looked out of
window at Amsterdam and you told me about ammonia.

Take up when you got out of Jail Jan 2 at 9AM, Dove had fled to
Ft. Collins. You went to Uhl's ranch, Bull, J. Holmes, found Joan
whoring in Denver, etc. Also maybe develope or adde theory of
sex.

Be man, not in style of writing, but in pride and presumption
and assurance in idea of writing, we are all peers if you are not the
master at least; not child. No be fraid of winning world, by quality
merethinking as you do, being self.

One thing: whenever you blow "alliteratively", by repetition of
letters, hardy herman, hamstrung herman tit tom tight tom:
beauty of music lies not in insistent repetition of letters h or t
(whatever being used) nor in repition of rhymed syllables (*t*antal-
ized *t*ipplers *t*rooping to *t*riumphant *t*rash), but in rhapsodic (not
nervous) fluid combination of vowel as well as first letter sounds,
in contrast as well as repetition. Too much insistent beat is only
nervous, not musical.

> I dont write a poem
> Take ten triumphant temples
> Teetering on Toad town,
> snickering snakily so slow,
> aping abbots along alleys.

There is such alliterative poetry (Piers Plaoughman):

and with his mouth so meekly	mercy on them besought
and pity on the people	who pain on him had brought.
Here may you find example	by God himself may'st see
how he was meek though	and mercy granted free

mighty   and hanged him high on tree.
to those his heart who pierced   thy heart may teach it thee.
And tis a natural knowledge

see how much less straightlaced and relaxed that is compared to
your insistence (hallucinatory while screwing letters) that everything seem the same, so nervous. Be care for inside of word, vowel
(aeiou) combinations

if money mellowed in the   un ell owe owl
   bowel   ung yon ung ane
the hunger beyond hunger's   un ade ind ane
   pain   un oak ort owl
or money made the mind more   ade/oan inn ain
   sane
or money choked the mortal
   growl
or made the groaner grin
   again

also you force sentence phrase out of natural order and writhim,
and also out of even unnaturally pretty rhythm, dem de, for sake of
repetition of tit tat toe tit tit tit etc.

The above comment applies to nothing that is in the story itself,
but only to your nervous and exhausted blowing at beginnings of
personal letters trying to get going; look for rhapsody rather than
repetition, if you are dealing with just physical sound qualities
by themselves. Or if not rhapsody (like Hawk, coleman;) then gaity
and lightness of variation (partly Parker), or even flowing clarity of
sound (Lester); or brilliance of invention like Dizzy, etc. But not
Jacquet, the hang up. You don't need too, youre too fabulous a
story.

Be interesting to see how you would write poetry. Invent a
kind of poem your own (mine is suffering from being an old steal).

Plain facts is not the alternative to unsuccessful hung up music,
but musical facts is the alternative: "there are deathmasks piled,
one atop the other, clear to Heaven." How that line rises from hell
to paradise. ere are eath ile, op, eer eaven

Jack, incidentally, just discovered Our lady of the Flowers.

But finishe me the end of the tale today.

We ought to start a magazine: Bills junk book, your sex book,
jack's nigger book, my God book; maybe Claude and Holmes.

Write me a letter.

                                    Yours
                                    Allen
    we are apart and I would not be

                                    [San Francisco]
                                    March 17, 51

Hello Dear Allen;
    Once again we try to speak to each other, and its harder to do
than it ever was. I can't piss a drop, theres not a word in my head,
I'm leaky as hell. (is).
    All the crazy falldarall you two boys make over my Big Letter*
just thrills the gurgles out of me, but we still know I'm a whiff and
a dream. Nonetheeless, tho I blush over its inadequatcies, I want
you to realize the damn thing took up the better part of three
straight Benzidrene afternoons and evenings. So I did work hard at
it and managed to burn a little juice out of me and if the fucking
thing is worth any money thats great. For the same half-concious
impulse that made me not do any Nuerotica Automobilestuff (I'm
bidin' my Time) I hesitate to try and force that letter into anybodys
hands and tell them I'm serious about it. I pretend I would blow my
little plastic flute all day if the letter fell into print, but I can't really
feel it, so unless they'd give 50 cents or more for it; thank you and
forget any effort on its behalf. As for finishing it, a snap, a breeze,
I think to myself, but I wont do it because I can't even spare any
attempts at a letter to you or Jack since all the little writing I do is
on the novel. And that stupid novel is a horrible stinker, really a
fart.
    The real reason I don't write is because there is so much to say
and if I begin to get hung detailing everything, and thats just to
goddam much work. That is the truth and is why I fuck the dog
about letters. Knowing how important a pleasure they are will
crowd the shit out of my busy day (and I mean it, you don't know)
and fret out one or two or throo or foo or foodedo a month to you,

---

*A reference to Neal's 30,000 word "Joan Anderson" letter,
somehow lost. A surviving fragment entitled "To Have Seen A
Spectre," appears in *The First Third* (City Lights Books, 1971).

and that a vow. While I'm at it, about my alliterations with words:
why shit man, I know all about that old stuff you went to all the
trouble to lay down to me, and I appreciate it and realize you know
all about everything I could possibly ever put to you, but I like
their naievity and play with them as one will a vice that is passing
for good and one gentle blow can absent it forever anytime one so
desires; example; Doc Savage and the Shadow, I stayed with them
until Julian J. Frierby frowned at such rot and instantly they
dwindled so that I even lost the kick of smirkreading them. And oh,
blah, blah, I think I'll name him Julian Koalters Frierbee. Anyhow, your critizism of my letter was right as rain, esp. about
sentences forced out of natural context, my main trouble for sure.
Enuf on this stuff. And Lyric is supported on bubbles and what is
too foolish to be said is sung.

                                                            March 20, 51

    Going thru old papers happened to see this beginning of a letter
to you on ST. PATs of two years ago. We were both pretty well at
the bottom of our fucking barrel at that time and my few paragraphs certainly show it. On other side of page is 50 sentence
excerpt from 50,000 word appeal of Commander in Merchant
Marine, Mike Walton, to his insane Communist wife, Lorna. He
begged for reconciliation to this dumpy bitch, but she tossed him
over and made off with a really dumb nigger Buck and all Walton's
money. All very goopily felt by me.
    In you lovely letter of a few days ago you talk of poetry, as usual,
a productive pastime I have not formalized for myself yet. Because
you asked for a few lines I devoted exactly 7 minutes to the following ones and did it in the same sense of careless freedom I used to
make "Joan's Letter", but of course, the below is so awfully poor
I must try and explain it away by telling you I'm as destitute for
things to write to you as you are in things to send me; (incidently,
I didn't change a word and used the first one that came into
my head:
        I'm off on the wings of Tangierian Swells,
        For flowing from Fable on Fable comes the pattern of Belles,
        That pressure the mind and weaken the bowels, tis true,
        But not as other things do.
        So, I long to lick the Lymph Glands larder
        of bubblely juices, and harder tarter,
        And makee amends with a woman's Tits; and farter,
        and stick my neck in the noose of her garter,

A plaything's above it to which I'm a martyr.
                                                    Love, Neal

                                                    Paterson
                                                 May 7, 1951

Dear Neal:
Song: Sh. Str. to Child of Rainbow. Bk III
    Come, sweete Angel, at laste come out o' the fyre;
    I'll take thee, I'll hyde thee, I'll make thee mie desire;
    I'll be thyne olde lover, I'll be thy lost groom,
    I'll cherish thee nowe ere thou goe'st to thy doom.

    And now thou aret drunken, and now I abide,
    Knowing the death from which thou must hide:
    Since I have gone tombward for lost love of thee,
    Now in my death, thy death shall love mee.

    What deathe can destroye, time can recover:
    Many a love in the night finds his lover.
    What dreamlike ressurections I have knowne
    In my olde bodie; what flesh come back to bone!

    What unknowne, late and joyfull teares
    Fall from the blinde eyes of the yeares:
    What mournful knowledge is an olde manne's joy
    That was but vision to the ecstatic boy.
    Poem written a monthe ago expressing passing fancie, and
vision, non ultimate, of the return of love from the tombe of custom. P. III does'nt exist and may never, however, as above is my
onlie contribution to letters this year so far.
    But Jack Kerouac, however, on the ball, had last week finisherd
On the Road, writ in 20 days on one sheet of paper yards & yards
long, that he got from Cannastra's Apt. once. On the road is well
written, things happen like in my favorite quotation about restful
truth: What they undertook to do
           They brought to pass:
           Alle things hang like a drop of dew
           Upon a blade of grass. (Yeats in Gratitude to
                                          Unknown Instructors)
    I.E.: the writing is dewlike, everything happens as it really is,

with the same juvenescent feel of spring: the hero is you, you are
the hero, beginning with appearance on scene 1946. Jack needs
however an ending. Write him a serious self prophetic letter for-
telling your fourtune in fate, so he can have courage to finish his
paean in a proper apotheosis or grinding of brakes. He is afraid to
foretell tragedy, or humorable comedy, or gray dawn or rosy sun-
rise, needs help to understand last true longings of your soul, yet,
though he surely knows.
Truly what is too foolish to be said is sung.
You sure are a martyr to that plaything. And Diana called & said
your wife Caroline was due again. You can have my policeman's
badge, like in the Charlie Chaplin Picture. Congratulations; I
hope you have the pleasure of a boy-child now. And Jack said 2
nights ago, "he went back to the woman that wanted him most."*
I'm looking as usual for a job but got nowhere yet. Guess I wont go
to Mex. this year either. Helen Parker in town with new boyfriend,
headed for mexico. Mardine marrying weak Joe, am readying to
spark with dusty. Helen Parker with Van Meter's roommate Yale
Harrison, in fact.
Ideal image of you in my mind has replaced reality. But I send love
to the reality.
   As for Joan letter, dont underestimate yr. own accomplishment.
Even Frierbee, who was in town a month ago, reading it, raised his
eye brow in regretful surprise that it should be so fine. So finish
sometime. Do I understand that it is part of the mosaic of the
longer book? And how far have you got on that? Jack says you will
blow faster if you allow yrself to skip around and write what you
please when you please, what periods you want when you want.
Maybe you should allow yerself that pleasure, son?
   And having trouble publishing Bill's book (still not finished as
he decided to write more of shit.) But Doubleday already says "no
respectible publisher will put this out. Or self respecting, it was.
   Bill writes, cursing C. in a letter. "He's off to the coast with the
Indians building a boat with golden sails to match his hair. I hope
he sails away into the sunset and I never see him again." or words
to that effect. C. left G. in Denver & has been in Mex. some time.
   And Seymour, before departing for england, said "Jazz killed
itself" like cannastra, in bop.
   And I say let fury and passion crush our skulls, and rage ignite
our hair like safety matches. (sounding like Solomon, who once

---

*Jack told me this quote "he went back to the woman that wanted
him most" referred to Neal—not Jack.—C.C.

said, How often have I seen existance display the affectations of a
bloodthirsty negro homosexual.)
   You could gossip about Frisco to me.

                                    Seriously yours,
                                    Allen O' the Forest.
                                    /s/ Allen O' the Wood

                                    [San Francisco]
                                    May 10 [?] 1951

[To Allen]
   Now to answer what I can of your letter, and I must keep it
shaved down into short bursts otherwise I'll get hung with expressing full feelings on each matter, or come up with something
good enough to make me use another page, besides, I've got
things to tell you of my external life that I save for next time; this to
make you answer soon.
   Your poem fine as usual, but an illiterate like me can say nothing
about it, so, I'm reminded instead to ask you if you've ever written
a little takeoff on Hope's poem that begins "When first I Loved,"?
If you have I'd appreciate a forwarding.
   Great news that Jack's finished ON THE Road, I trust in his
writing, but fear for it because the theme of on the Road is too
trivial for him, as his dissatisfaction shows. He must either forget
it or enlarge it into a mighty thing that merely uses what he's written as a Book 1, since what he's done doesn't lend itself to stuffing
he should create another and another work (like Proust) and then
we'll have the great American Novel. I think he would profit by
starting a book 2 with the recollections of his early life as they were
sent to me and then blend that into his prophetic DR. SAX. Of
course, I'm sure I don't know what I'm talking about, but I do
worry for him and want him happy.
   Children, children, the pox of freedom and demander of money
that siphons off luxury, but an enormous sponge to absorb your
love and a bottomless pleasure pit into which I throw myself sometimes.
   What does cryptic line of your letter mean, the one that reads
"And Jack said 2 nites ago he went back to the woman that wanted
him most", ma, Pauline, Edie, or just imagination figment, huh?

Next year or two we might all go to Mexico together in my (then) station wagon. Tell Van meter I began letter to him and had passes (RR) for him, but decided RR just too awful for anyone, still not too late tho, I think. Also you asshole, if you love me even a little you'd get me some t from him or Brandenberg, or somewhere, I haven't written to ask because I've no money to pay, but in few weeks could manage same. Please, if possible without too much hassel. Also tell Van great stuff he gave me and thank him. Is he writing? He fuck Dusty much?

Re. Joan Letters; can do same anytime, not now tho.

I know of Chase and Bill from Al Hinkle who is back on RR and lives 5 blocks away.

Got latest Neurotica, (tell you of coincidence sometime) since Carolyn subscribed years ago, and dug Solomon and Chris MacLane; both off their frantic side nowdays, well aren't we all?

I have $200 C melody saxophone can buy for 65, old conductor owner will save for me (has since last Nov.) yet, since am about to lose car for lack of 35 buck payments will be at least fall before I start blowing on a sax. I'll learn tho.

"Gashouse McGinty" has fair Joyceian center part, but J. Farrell only farts, and too loud.

Give me plenty NY gossip if you can please.

Tell Jack I become ulcerated old color-blind RR conductor who never writes anything good and dies a painful lingering death from postate gland trouble (cancer from excessive masterbation) at 45. Unless I get sent to San Quentin for rape of teenager and drown after slipping into slimy cesspool that workgang is unclogging. Of course, I might fall under freight train, but thats too good since Carolyn would get around 40 to 50 thousand settlement from RR (god's truth, mabe more—only reason I keep job instead of driving Greyhound bus with gals to sniff at) one thing sure, I'll just keep withering away emotionally at about same rate as have last 3 years, so unlikely that I can become insane or kill myself because there can be no further explosions except cap-pistol blowoffs. Have attained a run-of-the-mill schizophrenia brought on by past dwelling on loss of love and guilt of actions, but it is still a petty watery bluegreen and can't fade into a real greyness until another 10 years of steady Proustian recollection of life. There is hope for some unhealthy blast sooner tho because my frustrations are at a near-record high. I'm afraid I've irrevocably slipped however and in my mediocrity have become precisely what Jack long ago feared was my fate; I am blank and getting more so.

Tho I'm tempted; no more Brother, esp. since called for them, also can boast letter mailed same day writ **N**.

[San Francisco]
5-15-51

Dear Allen;
Carolyn has varicose veins of the pussy, Cathy & little one have measles & I am going slowly blind in left eye from little black & grey spots that have multiplied from single 1950 one.

I have not written anything for a month. This is not particularly bad, that is, I didn't quit in the habitual doubt and depression. There is a dissatisfaction; a basic deeply disgusting impatience and feeling of overwhealming inadequacy with words. Especially acute is the awareness of my lack of ability, an almost entire lack I fear, to deliniate any character literarily. Yet, as I say, this last stopping was not too frustrating since it was acuated by a rational slackening-off (altho I'm the last person recommendable to slow down, Time and my personality makes that inadvisable; in my 25 years I've written only a rambling prologue, an even weaker first 20 pages and pitifuly few letters to escape the mediocre monotone of what I'm writing by assimilating "Tender is the Night"— F. Scott Fitzgerald and a little poetry to Freshen my outlook, now that my oolong is gone and to sustitute for too powerful dexedrine. Again too, the RR program makes writing difficult because I'm seldom in SF more than 8 hrs. at a time. To compansate I carry a note pad and write a sentence or two as I think of it, but these caboose-lines are always, of neccesity, the next ones of the book and have accumulated into a number of illegible longhand pages. Being not at home long enough to work these into a typewritten reality, I simply quit writing until suchtime as I can catch up. So I do have an inflexible body of swollen adjectives to attack and shall do it, tho the slowness of the labor quells my spirit. I may as well tell you why. It happens this way in my untalented case: Of course, I have in mind a rough outline which consists only of an attempt to recall my befuddled memories. To put down these happenings gives me the original impetus for each line—at best I write only from sentence to sentence and can't construct beyond this—and I begin to write. After the first statement is out, and often before, I get hopelessly involved in words to contain the increasing number of ideas. As I progress this morass becomes larger and my head more and more deeply engulfed in recurrent themes which are infolded in sickening profusion, While on the paper, in attempting to snatch all I can before I forget, I am soon so overextended—stretched grammatically and logicly to the point where any semblence of clarity is lost—that I am forced to stop. These bunched ideas cannot long be conciously retained as I write and are lost by being momentarily thrust back into the mind, each as they come except the immediate one pinpointed, and the sensitive things, once rejected for a second, shyly vanish in an unrelenting march of steady retreat into their Limbo while I'm floundering at sloppy deliberation in the choice of every new word, and thus damned up my soul is left to rot. The limit of my foremind to tap and drain into paper any flow from my residue of self-saturated thoughts is usually half a page at any one sitting. Naturally, the shorter the space of time between each diving-in the less satisfaction I could weave for myself and each continuing made more oppresive the friction generated by rubbing so familiarly against my blocks. When confronted with these bounderies I had once either often changed the subject upon which to think or didn't write at all, mostly the latter. Now, in my still inconsistent and inconstant fashion, I've burst thru somewhat (¿) so face bigger things. These are more of the straitjacket variety and perhaps approach your own problems of poetic thought, but that is no help and might be something else entirely. Be as it may, the way it happens is simply that a particular word one knows pops out for use. But we quickly learn not to be content with just any word and look for a second, or third, or fourth choice. (incidently, when I first began typing if I accidently hit the wrong letter to start a word I would, rather than erase, think up a word to suit the letter and as another and then another mistake came up I had soon altered completely both the meaning of what I said and the things which I was saying—with all the accompanying change in chain of thought). At last I come to the core of my writing faults, flaws in reasoning, windiness or too tight style, grammar troubles, triteness, etc, so shall put off for a minute any delving into our straitjacket problems per se, altho all is tied together. I give you detailed example to show that most of my inability to get on with the book lies in my slowness in selecting words, more properly I mean my slowness in fitting into a sensible sentence the words that select themselves. My primary weakness is that I try to crowd to much in, once a word has come to me, no matter how obviously poor, I am loath to leave it out of that sentence. Seeing it wont fit I set out to manufacture another sentence for it, in doing so I create more, etc. Let us look at this a little more closely. Right away I've got a surplus of cheap old common words. In the interval it takes to make the sentence structure a few more hit me and they force the sentence into a ridiculous bulge which I must prune pronto. To load each sentence with all it can carry takes time and the longer I linger the more abstract possibilities flit across my mind. Then I'm really in for it because I start switching words about like an overzealous brakeman with poor savey. A compromise must be reached and the slow decision on one is what puts me in the hole so muchoftenfardeeply. See what I mean, those four words just popped and I had to choose. To continue this asinine level of elementary writing frustration you are to turn back to the upside down question mark on last page. I was about to modify "somewhat" by using these words—to adapt an attitude by attempting to be attuned for each topic in a subject matter but when I began arranging the words I realized I was doing typical writing in one of my normal sentences and tho they didn't mean too much, even if poor (and they arenot good words, as can be easily seen) I was about to use them because each one had just popped out in rapid order and because they had come I felt it necessary to try and put them in after "somewhat". Instead I left them out, and its most unusual for me to leave anything out just because its stinking and thats why the ordinary level of my writing is so trite and shallow, and put in the question mark to call your attention to the space and put the words here for you instead of where they were intended to be placed when I wrote them. Enuf. Back to the straitjacket problem of control For me to cultivate adequate management of ideas so as to keep them and to be able to put them down clearly is an everpresent difficulty to my stumbling mind. Incidently, it was along this line of trying to save something for writing until I could learn to make it all one process of just thinking and putting down that thought, that I rationalized into the decision to buy my Ekotape recorder. The experiment has proved somewhat disappointing so was abandoned in its infancy a few months ago, but when I got 10 buck to get it out of the repair shop (magnetized by sitting next to a radio in long disusement) I will begin a new attempt with it. Now, if I'm on the novel I write longhand and type it up with a bit of changing as I go along, if I'm writing a letter I just type word for word as I think of them, unless I get particularly involved, then I write that sentence or two in longhand before typing. In this letter, except for the majority of lines 25 to 40 on the first page and one or two other single lines, I typed right along at my average (a little better than average, I think) speed of—well,

figure it up if you've the patience, I've taken exactly four (4) hours
of sitting here, with a couple of times-out to piss and quiet kids, to
reach this sentence, anyhow, it must surely be at least several
words a minute, I guess, huh? Right now my book stands much in
relationship to the above words I gave you that were supposed to
follow "somewhat" on page one. That is, I have a lot of longhand
junk that has each sentence in it crammed full of stupid words that
make faulty reasoning and poor flow because of the jampacked
verbs and adjectives. This makes for a whole stretch of pages that
are not only poorer than usual, but also has no uplifting line or two
to compansate. In other words, one sunday a month or so ago I
wrote all of this weak part in the sunshine of the backyard (sitting
on a piles-making square of concrete) and got horribly involved in
my nemisis of too many poor words. So there I'm stuck because I
can't throw it all away and can't satisfactorily patch it up. All I can
do is finish this part and try to do better on the following pages and
if I ever accumulate a great many pages I can either throw this part
out or graft it on elsewhere. So its really not too bad, as I said in
the beginning, it just happens to be where I am right now. Ugh,
OK, I stop for the sake of intelligence and apologize that the reasoning of this whole letter would give discredit to a retarded ten-
year-old. But I must say this as it seems apropos; I find, and for the
first time, that when I read F.S. Fitzgerald I'm dealing with a writer that I'm about equal to. Not yet, of course, and maybe never in
terms of word-use, but I know I'm in there already almost as far as
he ever was. I was amazed to discover that his writing reasoning
was nearly exactly paralelled by me. Not that I can approach his
style, nor do I much care to, in fact, strangely enough, it seems
somehow beneath me. What I perhaps mean is that I feel he and I
both try with about equal intensity. If I can't come to eventually
write as good as he did I fear I'll honestly be pretty much of a
failure, ego? no, truth. I realize he's not much and only extolled as
American (at least a dozen, including your pal Jack K. are better)
and I see him as a baby compared to Proust or Celino. I HALT
these digressions so that I may begin the next page clean. . . .

                                        [no signature]

Galveston
Sept 7 1951

Dear Neal—
Claude & I went to Mexico and returned to the U.S. A few days
ago. Bill was in South America on some expedition. We took J. &
kids riding all over to Guadalajara & Mazatlan—Mex Pacific
Coast.

Car broke down near Houston—I spending week in Galveston on
Beach, Claude flew to New York. He returns in 4 days by plane to
pick up me & car & dog.

Note in newspaper I saw tonight says that Bill killed Joan in accident with gun last night. "An American Tourist trying to imitate
Wm. Tell killed his wife while attempting to shoot a glass of champagne from her head with a pistol, Police said today.

"Police arrested Wm. Seward Burroughs, 37, of St. Louis, Mo.,
last nite after his wife Joan, 27 died in a hospital of a bullet wound
in her forehead recieved an hour earlier."

That's all I know.

I am sitting in a broken down shack across the street from the
Gulf of Mexico. I have spoken to noone since I've been here, slept
much, bathed a lot, walked around town, have an icebox.

Kells Elvins is in Mexico City. He is a great man, and on the
scene so there is someone around to help bill & take care of kids.

Claude & J. played games of chance with drunken driving, egg-
ing each other on suicidally at times while we were there. I left
with him from N.Y. at last moment after jack dropped out to go to
hospital for leg and finish book.

Hope everything's ok by you. Write me 149 W 21 Street N.Y.C.
care of Claude. I'm nowhere as usual, not doing anything though
this summer I worked for a month as a book reviewer for News-
week magazine.

My imagination of the scene & psyches in Mexico is too limited
to comprehend the vast misery & absurdity and sense of dream
that must exist in Bill's mind now—or whatever he feels.

All my love,

Allen

P.S. Spent several days in Huston this trip—remembering 1947—
but did'nt visit Hotel Brazos—went to look at Shamrock Hotel,
drunk

New York
Jan 1952

Dear Neal—
I am leaving in a few days on Ship—anywhere. I have trip card in N.M.U. & raise in rating (like Jack) to Yoeman—so get more money & do paperwork, dont have to wash dishes.

I hope you are having a nice new year.

I always underestimate both of you, and feel bad afterward—that is insult you for superficial reasons. Thus my telegram to Jack. Holmes's novel stinks.

Burford in Europe is big intellectual now, Co-editor with Eric Proter on *Story Magazine.* Imagine that!

I am living in an attic Room for 4.50 per week, make 65-70 per week and piss it all away, which is why I am shipping out, to get $1000 - 2000 to analysis or business or live in Europe or something.

I am writing again a little. I think of you all the time old Sweetheart.

I found a good poet in the village, seduced him, (don't tell) and am now feeling guilty again.* What a life.

Dusty went off to Lusk** but I would'nt be surprised if she appeared on the West Coast; or if I appeared myself, for that matter.

Hope your children & wife have a happy new year.

This is what I write like now:

> Blind Visaged worms of Time
> > Crawl over Hunke's face in Jail;
> Phil White hanging in the Tomb's
> > Labyrinth's last passage;
> Passionate Kammerer, stabbed & aghast,
> > Fainting under Love's Nightmare—
> > Drunken gaze;
> Cannestra's face in the windows underground,
> > Dragged yelling against the pillars of the
> > > Subterranean world,
> Skull broken under the Radiant Wheel
> > on the Iron Track—

I see Ed White on and off. Burroughs writes he's OK and out of jail & will beat rap. His and her parents have claimed Julie & Willie however. "If I keep this up I'll end up in Tierra De Fuego"

---

*Gregory Corso.   **Dusty Moreland. Lusk, Wyoming.

he said, "I've burned this place down & I have to get out of the
country further south"—Love,

                                          Allen
If a Japanese picture named *Rashomon* comes, see it, or a Mexican
picture *Los Olvidados*

                                                  New York
                                 10:PM: Thursday Feb 15, 52

Dear Neal and Jack:
    I am living in the same house as you saw on 15th St, Jack, but
now upstairs in the garret. Last night I had my eyes closed sleeping (half asleep) and thinking about Neal's birthday, which led me
to think of my own in 6 months—I will be 26 like Neal. It has been
occurring to me often that years now seem shorter, more fast to
fly. At 26 we are almost 30 actually, and I woke with a powerful
knock of awarenes at my heart, my eyes flew open, I saw time
flying like an enormous bird. We are getting to our age
of most power, our peak. I feel older and clearer than I ever did—
though at the same time more irretreivable isolated in the huge
dream of the world. I don't really see much future, since by now I
should be more *connected* to outside things, like $ and society.
Whatever I want, I still am not what I wanted to be,—none of the
many kinds of things I wanted to be—and perhaps will not. The
opening of eyes goes on.
    I will tell you about New York. Claude was married at a huge
party—enough of social details. Now he and C. live around the
block from Newman's store—they drink & throw things at each
other, just like always, only a little different since Claude thinks
now that he always has to make up one way or the other. I see him
every week. He says, "Why did Jack leave before the wedding
without saying goodbye." I say "He thought you were rejecting
him". He says, "Well, he sure thought right." But he has asked
me several times why you were'nt there, and what did you think.
He is just the same. He likes his Father in Law, Old Von Harz was
standing on his balcony a few doors down from Dusty's old apt. on
a snowey day, surveying the street. Claude came down the street
and threw a snowball at him, "right in the puss". Old Van Harz
said "Well you're feelin in high spirits but you could have broken

the French window". Claude then explains that Von Harz broke it himself a week before in rage, while tugging & pushing at it impatiently when it was stuck.

Burroughs has been writing. He is very lonely—write him, Care of Kells, Turf Club, Mexico DF. His boy Marker left him temporarily on a visit to Florida, is to rejoin him in Ecuador any week. I've been calling Laughlin* but no word yet. Still considering (seriously apparently) Bill says: "Meanwhile things seem kind of dreary around here. Several other people I like left about the same time. I want to get the case settled & clear out." His kids have been claimed by respective grandparents. No word of Hal.

I saw Garver (did I see you since then, Jack?) Who says Phil White killed himself in Tombs because he was up on 3 raps, tried to get out of it by stool pidgeoning on an old Schmecher who didnt sell to whores & kids only to respectable criminals. Thereby he got out of 2 raps. Last rap (non-narcotics) still hung him, was going to bring him to Rikers. But old Schmecker & the boys were waiting for him at Rikers Island. So hung self in Tombs. Like tragic movie. Said Garver "I never thought he had much character. But what else could he do, he was washed up as a junkie in N.Y." Said Burroughs (letter Jan 19) "He was so uncompromising and puritanical about stool pidgeons. He used to say 'I don't understand how a pidgeon can live with himself.' I guess Phil could'nt after what he did. Even so I still have'nt changed my opinion of Phil."

Dusty has returned and has new greater apartment with shy frightened mother at 19 Barrow Street—same place as Henri Cru used to live, right around corner from Louis' Bar. I dream of marrying her but don't have the force or money, and we don't love each other. We are great tired friends now—we talk a lot, sleep once in a while, but never screw. I am, myself, getting tired of sex. Which reminds me of a Limerick I used to know:

"There once was a young man from Datchet
Who chopped off his cock with a hatchet,
And said "Well, that's over,
But my little dog Rover
Is hungry. Here Rover! Now catch it."

The great line is the third. This reminds me of a joke I once told you. Carl S. and I were sitting around with a Subterranean in his old pad on 17th Street. The third guy was a young villager I had met briefly several years earlier—tall, thin, rather big boned, white faced and pale, with (as I remember) dark? hair. He was

*James Laughlin, publisher of New Directions books.

reputed to be one of the most intelligent people, an apocalyptic,
and poet. He said very little, was not surly, though, just very silent
and too gone hipwise to talk. So Carl and I embarked on a conver-
sational conspiracy—we told silly jokes, limericks, dirty jokes—
very neighborly like and relaxed & dull (including the above
limerick.) Suddenly John Hoffman (the subterranean, whose name
and fortune you know) started to tell a joke, in a very straight and
low voice—he had a lugubrious solemn voice, very deep and
weary.

"There was a cat who killed his mother—to collect on the insurance. They lived in an old house in Frisco and he did'nt get along
with her anyway. He wanted to collect the insurance on her so he
could take things cool for a change. But he knocked her off with
a hatchet and suddenly he dug that if he tried to collect on her,
he'd wind up taking a murder rap instead. So he decided not to
blow his top and he finished off the job by chopping up her anato-
my carefully; and every night he'd pick up a leg, or a shoulder, put
it in a paper bag, and carry it out to the city dump. So he got rid of
his old lady piece by piece until on the last night, he was beginning
to breathe easier again. He was walking down the street toward
the dump and he had in his paper bag her heart, the last of her
corpse. Just when he went to cross the street he slipped off the
curb unexpectedly & went down, falling right on top of the bag,
squashing it. He almost blew his top and picked himself up,
cursing, when all of a sudden he heard a sad, frightened voice;
"Did I hurt you, son?"

I remember how his story shocked me, it fell like a maniacal
bombshell, told in that solemn & world empty voice. That's the
deepest I remember of Hoffman.

I see you are digging Lamantia, who is a very interesting chap.
Neal, I remember, met him (and possibly H.) years ago at
Solomon's. Give him my regards, I am glad you know each other.
Of course he's cool—but did I ever tell you how, in the long space
of dreary time when Jack was away, & Claude up the river, and I
had not met Neal, I used to haunt the Art Library at Columbia, in a
post Rimbaud love, and read Surrealist Magazines. Well, I was
astounded one day, when in VVV (3 V's) a N.Y. Transplantation of
the style, a Magazine like View, I ran into the poems of 13 year old
Lamantia (1945-4)—and I even remember envying and admiring
him. I even remember two lines from a meaningless poem
                      at the bottom of the Lake
                      at the bottom of the Lake
a refrain of some sort. I followed his career vaguely, & ran into him

in N.Y. also 2 years ago with great joy at the widening circle. Now you have him around.

Send *me* some Peyotte. Who else you know? How about digging Henry Miller?

Carl is serious about Neal's manuscript. Neal, get to it, honey lamb. He'll give you money & you are a great man.

How I miss both of you, and wish I were there with you so that we could share hearts again. I know I am hard to get along with & proud—I insulted Jack before he left & felt many twinges of sadness—that's what I meant in the telegram. I only hope that you two are not laughing at me or mocking me when I am here away from your warmth. Write me, I think about you all the time, and have no one to talk to as only we can talk.

So I have been reading a lot of things—Balzac (Goriot & Distinguished Provincial) Herman Hesse, Kafka's great Diaries, Faulkner's Requiem & Soldier's Pay, Cumming's Enormous Room, W C Williams Autobiography, R. Lowell's Poetry, Goethe's Werther, Lawrence's Plumed Serpent, Hardy's Jude the Obscure; Gogol's unknown novels; Stendhal's Charterhouse, Anson's Essays on Auden; Holmes's Book, Genet's Miracle of the rose, etc. Genet is the most beautiful. He is also a great poet, I am translating a Poem called Le condamne a Mort (Man in Death Cell)—Maurice Pilorge, his lover says—a long poem—65 huge Dakar Doldrums—pornographic stanzas of Love—great as Bateau Ivre. In the Cell, he says—

1. "Ne chante pas ce soir les "Costeauds de La Lune" "
    (Tonite dont sing ι.~ the "Hoods of the Moon."
2. Gamin d'or sois ρ.utôt princesse d'un tour
    (Golden boy, go be a Princess in a tower)
3. Revant melancholique a notre pauvre amour
    (With a melancholy dream of our poor love)
4. ou sois le mousse blonde qui veille a la grand' hune.
    (or be the blond cabinboy up on the mast")
         (like Melville's dream)

The stanza before goes

Dis moi quel malheur fou fait eclater ton oeil
D'un desespir si haut . . .

Tell me, what cra,y unhappiness lit up your eye with a despair so high . . . etc.

Well there's a loι of great golden-obscene poetry—I cant have time to write it, like

"Enfant d'honneur si beau/corrone/ de lilas!

/Penche/-toi mon lit, laisse ma /queue/ qui monte
Frapper ta joues Doreé; Ecoute, Il te reconte
Ton amant assasin, sa geste un mille eclats"

(Child of honor so beautiful crowned with Lilacs
Lean on my bed, let my raised cock
Beat on your golden cheek; Listen, it tells you,
Your murdered love, his gesture of a 1000 insights)
and
Le chanson qui traverse un monde tenebreau
The song which crosses the shadowy world
Les matins solonnelles, la rheum, la cigarette, etc.
    solemn mornings   flegm   cigarettes
But the best is a long section calling on the sexual universe to
breake open the walls of the jail—
"O viens mon beau soleil, o viens ma nuite de'Espagne
O Come my beautiful sun, o come my Spanish nights
Arrive dans mes yeux qui sera morts demain
Arrive in my eyes which will be dead tomorrow
            etc.
O viens mon ciel de rose, o ma corbeille blonde.
Visite dans la nuit ton condamne a mort
Arrache-toi la chair, tue, esclade, mords,
Mais viens! Pose ta joue contra ma tete ronde.

Nous n'avions pas fini de nous parler
    d'amour.
Nous n'avions pa fini de fumer nos   Gitanes are the
    gitanes.   cheapest cigarette
On peut se demander pourquoi les cours   on the market
    dondamne
Un assasin si beau qu'il fait palier le jour

O Come my Sky of Roses, O my blonde Crow,
Visit in the night your man condemned to death,
Tear apart the Flesh, Kill, ascend, bite,
But Come! Lean your cheek against my shaved head.

We didn't have enough time to finish talking together about
    love.
We did'nt have time to finish smoking our cigarettes,
I've got to ask why the courts condemned
A Murderer so beautiful he made the dawn pale.
(My translation is not above, that's just a literal.)
    Well, so much for that. Dig the French tho.
    Also I have been writing poetry again—I think my sterility of

last 2 years is over. I enclose, in ink, a long ballad. I wrote it in
stanzas

> I came home from the movies
> With nothing on my mind
> Trudging up 8th Avenue
> To 15th, almost Blind etc.*

but have collapsed the lines for experiment in this copy. The
(1) marks the end of the line. 2 long lines = 1 stanza, or 4 short
lines. The poem is unfinished. See appendix I & II

Also	*An Interesting Couple*
	"When the movie was over
	and you and I walked
She	Up Times Sq. with each other
	We hardly even talked.
	What was it we said?
	What was it we thought?"
Refrain	Lover said to Lover
	Naked in the bed.
	"While walking I wondered
	If I had by heart at last
	The speeches I blundered
Me	Reciting in the past.
	I said I was sad, instead,
	and my heart was self-aghast"
Louanne? Dusty?	"You said you were sad so sweetly
	I wanted to be your whore
	So I undressed completely
she	As I never had done before.
	Forget what you left unsaid,
	Say you are sad once more."
	"After so much sorrow
	What more could a lover say?
	I only thought to borrow
Me	speech of courtesy,
	hoping you'd hear instead
	The Wild Man in me."
	"O but a beast was talking
	When you said you were sad.
	I saw an animal walking
she	on the pavement at my side,

*See poem which follows letter.

> And I let myself be led
> To a Roaring Subway Ride."
>
> "Yes I understand
> You want me to make
> a physical demand
me   my soul cannot fake
> Well, my loins are heavy as lead
> Like a heart that must break."
Refrain   Lover said to Lover
> Naked in the bed

John Holmes' Novel* is No good, I believe. I was shocked when I got his eyedea of me. But maybe I'm so prejudiced. John Hall Wheelock, his editor, says that Holmes' conception is of a real poet, and that the poems (imitations of mine) are profound mystic poetry. Whore! Whore! Whore! as old Bull uster say; or how wondrous doth the Wheel of the World turn! But I say Wheelock is a fool, and Holmes because he talks nice & treats self badly in Book, as badly as me or you, is not so much of a Fool.

However Marion & John have actually separated. He lives somewhere else now. I went by to see him, he was'nt home, I have'nt heard of him since. I wait developements.

I've been spending weekends out at Alan Ansen's house (816 Bryant St. Woodmere LI—you and Neal drop him a hello Valentine)—and am acting as his agent. He's also writing a strange literary but very sad novel about a spectre of a party at Cannastra's Perhaps I will be able to get Auden essays in book by him through Mardeau's publisher (Goreham Munson, an old-time midtown Ninny.) Ansen sends regards to Al Hinkle. So do I, thank them for the pretty Christmas card they sent me.

I love a great new group of Subterraneans—I pointed out one Bill Keck, the N.Y. peyotl connection, to Jack. See if Lamantia knows him (and Anton, Norrie, & Stanley Gould of course) and I see Peter Van Meter, & may move in with him while I'm waiting for a ship.

I registered Jan 7 with NMU, have a tripcard as a yeoman, but have been going to the Hall, and no tripcard yeoman's job has come up. That's all besides reading writing & socializing that I've been doing—I go there every day from 10/AM 11-/ to 3 PM. My registration is running out, I dont know *what* I'll do, except hang on and really make a ship, as I do want to. I don't know how you would do if, Jack, you came east. Norfolk, of course, perhaps but

*Go by John Clellon Holmes (New York: Scribners, 1952).

who knows what's going on in Norfolk? There are very few tripcard yoemen in N.Y. but still no free jobs.

As for Wynn*, Jack, the whole thing will be easily resolved if you: 1. Write A.A. Wynn (Jollson) a note of 2 paragraphs, saying you are working on the novel and feel sure that a first version of it will be complete on (_____) you fill in date, but not too near, give yourself at least 1 year to integrate your notes & ideas.

Tell him in as *few* words as possible and in as *least* alarming manner as possible that you have changed your plan or method of approach somewhat, but like what you have as a result.

And say that of course you know he will have the final say—so on publication, you have that in mind and feel sure that you and he will see eye to eye on completed manuscript, and you are of course willing to make revisions as he suggests, compatible with your own idea of integrity of structure.

On this basis (knowing that you may have to do some re-integrative revision, or that is, have to sweat out a little extra work,) tell him that contract as proposed by Carl is O.K., and that Carl knows how you want money apportioned. (Carl has'nt showed him your other letter yet)—(and also Carl will consult with Eugene** on legal details—that's all there is to it. Let's see you rejoyce with the Ball of God. Send the letter, if O.K. by you, immediately, and you'll have contract signed & O.K. in jiffy & be free to do what you want & finish book.

It sounds O.K. to me as discribed in Carl's letter, broken up sections and all—just like last Faulkner Book (All I wonder is if you're trying to escape (as I always do) the sweat of patient integration & structuring which you slaved over on T. & C. This my aside, is what Carl is worried about.) Aside from that Book sounds O.K. as it is if it is as you describe it.

Please also write Laughlin (New Directions) 333 - 6th Ave. N.Y.C.—a short note telling him how much you like Bills book† recommending it for prose & great Archive value, and telling him

---

*A.A. Wynn, Carl Solomon's uncle, publisher of Ace Books in New York. Solomon, who was then employed at Ace as an editor, managed to get Jack Kerouac a $250 advance for a novel they never published.

**Eugene Brooks, lawyer-brother of Allen's.

†*Junkie* by "Bill Dennison" (the then-pseudonym for William S. Burroughs). The book finally did appear from Ace under the pseudonym "William Lee."

you're out of town & I'm Denison's connection here for moment. I
wrote him 6 page letter (to Laughlin) telling him why it's great
book. I have revised version Bill sent up 2 weeks ago,—smoother
now, not so wierd Reichian. Great book. If Laughlin no want, we'll
peddle it to cheap paper cover 25¢ Gold Medal or Signet books,
like "I, Mobster."

How or when will I ever hear your records? I sit here & my soul
lacks you Neal and you Jack. I hope my ship goes your way to
Frisco. I dont want ever to fade from your minds.

Love, Allen

I read this over and it sounds so weak & matter of fact & hung up
on details so as to bore you, while I see your bloody-red clouds of
the western flood & Pacific riding by me here to the Atlantic. Send
me a smoke signal from the cloud factory.

> Put a kiss and a teár
> In a letter
> and I'll open and cry
> over you.

> Put a sperm and a wink
> on the paper,
> and I'll come when I read,
> I'm so blue.

> Put a throb of your heart
> In, "Yours truly",
> With your names writ in blood,
> "Neal and Jack",

> And I'll open my palm
> With my penknife
> And send you a bucket-
> Full back.

Done in 3 minutes 2/14/52
A.G.

TITLE
3456 W 15th St.

I came home from the movies with nothing on my mind,
Trudging up 8th Avenue to 15th almost blind,
Waiting for a passenger/ship to go to sea.
I lived in a roominghouse attic near the Port Authority,

An enormous City warehouse/slowly turning brown
Across from which old brown stone's/fire escapes hanging down
On a street which should be Russia/,outside the Golden gates
Or back in the middle ages,/not in United States.

I thought of my home in the suburbs, my father who wanted me
     home,
My aunts in the asylum/and myself in Nome or Rome.
I opened the door downstairs & Creaked up the First flight.
A Puerto Rican in front/was laughing in the night.

I saw from the second stairway the homosexual pair
That lived in different Cubicles/playing solitaire,
And I stopped on the third landing and said hello to Ned
a drunk old man like father time/who drank all night in bed.

I made it up to the attick room/I paid $4.50 for.
There was a solitary/cockroach on my door.
It passed by me. I entered./Nothing of much worth
Was hung up under the skylight./ I saw what I had on earth.

Bare elements of Solitude/: table, chair & clock;
Two books on top of the bedspread,/Jack's Word for Paul de Koch
I sat down at the table/& read a holy book
About a super City/whereon I cannot look

What misery to be guided/to an eternal clime
When I yearn for sixty/minutes of actual time.
I turned on the Radio/voices strong and clear
described the high fidelity/of a set without a peer.

Then I heard great musicians/playing the Mahogany Hall
Up to the last high Chorus/my neighbor beat on the wall,
I looked up at the Calendar/It had a picture there
Showing two pairs of lovers/and all had golden hair.
I looked into the mirror/to check my worst fears.
My face is dark but handsome/It has not loved for years.

I lay down with the paper/to see what Time had wrought:
Peace was beyond vision,/war too much for thought.
Only the suffering shadow/of "Dream Driver Boy, 16"
Looked in my eyes from the Center/after murdering High School
     Queen.

I stripped, my head on the pillow/eyes on the cracked blue wall.
The same cockroach, or another/continued its upward crawl.
From what faint words, what whispers/did I lie, alone apart?
What wanted consummation?/What sweetening of the heart?

I wished that I were married/to a sensual thoughtful girl.
I would have made a wedded/workman like tender churl.
I wished that I were working/for $10,000 a year.
I looked allright in business suits/but my heart was weak with
    fear.
I wished I owned an apartment/uptown on the East Side,
So that my gentle breeding/nurtured, and had not died.
I wished I had an Aesthetic/worth its weight in gold.
The myth is still unwritten./I am getting old.

I closed my eyes and drifted/back in helpless shame
To jobs & loves wasted/Disillusion itself was home.
I closed my eyes and drifted/the shorting years ahead,
The walks home from the movies/the lone long nights in bed,
Books, Plays, music/spring afternoons in bars,
The smell of old Countires/the smoke of dark cigars.
                  *unfinished**

New York
[Early 1952]

Dear Jack: and Neal:
    I finally got up off my ass and went down to MCA and found
your ON THE ROAD chapter mss lost, forgotten, and gathering
dust on the bottom of a dusty closet, the one dusty closet in that
huge emporium of talent, all brilliantly lit, efficiently manned by
career girls, and decorated with the nicest antiques all over.
    Is Neal continuing writing?
    Carl has the chapter and will send it to 29 Russel Street. If Jack
has left for Mexico either forward it immediately or send it back to
Carl, immediately.
    Eugene is reading Spengler.
    I took the peyote, but got no technicolor visions. Will try larger
dose, though had three plants. Got an all day kick like combo
benny-tea. Painted picture and wrote thoughts.
    Jeepers, where is Jack? Have'nt gone out to your mother yet,
nor to Melton Pippin, nor heard fate of Empty Mirror (my book)

*Kerouac paraphrases this poem in *On The Road*, or somewhere.—A.G.

nor yet signed Bill's contract, nor shipped out. Seen Peter Van Meter and other subterraneans, seen dusty, Claude, Bob Merims, Columbia Retinue, Stringham, no Holmes, seen Adams (poor creep working in a bookstore downtown), no Kingsland. Ain't got nothing to do but figure out how to make things happen.

I would vote for Harriman or Douglas and Douglas for Prexy U.S.

Send me postcards.

Glop,
Allen

Paterson
[May '52]

Dear Neal and Caroline:

Recieved a monumental letter from Jack in Mexico, he's at Bills. Carl sent on Jack's 23 pages beginning on the road. Send them back to me here immediately please, Jack says he'll send rest very soon, and need to insert.

Jack says you are mad at him or tired of him, Neal, is it true, and also, if you got patience send me letter summing up general situation for him. I am afraid for him in Mexico, it is a kind of lostness, too, though the things he is doing there are more close to an alone rolling stone—he's smoking with mexicans in mudhuts—I got a sense of absolute freshness or originality in his voyage outwards from world, as if he were really exiled from known world. Can't explain. But write me what happened, in sum, and make sure to send me immediately the chapter.

Nothing else now, miss your contact. He says you are busy and obsessed with "complete all-the-way-down-the-line materialistic money and stealing-groceries Anxieties," etc. etc. also said he was happy there.

What is state of your writing? Write me or Carl on that immediately. I am trying to arrange for issue of Burford New Story, I'll edit it and publish us all together alone at once, so want to use whatever you got. Jack has some—your letter of 2 years ago?

Love,
Allen

Are you in Frisco even? What's going on around there anyway?

[San Francisco]
May 20, 52

Dear Allen;
    You're the same great wonderful guy and I'm more of a bum
than ever so, tho I love to get your letters, I can't think of a damn
thing.
    I meant to tell you that I was struck that your reaction to some-
thing was exactly similar to mine about whatever the damn thing
was; coincidence.
    Just finished 7000 mile car trip SF, S Barbara, Los Angeles,
S Diago, Nogales, Elpaso, N Orleans, Nashville, K city, Denver,
Albaquerque, SF.
    Back on brakie grind until Dec. will write on book if can get
started. You can publish my Joan letter, I'll polish it if necessary.
    Why don't you come out here? nice place if one likes it. Be
brakie and make lots money. Or write in attic and make love to wife
and me.

                                           [No signature]

                                           416 E. 34 Street
                                           Paterson, N.J.
                                           30 May 1952

Dear Mrs. Cassady:
    How is you, after all. I know I have always been a beat cock-
sucker in your imagination; but I never meant you no harm personally. In fact as I see things now I think maybe you been through the
mill bad, always been sorry I contributed to the privation; but in
extenuation my part was very small in fact it was jess part of
everybodys fate. Too bitter to forgive, I hope not.
    Take care of the children (that means Jack too and Nealo) as
everybody will all ultimately be saved, including you, I'm sure, in
fact I think that's happened to The Cassadys already, however
much as Jack says Neal is half deaf and walks around unlistening
like a Zombie and is a most unreassuring character, always
seemed he was listening to his sores.
    I plan no immenent invasion of Frisco but would like to some day

and hope I will be welcome to you and we can be friends. You always seem alright to me. Jack likes you but is afraid of you. (you know?). I wonder how you feel about him.

Yours,
Allen the Stranger

New York
July 3, 1952

Dear Neal:

Why'nt you answer my last letter? Too flip?

I have your manuscript beginning of novel from Carl. I would send it to you but I think there's a chance of publishing the section beginning with your own remembrances (excluding the historical preface) in the New Directions annual anthology. I'll give it to them, they may not take it, or they may—we'll see.

I reread it incidentally. I thought the parent's intro was too tight and in a way dull, except for moments like the porch—or Harper's dump house. Maybe it's the strain of point of view or strain of writing; and maybe as it is it would still be appropriate for a beginning when the whole thing is done.

The main body, where you begin with yourself is very good and swings and is actually interesting to read (to a total objective outsider's eyes). I think it's ripe enough to try to publish as is.

I don't know where your long autobiographical letter is—has Jack got it? or you? I dont, maybe you know who does.

New Directions took a few (2 or 4) of my poems—ones which were prose-poems, in paragraphs—for this same annual.

I have'nt heard anything from Bufford at New Story, he must have thought I was crazy maybe. That's O.K. as I have new U.S. Connections slowly opening up.

I am writing Kenneth Rexroth today. He lives in Frisco, believes in Williams, has a lot to do with New Directions poetry selections, and with a big new international magazine named *perspective*. Lamantia (Philip) gave me his address. I ask him to publish my own poetry and Jaime De Angulo's (great poems) in his connections. If he says he'll try, I'll send you my book (with W.C.W.'s introduction) for you to read and then deliver to him by car if you'll do it. He's an old guy, not really great as writer, too hung up on booklearning, but he does dig all the young subterranean cats like Lamantia.

I saw Lamantia for an evening—he's a nice boy like I thought and intellectualy experienced but he's not big enough and is all hung up on being a cabalistic type mystic. He's no ignu, but nice. He could'nt give me much account of your visit, which I tried to get from him—sure sign of lack of soul on his part.

Carl and I may also start our own magazine, and call it *Crazy*—; but only hi-class stuff in it, no Lamantia bullshit about the green guts perched on the churchpole and "real reality redness of the real" on peyote. That dont say nothing much. Lots of young kids like us got the right idea but don't have no reality in what they put down on paper.

Jack's book arrived* and it is a holy mess—it's great allright but he did everything he could to fuck it up with a log of meaningless bullshit I think, page after page of surrealist free association that don't make sense to anybody except someone who has blown Jack. I don't think it can be published anywhere, in its present state. I know this is an awful hangup for everyone concerned—he must be tired too—but that's how it stands I think. Your tape conversations were good reading, so I could hear what was happening out there —but he put it in entire and seemingly un unified so it just skips back and forth and touches on things momentarily and refers to events nowhere else in the book; and finally it appears to objective eye so diffuse and disorganized—which it is, on purpose—that it just *don't make*. Jack knows that too, I'll bet—why is he tempting rejection and fate? fucking spoiled child, like all of us maybe, but goddam it it ain't *right* to take on so paranoiac just to challenge and see how far you can go—when there's so much to say and live and do now, how hard it is albeit. Jack is an ignu and I all bow down to him, but he done fuck up his writing money-wise, and also writing wise. He was not experimenting and exploring in new deep form, he was purposely just screwing around as if anything he did no matter what he did, was O.K. no bones attatched. Not purposely, I guess, just drug out & driven to it and in a hole in his own head—but he was in a hole. I dont know what he'll say when I say this to him—he comes back to N.Y. this week or next I think—and how he'll make out, with all this shit to shovel around, I duno. I will try to help but I feel so evil when I not *agree* in blindness. Well shit on this you git the point.

Bill's contract is signed & sent down to him, so that's all over. I

Visions of Cody.

have'nt heard about my own book.

My unemployment compensation is running out; Dusty and I are separating residences (on friendly basis); I will be poor again in 2 weeks and don't know where to turn. I started trying to get back to work kicks yesterday, but nothing's turned up and I'm feeling -weak. I guess I will find something by next week however, I have to, and I feel it closing in on me.

I will stay on in N.Y. longer. When I begin wandering in space, and among the suberraneans, and into the hung-up literary corridors, I get hung up on everything but the real pressures—money, love. Anyway I want to set myself up independent again, with a small apartment, a steady secure job, start laying again. With dusty I seldom lay and it is no good really, though I like her alright.

I still have love longings and yet have not in my lifetime founded a relationship with anyone which is satisfactory and never will unless I change and grow somehow out of this egoistic greyness and squalor. Drifting like I am or could would leave me with no hope but stolen fruits. I had begun to get hung up on the metaphysical Image and the subterranean peyotelites here—Must stop *playing* with my life in a disappointed grey world. Maybe go back to analysis. I am miserable now—not feeling unhappiness, just lack of *life* comming to me and comming out of me—resignation to getting nothing and seeking nothing, staying behind shell. The glare of unknown love, human, unhad by me,—the tenderness I never had. I dont want to be just a nothing, a sick blank, withdrawal into myself forever. I cant turn to you for that any more, can't come to Frisco for you, because how much you love me, it is still something wrong, not complete, not still enough, not—god knows what not—you know how I was before and what I am, my hangups—do you think that is all I shall get ever, so that is why I should come out? Maybe that is not bad idea but I still want to seek more. I suppose maybe I'm looking too hung-up at a simple sociable proposition.

I guess that's true, too—I have'nt reread this—but I started off trying to say what I'm feeling. I just *want* something, beside the emptiness I've carried around in me all my life. Bliss of tenderness I think of, but that's too monomaniacal and soft-hearted—maybe I should go out of myself somehow here & keep trying to get back to life.

So anyway I will I guess stay here and live it out like a man. What this does'nt sound like.

I am real tired, but it is sleep-fatigue, not work fatigue—I live in an inactive lethargy of thinking and running around and doing everything but what I need to do to keep myself comfortable and happy.

Well write me, I would like to hear from you, dear Neal.

Yours,
Allen

Whatever this letter means I have just given you the picture as it runs thru my mind.

Maybe a change of scene would be good. I may come out there yet. I suppose someday I'll regret not just jumping out there on a rainbow.

San Francisco
July 10, 52

Dear Allen;

First, always, I'm stuck by the intelligence in your letters; your reasoning in all their statements is usually sharply simple, due to the conciseness of focus, yet is often nearly 100% correct, esp. about people. In particular, your understanding of Jack and myself when I think of it coupled with the genuine interest your soul engenders for your letters, and indeed, operates the entire lever for your powerful wise attitude toward everything in general, makes me know and feel most pleased that you are the most sincere, close and best friend that we ever had.

[No signature]

P.S. I have the Joan Anderson letter and before anyone would publish the beginning of my novel it would be easier to persuade them to publish it.

I'll deliver anything for you. You're right about Jack's and my book. We're moving to San Jose as soon as I find a place. Jack's with the Indians permanent and said to send you any messages for him. I wrecked the st. wagon and must get a new one. Jack's for Taft, 'igh, your Harriman's O.K., but it makes not one whit of difference who gets it, says I. Carolyn wouldn't trade me for anybody and the same goes for me.

*Jack Kerouac joined the Cassadys soon after their move to San
Jose (so Neal could be closer to the railroad).*

San Jose
Oct. 4, 52

Dear Allen;
   I've never written a letter, or learned to type, epypupipwe even
so, with my thunderbolt eye I see my children and me. We are con-
valescing MY sweet Cathy from Osteomyelitis of the left leg. 200
plus doc and medicine and hospital, ugh, no insurance and I live
in front of an insurence agent (whose son is beside neal and John
allen and jamie helping in the convalese) from whom I wouldn't
buy, but I got a whole closet full of weed thats grown for six
months and is hanging its beautiful curly head medusa-like and
downward but curled under since its 6' and some inches lengh
cannot come full unfurled beneath the 5 foot height of the shelf.
Jack refuses to smoke (almost) Carolyn knows and satisfactorily
proves to even me that it has surely made my mind fully blank, still
I do get very very hi, still stoned and happy. Jack is, almost needless to say nowdays, not happy, perhaps is quite unhappy. I could
fill up much copy with seperate items of interst about bro jack, I
am worrying about the boy, but I don't, can't quite, have never
managed to tell him adequately. thiz and much else of trivia
bothers him yet I'm not really quilty since everybody should know
that all of us are usually trying to make it as easy as we can, I mean
trying to get by in life and feel a little peace in the belly and its
hard as hell to do, at each moment, the actions and vocalizing that
other people demand deserve and need. Jack's the lonely fucker;
of Carolyn, who blows him; he was almost capable of going 3 ways,
but hope for that is about given up since he's so morose all he talks
of now is moving from up here to way down there on skid row 3rd
street, to be near work (he brakie now too) and write. It seems to
be all my fault but why bother, its nothing that one can explain,
esp, a moron t head who locks his tongue while his heart pounds
watching people, and the sound of their voices! like in these
marvelous moments which are happily coming so often nowdays
(despite the external pressures to deny my soul its precious
privalege both those of job and home; keeping alive—falling under

the wheels of the boxcars, staying unfired—ten demerits for derailing an engine which ended so much on the ground that it fouled the Eastbound main in the face of all the homeward bound commuters forcing me to flag to a stop trains number 78 to 148; the one wish, so strong that now its become vital, of Carolyn that I could stop blasting, altho she gets hi with me and unlike Jack who goes to sleep or broods after being insulted, tho unintentently, shes sensual and lazy tho) when I'm driving to 50 mile away frisco and filling up all the weeded air my lungs will hold and just before and during release of the minute and somes seconds held breath, which has been exhausted of its vegetable qualities by my eager sacs extended lips, at which instant the mystic spin developes at the heads peak and dives downward to the toes traveling along the nerves with a relaxing rush and the floodgates of amazement are open and every sight astounds and mystifies to manufacture a thought that startles one into exclaiming aloud a big soft "Oooooohhhh!"

Send me my "First Third" please, before thanksgiving maybe. I understand you bugged Jack in NYC, me too, I guess, in San Jose 27. We moved from S.F. in August, the 75 a month 9 room, well built house began as an estate, became a rest home before the mexicans prior to Cassady got it. The landlord is the estates lawyer in Boston, Mass.

HOWS LIFE EAST//?????????

I saw a priest as a personal favor for a religious brakie friend, I knocked him with my account to god for t, esp. since father Schmit is head of Catholic dept delving into dope (he accompanys government agent in old chlotes once a week to "dopedens" talked for an hour to J. Edgar Hoover, witnessed gang murder on 106 and Madison below Malcolms window. The church digs this stuff to know how to combat devil with youth clubs where the play pool, drink cooffee and dance and coo in blue lit hall with great jukebox, I wish I were young enuf to join, the most are only 17 and watch you, with moist eyes under fluttering lids imply as good a piece is wanted as can, by then, begin; or as it was 69?

Love, write soon & good. Thank you, Buddy.

[no signature]

New York
[Late 1952]

Dear Caroline:

Jack's attitude:

a) As I haven't got all his letters here, I'll send on an anthology of statements apropos his relations with Neal when I assemble them. What *I* think about it is, Jack loves Neal platonically (which I think is a pity, but maybe about sex I'm "projecting" as the analysts say), and Neal loves Jack, too. The fact is that Jack is very inhibited, however. However, also sex doesn't define the whole thing.

b) Jack still loves Neal no less than ever.

c) Jack ran into a blank wall which everybody understands and respects in Neal, including Jack and Neal. It upset and dispirited Jack, made him feel lonely and rejected and like a little brother whose questions the older brother wouldn't answer.

d) Jack loves Carolyn also, though obviously not with the same intensity and power as he loves Neal, and this is acceptable and obvious considering all parties involved, their history together, how much they knew each other and how often they lived thru the same years and crises. Jack is full of Carolyn's praises and nominates her to replace Joan Burroughs as Ideal Mother Image, Madwoman, chick and ignu. The last word means a special honorary type post-hip intellectual. Its main root is ignoramus from the mythology of W.C. Fields. Jack also says Carolyn beats Dusty for Mind.

e) Jack said nothing about sleeping with you in his letters.

f) Jack thinks Neal is indifferent to him, however only in a special way, as he realizes how good Neal has been to him and that Neal really loves him; but they couldn't communicate I guess. However, he would love to live all together with everybody in Mexico, I believe. He would claim right to treat Neal as a human being and hit him on the breast with balloons. I will transmit all messages immediately.

g) I did not think (even dream) from Neal's note he is bitter. I was surprised to get his invitation to visit, and thought it showed great gentility in the writing and the proposal which I accept with rocky belly for sometime in the future. Had I money I would fly out immediately for weekends by plane.

h) Perhaps Neal wants to feel like a crestfallen cuckold because

he wants to be beat on the breast with balloons. I well imagine
him in that position. Neal's last confession is perhaps yet to be
made, tho his salvation is already assured . . . however nobody
seems to take seriously the confessions he has made already and
continues to do so, which have always had ring of innocency and
childlike completeness and have been all he knows, which is more
(about himself) than anybody else knows anyway. I believe Neal.

I include his preoccupation and blankness (preoccupation with
R.R., household moneying, etc, as final confessions of great merit
and value, representing truth to him.

What further sweetness and juiciness issues therefrom no one
knows, even him; there is no forcing anything, guilt. (He does not
know?) He is already on top of the world. What to do with world is
next problem.

Jack probably feels no remorse, just compassion for Neal.

I don't know whether you do or don't want to make Neal feel
jealous . . . it's a question for you to answer, but perhaps it is
not important to answer it, or it can't be ultimately.

Jack's Mexican plans may or may not go through. Mexico may
be a good idea for all of us when we become properly solidified.

Love is not controllable; it can only be offered and accepted . . .
you know . . . under the right conditions. As a matter of general
course I accept your love and return my own, but it will take a
moment of soul-facing and intensity to actually communicate other
than words and hopes and general feelings. I don't *know* you like I
know Neal, and love is only knowledge. Don't get me wrong. This
is no rejection of your desire to come in the middle of the hazy
circle, which itself knoweth itself not. Let us arrange all elements
to be physically present then.

I am not shipping out I am sure after all.

The moment is ripe for me to be in S.F. South America with Bill
and maybe Jack and in N.Y., and I can't be in all three at once. I
wish we were all together however. How have we become so
scattered?

What we must make plans to do is all meet somewhere where it
is practically possible for us to live, under our various pressures,
when the practical time comes. Shall we not then keep it in mind to
try to arrange for a total grand reunion somewhere for as long as
it can last?

I am definitely interested in going to bed with everybody and
making love . . . however also I want to say my sexual life has
changed a little and with Neal I want him to make love to me. This
is something I know, as if the jigsaw puzzle were falling into place.

He understands that.

The mileage is too great; we are being tossed around in the cosmic mixing machine. I will make what arrangements I can think of.

Love, Allen

PS Neal: Write me a letter about sex.

A.

New York
[Jan. 1953]

Dear Neal:

Jack is back here. Have seen him not much though. He's at mother's house hiding out, comes in to see White, Holmes, self, seldom—never except thru my arranging—Claude. Came in in time for New Years, cried drunk & high in cab at dawn on way home from Newman's recording studio. Could'nt tell why crying, except general recognition of time past and self back in N.Y. older and (no?) wiser. But he and I not had long sincere talk, we joke a little, at each other's expense, and I feel there's some underlying battle somewhere lurking. He writes very hard and long solitudes, and that's good, while I am dissolute and beat as far as creativity & life splendidness which beatness he sensing as one senses the wrinkles of age in me, he begins to avoid. Which makes me further selfconscious and defensive and cooler with him. Also he always all hung up on noise, noise, music bands, tea, excitment, organizing—have feeling he does'nt respect presence of individual he's with (me) and is creating artificial excitement—when after all this time I want to talk about old life and new, in old terms and new, find new terms together. But he solitary and overexcited—won't talk—though of course knows, sees what I am thinking, and says: "I want to see you and talk to you 4 times a year." However I am impatient, have waited years to talk and now he's too busy flitting from soul to soul like hornet-bee whenever he comes to Manhattan.

This condition of withdrawel from life I find a general condition for self so cannt blame him, but feel he's avoiding me nonetheless.

Through Holmes's arrangement he is making out, has option and advance from New Pub. Co for new novel with vague possi-

bility of Dr. Sax being published. I think his writing except for preoccupation with self as subject matter is advancing greatly.—preoccupation with self's helpless sense of loss of Parents and youth
innocence. Maybe right preoccupation but wrong lament lament
lament for him. I keep thinking he has no adult Claudesque
society & marriage world to write about, and keeps repeating
lament for Mother. New book about 17 year old Mary Carney love
affair. I repeat, no less a great writer.

But who am I to complain about all Jack's rich adolescence and
timewoe when my complaints echo year after year in and out of the
dusty sub basements of my own lifetime, "and curse deaf heaven
with my bootless cries."

Considering the general sense of change and deprivation (no sex
in months hardly, maybe once with colored cat) of mutual life I
feel: I thought tonight (which inspires this letter) how brave and
inspired you were to have in last few years to have come all the
way seeking to N.Y. for such short periods. I did'nt sufficiently
value the sweetness and pathos of your attainment (the 3000 mile
trip) while we were walking (remember?) down Fifth avenue after
you met me at my office at the Empire State Bldg. So I have had a
few times in last months—or years, wish to gather a few dollars
together and go on beat beggarly pilgrimage to see you, but do
not—I keep thinking the time is'nt ripe, I'm not finished up
enough with trying life here—but really do not (as I thought just
now with tears in my eyes) because of the cold skull and further
fade and drift of us away from each other when I might get there—
which destiny seems like woe, too.

Goodnight old neal, this is the first time I've spoke in long.

Love,
Allen

Will write otherwise sometime soon. Hope you cracked that
book of Klee. I thought Caroline might like it—a breath of old
bennington culture, also. I finally got a phone—OR-3-4967—. You
have one? I'll call you up some night. When are you home?

Dear Neal:

Where shall I start again? So long a time. I hardly remember you, who are you? Insult number 1.

& Mannerly came to town. While back. I wanted to talk to him one day while here and vainly phoned him—saw him nite before briefly with Jack in San Remo. In fact wandered over to his hotel Biltmore (really to sound him out on advertising jobs if he knew anybody in NY in the business): and saw that hotel, right near Grand Central for the first time—a tremendous peacock'd lounge I had never laid eyes on. Filled with young Princetonians, pretty well bred young lasses in silken threads with a cocktail-hour—but from the nice country seat standing about waiting for Collegians to date them richly a la privileged New York. But the lounge was I tell you positively enormous, like one of the darkened halls of a continental heaven, with great marble pillars enclosing an open space vast as a grand ballroom, whereon were located an hundred small tables filled with cigarette ash trays and cocktail glasses and *young* people who looked as if they didn't have to wonder where their worldly fortune was coming from: their fathers owned the hotel. Anyway, I didn't get to see Mannerly, he was avoiding me. I didn't realize till Jack told me some days later that he was aware I was searching for him. Believed Mannerly was rejecting me: his last vision of me, still standing lone and somewhat elegant dressed at the 3:00 AM bar of the San Remo in the Village, weary with a book under arm, after years, suddenly come upon like a changeless spectre of other days of dissipation, but now lone and apart: come upon me from uptown he accompanied by Jack, White, and young new dandy from Columbia—a *new* fresh generation ready with sweet but knowing eyes to supercede our own with romance.

Jack told me in note few days ago about your accident. I groaned when I read. But aren't you fortunate having wife and children around to care for you in pain and distress? Oh old father: What happened (but not in T-hi incomprehensible detail) Are you getting compensation? Maybe you can read or improve your knowledge with the leisure. I'll bet you sit around blasting and coughing all day.

Someday yet we will be of all one family.

Now, I am on a new kick 2 weeks old, a very beautiful kick which I invite you to share, as you are in a city where you have access to

this kick. A prelude: I was working in a literary agency for 2 weeks
and got fired for poor typing (tho you'll notice that thru the experience my typing in this letter is mistakeless and neater—I go over
and correct instead of being a slob). So after making preliminary
financial arrangements (all taken care of: I work for Gene during
unemployed periods, do little work, live easily $$-wise, maybe
will continue this way awhile tho I have old market research jobs
to go back to if I desire—nice security at last) I rushed over (3
blocks) to the Public Library Vast branch 42 St and went to the
fine arts room and took out a dozen volumes of Chink painting,
which I never hardly laid eyes on before in m'life. True, I had
attended the Met Museum of Art show of Jap paintings, which
opened my eyes to the sublimity and sophistication (meaning
learning and experience, not snideness) of the East. But as far as
Chinaland went, I had only the faintest idear that there was so
much of a kulcheral heritage, so easy to get at thru book upon book
of reproduction—coolie made volumes sewn together on fine linen
paper by laundrymen in Shang-hai or Kyoto (Jap.) decades ago
before the first world War even. That is to say, tho China is a bleak
great blank in our intimate knowledge, there is actually at hand a
veritable feast, a free treasurey, a plethora, a cornucopia of pix—
pictures, like children love to see—in good libraries and museums.
So this gets me on a project and I am now spending all my free
time in Columbia Fine Arts library and NY Public leafing through
immense albums of asiatic imagery. I'm also reading a little about
their mystique and religions which I never did from a realistic
standpoint before. Most of that Buddhist writing you see is not
interesting, vague, etc because it has no context to us—but if you
begin to get a clear idea of the various religions, the various
dynasties and epochs of art and messianism and spiritual waves of
hippness, so to speak, you begin to see the vastitude and intelli-
gence of the yellow men, and you understand a lot of new mind
and eyeball kicks. I am working eastward from Japan and have
begun to familiarize myself with Zen Buddhism thru a book (Philo-
sophical Library Pub.) by one D.T. Suzuki (outstanding 89 yr. old
authority now at columbia who I will I suppose go see for interest-
ing talk) "Introduction to Zen Bhuddism". Zen is a special funny
late form, with no real canon or formal theology, except for a mass
of several hundred anecdotes of conversations between masters
and disciples. These conversations (called Zenzen I believe) are
all irrational and beguiling: such as "I clap my hands, o pupil, you
hear the sound. Now, answer me this what is the sound of my right
hand clapping alone in space?" Or anecdotes of actions such as:

"Two groups of monks arguing over which wing of monastary should have posession of a kitten. So head man says: Anybody can give me a real good reason they can have the cat, but if no one advances a convincing argument I chop cat in half and give each side half. So everybody comes up with big loudmouthed arguments and he chops cat in half. Next day into monastary comes young novice who spent week wandering in forest looking for his soul. Master say; This what happened, what would you have said to get cat? Novice look at him, take off shoes, put them on his head and walk out of room without further word. Master say: had young novice been here yesterday that cat would have been saved." This is incidentally all very Carl Solomonish. Also story of great monk who never spoke but just held up his forefinger and everybody got the idea, no matter what they asked him. So there was a little boy running around the court seeing this, and soon the boy began running around, and whenever anybody spoke to him, he'd hold up his forefinger and lay his point across just like that as cool as you please. Well one day the monk saw him do that in the court, and he reached to his backside for his machete and WHOP! off went the kid's finger. The kid grabs his hand with a look of astoundment and surprise and opens his mouth to let out an agony-howl and the master suddenly lunges forward in front of him, zonk, sticks up his finger in the air, and stares right at the kid. End of joke, except that the kid grew up to be a famous and holy monk on the basis of this lesson.

Well anyway, to continue, all these Zenzen, or conversations or anecdotes are given to the Zen novitiates, and made up as they go along sometimes, until the novitiate is completely beflabbered intellectually and stops thinking. Meanwhile all along while he's been shooting his mouth off like anyone else trying to explain the sound of one hand in the air, and other rediculous questions metaphysical and otherwise, till now. Then he gets the point. He begins to look about him. If he says "What is the Eternal?" the Zen master answers "That bird over there", or "my left foot". If he says, "Tell me, master, Why did Gautama Buddha walk all the way from India to China in the year 0450 BC?" the answer he gets is likely to be "Buddha never made no such trip, what you talking about boy hah?" So now he begins to look at the water fall. If he keeps asking silly questions, he also is often insulted like Cannastra insulted girls, or slapped around, or pushed off the monastary porch.

Then finally one day he gets the Big point and has what is known as SATORI, or illumination. This is a specific flash of vision which

totally changes his ken. Then he's graduated, goes off to hiding or
into the world, does whatever he wants in the earth.

Zen also says "There is no god." and "god is big toe" and "I
am god" and "don't presume to think you are god." That is there
idea of God is very interesting: they refuse to have a theology or
admit that one exists, or anything verbal at all. That's the point of
these anecdotes; to exhaust words. Then the man sees anew the
universe. The kid in the story had satori after losing finger,
at that moment. Satori also comes oft by accedent or after monk
gets slapped or nose-tweaked.

Interesting is that this is not a small sect but the great formal
final religion of the last 1000 years in China & Japan—the basis of
all later great post 500 AD Jap-Chink art.

Here followeth poem based on a famous painting, with notes:

SAKAMUNI *1 COMING OUT FROM THE MOUNTAIN

>   Liang Kai fecit *2
>   Southern Sung *3

In robes of rag, eyebrows grown long with weeping
and hooknosed woe,
>   dragging himself out of the cave
barefoot by the shrubs
>   wearing a fine beard
unhappy hands clasped to his naked breast
>   humility is beatness
>   humility is beatness
stands upright there tho' trembling:
>   4*Arhat who sought heaven
underneath the mountain of stone
>   reentering the world a bitter
wreck of a sage the flash come
>   earth before him his only path.
Sat thinking till he realized
>   how painful to
>   be born again
wearing a fine beard
>   we can see his soul
he knows nothing, like a god
shaken:
>   meek wretch:
>   humility
>   is beatness
before the absolute World.

*1. A name for one of the later forms of Buddha, I think
*2. Liang Kai made it, painted it—latin, Pound identifies things thus.
*3. the period—don't know when—about 1150 AD it was painted
*4. asiatic name for Sage or Mage or Saint or Holyman.
Apparently this man immured himself under a mountain till he should be wise.

Well now anyway, all this religion aside, Neal: in San Francisco, I understand, you have a great deal of oriental art in the museum—whatever it is called. Really, go there and look at the Chinese and Jap stuff carefully—if you can move out of house—believe there are wheelchairs for such cripples as thee. My opinion is, it is a great area of pleasure.

Remember incidentally, that green symmetrical head of christ crowned with thorns by Carlo Crivelli we once saw high in the N.Y. Museum.

I am incidentally all hung up on looking at paintings, all sorts. And I daily grow hunger on Orient. Today I heard a remarkable record of Ghandi speaking before vast New Delhi All Asia 1947 mass of people: saying something intent in weak voice about asia teaching West the way of peace. Then crowd begins to applaud, and he says as if speaking to children something like "No, please, no, (in a voice so intent and weak as if he were half dead and urgent) I am trying to tell you something which I want you to understand in your hearts and if you interrupt with clapping that is not what I want I am trying to reach you etc." Well anyway he mentions in this speech the great Teachers and speaks of Buddha, Christ and (of all people,) Zoroaster. Who the hell that is I don't know. Shows you, how ignorant we are of the real powers of spiritual history—Zoroaster in West is a vague magical name, somewhat of a seance joke.

Needless to say I am as usual all hung up in every way on the wrong kicks—now I don't know what I'll do about Job again in long run—maybe I should become a social bum like Jack (which I am halfway already without his accomplishments) or look and still make the social effort to adjust etc. And I still at this old age am torn between various kinds of sexual impulses which I dont, cant satisfy.

Did you see Bill's book? If not tell me, I'll send thee it.

And much more of the youthful flower of romance has drooped & died. Amazing how truly ageing is a process of horror and disillusioning for me, tho once however mad I was, I never dreamed it would be like this. Also amazing to realize how truly we create our own world and world-delight and romance out of our own hearts. As if youth's sweetness, once gone, can be recreated in another elder form of activity and delight through the realization that the feeling we have for existance is up to us to choose. One choice I made before was empty mirror. Now I will make another brighter and fuller. Amen.

Well dear Neal, how are you? I sometimes see you afresh, a great erotic and spiritual existance, after all the dross of history is washed down the drain and you emerge pristine as I first knew you shining and triumphant like an angel rejoicing in the strength of your own imagination, your own self-creation fostered in the sweetness of naked idealism. I'm beginning to think that that isn't lost, after all, while we can imagine it—or its equivalants standing over and correcting the material shape of our existance. Dread material shape. The land of blessedness exists in the imagination.

A poem on this subject is coming up.

How is Jack? Can you tell him to lay down his wrath? I saw him do that a few times this year and he shone through his own flesh untroubled and tender.

Write me a letter if you feel like, or better still make a long tape recorded letter and send it on here in a package—I'll get a machine and play it. Or if you have nothing to say dont worry and don't try.

Love,
Allen

206 East 7th Street
NYC Apt. 16, NYC

San Francisco
[May 1953]

[To Allen]

I might come to N.Y. next June, after a May 30th stop at Indianapolis & tho I know its much to far away for plans I hope to see you & regain again something of the spirit of old, if only over bottle.

You really are a poet, you know, as shown by your continued interest in same; who else but a poet could look for hours at mystical & metaphysical pictures & rhymes not impatient I,

except hi

tho you might discourage often and/or deeply, remember the

thing, whatever it is, that makes it worth it; to me reading alone is almost enuf reason for continuing the struggle, but perhaps that's due to the flat-on-back weeks in Hospital, where that was all one could do.

chipper case they call me.

Love, N.

San Jose
[June 53]

Dear Allen;

Jack has quit the RR and got himself a job washing dishes on a ship bound for Alabama, maybe New York, then Korea and—if he stays on, which I'm personally sure he wont*—then a continued shuttle between SF and Korea. So that takes care of the wandering minstrel for a while, except that thru his own lack of scheduale (not doing what one expects him to do) he missed the huge 18 cent letter you sent him and so he agreed to send an adress to me and I will forward it, after reading it as he said I could; right now its in a nigger hepcat's room and will be for two weeks more before I retrieve it.

I got a bone chip still unassimilated in my healing foot so will have another operation next month and tho I have a walking cast on now I can't walk because its ill-fitting and the ankle itself isn't ready anyhow, etc.

I might here remark that your last letter to me was a real fine one and I wish only that I could answer you in kind (good descriptions, intelligent questions, keen insight into me and life, interesting new kick, etc.) but I find it much too hard to even get out half a page a month on my book so you can see I'm really exerting myself, tho its taken 3 weeks and more to complete it, to get this letter off to you and still make it more than just a one paragraph note, tho I realize its not much more than that and not clear or pretty or anything—it might be moreso if I rewrote or thought it out as I went along but again that would make me work as hard as on the book and we both know that is taking too long, indeed threatens to strech out another ten or 20 years and might better be called "The first Half" or "All Of It", so I ask again please

*He didn't.

excuse, understand and write to me oftener and anyhow, throwing
yourself into a letter as only you can and despite the fact that I
don't, as much as I should anyhow; the real fact is that I can think
of nothing to say that matters for my mind is blank. Take heart,
dear Allen, and write again.

                                                    Neal

                                                    New York
                                               June 23, 1953

Dear Neal:
    Your letter arrived on June 5, a little late for my 27th birthday,
this ought to arrive a little late for yours (is it late June?) I enclose
a small birthday present, a book of mystical pictures which are self
explanatory & very amuzing (10 Bulls) I think I mentioned it as
part of Zen stories, in last letter.
    You never answered my question: what size tape record. or what
make you have, intend sending a tape.
    Speaking of which, I saw Newman (Jerry) the other night and he
told me he's issuing another series of Ch. Christian-Gillespie-etc
records, 3 in number, and one side he's christened KEROUAC.
Neat Bop name, too, what? Nobody will know what it means. He
said he thought of naming one Ginsberg, but that didn't sound so
hot. I was secretly disappointed.*
    Did you ever retrieve my letter to Jack, which you gimpily let out
of yr. hands? It was a letter, plus another older letter undelivered
for reason of address fuck up both mine & Jacks, plus notes for a
poem, a new long poem I'm finishing (and will tape recite and send
to you, since you are a chief character in it) plus a set of Power of
attorney forms. Jack asked me to peddle Sax and Springtime
Sixteen** (the last book), so I sent him those forms, and can't
proceed without it, officially, though I am doing the best I can.
Unfortunately the female member of the K. Family (Mrs. Gabe of
Richmond Hill) is also hard to reach, and she has the mss. Yes of
course read the letter when you ever get it from the unidentified
darkie. Jeez.

---

*Jerry Newman was owner-producer of E.S.P. records.

**An early title of Jack's "Mary Carney" novel, finally published
as *Maggie Cassidy.*

"Hopeless and so horribly sick of trying to rise, mind." is a nice rythmical sentence.

In new poem I am beginning to explore some of the uncharted verbal rhetorical invented seas that Jack (& yrself) sail in. More I think of it the more interesting Jack's blowing is. After my Empty Mirror, which for me strips yakking down to modern bones, I would like to build up a modern contemporary metaphorical yak-poem, using the kind of weaving original rhythms that Jack does in his prose, and the lush imagery. I been dry too long. The GREEN AUTOMOBILE, which if you've seen letter to Jack, you know of, does this, at least begins this.

Mainly I discover life so unsatisfactory that I am beginning to use my imagination (as one uses it to make believe stories or heated dreams) to invent alternatives (in the imagination) (Which the Green Auto is a vehicle for). For that (imagination) seems to me in my state present to be my temporary only value salvation and Good.

I almost, almost, took off, at last, toward California, after your letter. I just did'nt know what to do. I had been reading chinks Japs for a month or more, fallen off with a girl I'd been seeing, didn't want to look for a job. I was imagining (in green auto) taking off, and almost did. On a long pilgrimage, thinking to take several months hitching around all over the US, everything I've never done alone & leisurely, winding up in California. Starting "over" somewhat try to get job or career there. Well enough. Would have been O.K. but something defeated, I can't get over feeling I should try to make something of my talents or whatever in N.Y. Been like giving up to become lifelong bum-cripple-hungry-jerk. Anyway temporary salvation came in form of an unexpected call from the N.Y. World Telegram where I've now been working as copyboy at $45.00 per week easy hours, short days, for 8 days. Don't know what future holds. I get some extra money for typing work for my brother & have cheap rent (33.80) so I have enuf to live on easily & beer. I suppose my schedule calls for several years application and getting ahead, don't know if I can or am fit to as usual but will (as of now) try to. Anyway my trip is off. If it ever comes to exhausting my possibilities in NY I will go, and see you then; or if make out well, will see you in style. Ah dreams.

Many chinese poems are occupied with subject matter of old friends way far from each other over boundless chinese provinces (foot travel those days & thousands of miles, so that a reunion was a terrestrial event): or are enclosed in actual letters. Example:

by Po-Chu-I 772-846 AD (Arthur Waley Translation)
DREAMING THAT I WENT WITH LU AND YU TO VISIT
YUAN CHEN

At night I dreamt I was back in Ch'ang-an;
I saw again the faces of old friends.
And in my dreams, under an April sky,
They led me by the hand to wander in the spring winds.
Together we came to the village of Peace and Quiet;
We stopped our horses at the gate of Yuan Chen.
Yuan Chen was sitting all alone;
When he saw me coming, a smile came to his face.
He pointed back at the flowers in the western court;
Then opened wine in the northern summer-house.
He seemed to be saying that neither of us had changed;
He seemed to be regretting that joy will not stay;
That our souls had met only for a little while,
To part again with hardly time for greeting.
I woke up and thought him still at my side;
I put my hand out; there was nothing there at all.

Same poet wrote, later:
Longing for each other we are all grown gray;
Through the Fleeting World rolled like a wave in the stream.
Alas the feasts and frolics of old days
Have withered and vanished, bringing us to this!
When shall we meet and drink a cup of wine
and laughing gaze into each other's eyes?

Gets more sad as time rolls by: another later note: (these all different poems)

DREAMING OF YUAN CHEN (Now 8 yrs. deceased, Po Chu I now
68 yrs old)
You lie buried beneath the springs[1] and your bones are
mingled with the clay.
I—lodging in the world of men; my hair white as snow.
Lu and Yu both followed in their turn.
Among the shadows of the Terrace of Night did you know
them or not?

[1]reference to the Yellow Springs, or Chinese version of
Hades, underworld of dead at the sources (possible of yellow
river of earth).

Claude recieved a card from Jack in Panama—I presume he's
with the ships. If you know how to reach him let me know, I need

his address for Dr. Sax Sales.

Do you have personal signitures on yr cast? like in High School? I tell you these pictures of me & Gotham life built up in various works are sheer manic slander. These people have nothing to write about but the gossip of others, etc. Jack has infected you with his anti-semitic paranoia he inherited from his mother. Can you imagine that the author of the Green Automobile goes around gossipily betraying you to ex-wives? This is something. I'm ashamed of you. Be that as it may, shot in dark and all, I am really much more discreet than you can begin to realize. You can only realize the absurdity of my position when I tell you I recieved (from Diana) exactly the same admonition as from you when I last saw her by accident after a lapse of perhaps a year or more, a month ago. I babbled nought about you, and vice versa. This is irritating, these admonitions, comming at me from every side. And Jack from Mexico, a year or more ago, wrote me a poison pen paranoid letter winding up with threatening to come up to N.Y. & beat me up if I did what he suspected me of, namely, communicating his where-abouts & betraying him to his wife. The sheer gall. It is true I make or keep so many secrets I hardly remember what's supposed to be secret from whome in this labyrinth of paranoia, but surely I can be given credit for the primary grownup tact of knowing what's proper & wanted with your ex-wives. Well! As for Holmes version, he is nothing but an emptyheaded idiot & he makes everything sound like rattlebrained gossip. I really feel misrepresented. Nothing brought home the dank truth of the passage of time to me [more] than your unfortunate remarks on this score in yr letter . . . I really saw serpents. So for gods sake write, write freely.

Now while you may not have me pegged (I excuse it since you haven't seen me for so long your mind wanders occasionally on the subject) you sure have Jack pegged, I'm glad to read. Really when you write like that it's like emerging from the mist.

Really he could publish some of his novels *now* if he tried—took the trouble of keeping in touch with me or an agent. They don't even believe he wants sax published, his agents, and insist I get a note to the effect that he definitely does, before they'll do more. Then they are perfectly willing to try, and *think they can.* That's why it's a shame my letter never reached destination.

Speaking of yr. description of him jumping off the deep end, strange that after all your wanderings you should come on so full of fatherly warnings—I understand & agree—particularly the side remark—"all I've ever tried to do is to make him less hasty to throw it up on the chance that a fatal dissatisfaction might set in on

him because he was not warned." Ah, would that he would understand the tone and content of that. You should maybe write a novel
of such fatal dissatisfaction—your own (what is yours? any or are
you redeemed by your early settling down? what would you have
wanted to do ideally?) Reminds me of Hardy. On this score might
I add I miss the advantages I might possibly have had had I come
thru Columbia clean and with the institution squared away, fellow-
ships honor teaching, scholarship (mine limps and is cruder now
that might have been). Remember John Hollander, columbia
Poet—he is an honored scholarly instructor in Illinois, will be
published in Kenyon Review this year (poems) and growing
worldly with years. My isolation is not of my own choice
the last few years, but consequent on the path I chose or was
chosen by Fortune for me. Cannot tell yet what I'll make of it. Most
horrible shudder of later years was a chance remark to Carl or
someone about me by Hollander, 2 yrs ago: "A lot of people (up
here) have given up on Ginsberg" (up here—columbia minds).
Sort of a shoddy fate, if accurate. Agh.
        I admire your routine, how is Carolyn?
        I will send you poem (Green Auto) when finished. If get fired
again will come out. If not will make it. By the way, what's yr
phone number? I might get drunk enough to call you some evening.
        I telegraphed to Eisenhower last week: it cost me $2.00:
"Rosenbergs are pathetic, government Will sordid, execution
obscene America caught in crucifixion machine only barbarians
want them burned I say stop it before we fill our souls with death-
house horror." Did'nt do no good. Terrible scene. — Allen
                                        Love,
                                        Allen

                                                    [San Jose]
                                                    June 29, 53

Dear Allen, Oriental ogler;
        Thanks for oxherd pictures, I like much. My birthday Feb. 8.
Tape recorder is Ekotape, Your letter to Jack he has by now at:
JLKerouac, care of S.S. William Carruth, Transfuel Corp. 25
Broadway The Apple (NYC), letter not delayed by me but by it, I

mean him, the thing from another world—of his own making, in
which he'll allow only himself. Above unwanted marks of hand etc.
make by son John Allen during moment typewriter untended.
Haven't seen letter, so don't know of Green Auto, would like to.
How does one investigate verbal seas? would like to myself if knew
how, and not too much work.

Anytime you need great climate—winter average 55, summer
69—sunshine 364¾ days a year—beautiful country with oncean on
right and mountains on left—rich people, of U.S.! 3003 counties
mine, Santa Clara, ranks 19th in per capita wealth, produces ¼
billion lbs. of prunes a season, rich land with apricot, fig, almond
and walnut trees in my back yard, blackberries too, nine room
house ancient estate, then rest home, then Mexicans got it then
Carolyn who clean up their mess and make great castle of it. Etc.,
then come on out here to the west where men are men and the
women are damn glad of it. Oh yes, and quince tree too, in front
yard along with another almond tree and beautiful gigantic palm.
roses etc, etc, even old tea-weeds in vacant lot next door. and there
is a great private room for you with great oversize desk, this
machine, Ekotape, radio-clock, coffee table, etc. french windows,
wierd lights, you see, the next 90 days I have absolutely nothing to
do, will be going to beach, driving up and down country, etc, and
if you came now—esp. to escape NYC heat—we would have great
vacation with no money worries, much time for everything, if you
don't come out here now, on bus for 50 bucks, which in one month
alone you will make up by having free rent, food, recreation, etc.
you would not see me except about 4 or 5 hours in 36 or 48, because in about october I'll return for RR work for 2 or 3 months
before being laid off, or very slow work, until the third month of
1954, begin gradually busier season until Xmas. So, if you aren't
here this summer, come next winter, lowest tempature is low
forties, between January and april or may. do you best in this
cause life so simple good and easy here that it's actually unreal
seeming, like a joke or dream, no reason for worries, tho from old
experience I try to, and all troubles of world like mirage one reads
about only to keep abreast and pass time. If you want to suffer in
frantic east do, if want calm and midget auto races, do come. ball
games to see, parades, archery, grammer school across street, jr.
hi, block away, big new moderistic San Jose hi directly in back, so
all year I watch from garage roof, sport football, baseball, track,
hi jump, broad and pole valut, etc.

No personal autographs on cast except Ike's and Joe Stal. Very
true what you say about you and Gotham Life, much sorry please

accept my apology, I knew what I said not true even as I wrote it for sake of faint and false fear I thought I should have, thank you. You always very accurate in apprasal of people and situations, your chief attribute, in fact. Glad to hear about John Hollander, always knew he'd make it that way tho, funny, had no doubt of his success at all. this damn tiny paper, can't write since always tempt to chop up every thought by supposedly pithy sentences, do not work because instead one just feels free to be sloppy in ideas as well, so no thinking, no good letter, only thing put down in here is first word that arrives in head. Great telegram to Ike, too bad, I agree with you, did so to everybody long before you letter came. My phone number in San Jose home here is: CYpress 7-0295, make it station to station since I'll always be home as long as there is anyone here to answer for (I mean phone, not that last for)

Enclosed find carbon of letter sent to H. Chase at old denver address I doubt if anyone there anymore so wasted effort unless happen to have parents forwarding address, I understand Hal's father is dead, but I no mention in letter.

Took cast off this week, put ace banadage on, told me to walk, but can't since foot too far out of line and tendons unbendable, etc. Final removel-of-bone-chip operation yet to come. How's your brother, mother and father, W. Carlos W? Ezra P. T.S.E. W.H.A. D.T. C. Shapiro and C. Sol. and A. Gin? Did you know flying saucers are Bees (honey, you know) from Mars. Did you know I have one dose of scophilimine (twilite sleep they give mothers in childbirth) from black Mandrake plant which even most ardent Hunkies say about that "Once is enuf" have had for almost 2 years now and still haven't found the 36 to 48 hours of free time necessary to indulge. Save till you arrive to hold my head and direct my feet toward pisser.tytyui is Hello from Jamie (middle kid) afterreward making up for spank; she just spilled my beer but that not cause of spank which I don't know she (wife) did it outsidejustnow. Yanks and Giants for pennents, war within 3 years, Ike win again in 56, 4 minute mile by Wes Santee of Kansas State, 60 foot shotput by O'brien of USC, 200 foot discus by Innes of USC, finish of FIRST THIRD in 55 at Xmas, Death of Kerouac in 1970, Cassady 76, Ginsbery, 2000, Claude before you are, B.B. same year as Jack, and everybody rich before IT comes hard for JLK, NLC, Claude and Burroughs, easy for you, buttaketolong. John Allen Cassady is and will be the greatest thing to every hit the world, and remember, like Drew Pearson, I'm 83% accurate.

[no signature]

New York
September 4, 1953

Dear Neal:

I was wrong not to have written since your last letter so long ago, so much more so since you invited me out (and I was perhaps near before the Telegram to going)—but the thing is there is such a kind of confusion and hesitancy about life-moves in me that I kept putting off. (writing—that Is the fantasy of saying, "Yup" was so tempting)

Notwithstanding your desire for correspondence in bed or at home and the realization that this was a convenient time for me to appear—so I admit I didn't jump like an angel should (with wings yet across continents). Yet there'll be days when I'll be rich & fat maybe to take planes and arrive one christmas with presents for all. (or come on crutches one easter-crucifixion day beggared & sore & older). I jess dont want to pull up stakes & move my ass yet I guess. Not that I'm doing myself *so* much good here. But enough of this.

I enclose a writ copy of the as yet unfinished GREEN AUTO-MOBILE, which shows you that though this letter is late I've been writing it, in other forms. Unfinished: you will notice a gap of left out explanation after "I cannot here inscribe" in the text. That refers to the Texas vow, etc. which I've been rethinking & trying to understand just what I was getting at then, (though from Jack's taperecorded conversation with you I gather that it meant then (& now) so much less significant to you than me. I intend to try & idealize it and make a legend of love out of it—a purely imaginary thing which exists and existed only in my own mind which since it has a beauty of its own I intend to clarify by hindsight and make eternal. The point of this poem is to rewrite history, so to speak, make up a legend of my poor sad summer with you, and try to create some recognizable human-angelic ideal, ideal story, too.

Jack said, t'other day, "Why do we always say angel?" & I grubbed around saying "waaal you gotta say something, et. kaff kafetc." So now I'm at a loss what I mean when I use that trite word. However the point is I am using my wig to try to figure out a fictional relationship which could be truly discribed as angelic, for this poem.

Boughrrouhs is in town, here a week now, to stay a month. I haven't seen him for six years. Peculiar how my memory served me well—he is really exciting to talk to, more so for me than ever.

His new loquaciousness is something I never had the advantage of.
I am older now and the emotional relationship & conflict of will &
mutual digging are very intense, continuous, exhausting and
fertile. He creates small usable literary symbolic psychic fantasies
daily. One of the deepest people I ever saw. He is staying with me,
I come home from work at 4:45 and we talk until one AM or later,
I hardly get enuf sleep, cant think about work seriously, am all
hung up in a great psychic marriage with him for the month—
amazing also his outwardness and confidence, he is very personal
now, and gives the impression of suffering terribly and continu-
ously. I am pursuading him to write a really great sincere *novel*.
He is going to Tangiers (so's Garver, maybe also Jack later. By
sincere I mean pour himself forth and use his mind fully & create
an enduring story of truth of life. Will write you more about him
later. He said he changed his mind finally about you and now likes
you as of last trip he saw you—thought you were sincere and allright, etc.

Jack here is worried you dont answer his letter, thinks you've
rejected him & wants word from you. If you talk to him straight,
whatever you think, he will accept, so do. Did Hal answer? He's in
Denver now according to White thru postcard to Jack—has a
convertable.

Cant get ahold of tape yet. Claude has a baby boy. . . .

The new impression of Bill that I get is that he is very great,
greater than I ever realized, before even.

Jack finally (with Bill) in San Remo met Gore Vidal, & Jacklike
got drunk and boastfully queerlike—& went home with him &
couldnt get a hardon & fell asleep in his bathtub.* I am handling
J's books—so far successfully & ON Road will be published except
for whatever slips there are between cups & lips. Otherwise,
except for the romance of cocktails with his publishers, my worklife as copyboy is grubby.

Love
Allen

---

*Differing versions of this incident were recorded by both Vidal (in
Two Sisters) and Kerouac (in *The Subterraneans).*

New York
[Nov. 1953]

Caroline:

From the enclosed note you see what I want to do. I hope it will be welcome to you.—I feel very well & full of vigor and have a whole load of projects both for living & writing—and depend very much in the immediate future on your welcome & Neal's—please try to swing it. It will work out well. Also get Neal looking around the R.R. and if there is nothing there let me know what kinds of jobs there are in the S.F. area in general circulation. I mean inform me on work conditions there. Maybe I'll wind up on a newspaper— I have possibility of one in Santa Barbara if all else fails—so far away but want to be in Frisco Area of course to live in the Cassady household—and I also have a lot of friends & connections at Berkeley I want to see.

As ever,
Allen

Neal:

P.S. Enclosed find great picture of Bill in my apartment. I have pictures of everyone newly made.

While staying with you I plan to be working so will pay you board or whatever it costs & not be a $ drag—also I want to *save* money $30—maybe a week for money to travel further—Europe, Tangiers etc. Possibly—I dont know what eventuality I may even go to school again out there tho I doubt it (though did wish to learn Chinese earlier this year.)

Let me know return mail what your plans are and how you like this.

Also Jack (now in a better mood) is casting around for plans and wants to know 1) If he can work anywhere, Yuma or Elpaso or where?

2) Do you still love him? If everything is O.K. I think he can be pursuaded (merely by a little push) to join us there Jan. or Feb. or early in '54 sometime.

He and I plan a mutual publishing venture—to issue books (1000 or less copies) cheap, at a loss, for the sake of getting our total works circulated—an old traditional custom by the way of course.

I am all excited and collecting mss.

Allen

Also I need travel & about a month's peace & quiet (away from

work & thoughts in N.Y.) to type my second book—or third whatever the count is.

Huncke just called on phone. Will say farewell to him tomorrow.

Alan Ansen (who never was out of 50 miles from N.Y.) is off to
Tangiers with Bill who he thinks is one of the great writers of
XX Century (a vast & unnerving exaggeration but very charming
of him to respond).

Is your invitation still good?

I should leave here in 3 weeks or perhaps later, perhaps not
(Have to pay bills, get rid of apartment & frigidaire etc) (wait for
Bill to exit) and should arrive soon after the middle of January depending how much I want to tarry in travel. I will ship a trunkful of
clothes & books ahead of me, and papers—you can open & read
what you want. Will travel lite naturally.

I am really ready to leave N.Y. as I have been saying I have not
felt previous to this—partly natural circumstances of lousy jobs,
partly Bill's catalytic arrival here, partly wash up of our publishing
plans (and commercial future there—thru with Jack's & Bill's
work I have been agenting) I ever had.

P.S. Enclosed find also unsent dull letter of last month.

New York
November 14, 1953

Dear Neal,

Bill is sitting across from me fixing himself up and he is going to
Tangiers in a few weeks—been here a month—full of imaginative
routines—he and I been having period together in N.Y. His second
novel is all thru—I'll bring a copy of it with me to California. Much
greater than Junk.

I am coming to California soon and am making plans to travel
now

—"I am trading" is saying bill "on one of the most appealing
characters in literature the incorrigible old reprobate."—That sort
of thing all day long.

Forgive the handwiting but my typewriter is out with the
secty's who is typing up Bill's Book.

NOW: I am leaving New York inside of a month—plans are not
yet formed (tho *sure* it will be): I will take my time getting there as

I plan a *long* trip across continent, down south (hitchiking) then to Monterrey Mexico then to Mazatlan on the East Coast, up to the border by bus and thru Grand Canyon, Las Vegas, Los Angeles perhaps. I may stop off here and there in New Orleans to work for a week and replenish my cash. I will start out with $100 or so and will also send you on another $50 to hold for my arrival so I will not be beat.

I will stay in California I know not how long—years maybe.

Temporarily I want to stay with you *and* you must try to get me a job on the Railroad as a yardclerk or something (even Brakie though we know I would be scared of that but could try if necessary).

I want to make some $ to move—can I make $70 as a yard clerk? And can you get me the job? Jack suggested it, I don't know. If not I will have to look elsewhere but will come stay with you anyway.

Too much to say right now—Green Auto I will bring or send later.

Jack's novel is rejected, I think for good.

Our plan is to save money & publish self, Bill, Jack & you if ready as soon as save $1,000 by ourselves—plans yet to be made but can and *will* definitely do. I have great enthusiasm for what I can do, with Jack & Bill—whose *sublime* work on South America will never see the light under the present structure of publishing in N.Y.—I am sick of staying here and *must* leave—for every reason especially that I want to go where it is sunny and the child I am can be happy.

But I will be alright working naturally etc.

[no signature]

San Jose
Nov. 20, '53

Dear Allen;

For reasons better left untold, since they are so diverse and elaborate as to defy putting here, I am not forwarding the long 4 page letter which I've spent the last two days writing to you, and Jack; perhaps I'll save to show it to you and he when you arrive. I have a job for you or Jack or both of you if it would be too much of a drag for either of you to sit on your ass for 8 hours a day—one

could sit here on parking lot in AM the other in PM—for I'M running a lot so slow all I do is sit and collect, the customers park their
own cars. I think it will be a real kick to see you, a man who can't
drive, a big important parking lot manager, ten bucksaday plus
lunch money six days a week and all you do is sit and read or write
and play with yourself, thats what I do anyhow. So there is your
job.

Now fortunately you'll arrive after the xmas rush so I'll hold the
job till you get here than I'll go back on RR, don't worry about it,
an easier job you've never had, Cathy, my oldest kid, could run the
lot except that she's not quite conquered sums yet, and, of course,
the strict child labor laws.

Do not send me any money nor fear for living expenses nor feel
you should in any way pay your way at my house because I've got
plenty enuf for all of us including Jack and will have even more,
much more than all of us put together have ever had, in the springtime, so I repeat you wont need a single penny when you get here
so I advise spending *all* your loot on a bus ticket and get here
broke, now please do this one thing for me as well as persuade
Jack of all the hundreds of reasons for accompanying you—whom
I hold responsible for presenting to him in such a powerful fashion
that it will be quite impossible to refuse us his warm companionship.

                                                  [no signature]

                                                  New York
                                                  Nov. 24 1953

Dear Neal & Caroline:
    I recieved your letter—thank god you wrote so soon—thank god
you said yes—Everything dependent on you yes—Good you have
the job.
    Am writing while waiting for Jack who will add a note to this—
now here is my plans (made while waiting for your reply.)—
    First I am definitely comming out there, there's no question.
When is the question. I am worried, seems from your letter there
is a time need (And I dont want to hurry & worry about time) for
me to get there right after Xmas—but I am not sure from your

wording how definite and urgent this need is, in order to get the parking lot job (a fine job—that's allright)—*BUT*

Now think of this—

I have about $300 or will have, and am anyway sending 50-100 ahead for kitty for kicks, etc, security.

Before recieving your letter, I had made a *vast* grand plan for travel which I *need* for my art and soul's sake—when you see the extent of my plan and it's simplicity you'll realize why I really should go thru with it before getting out to Frisco *if it is at all possible* as far as your parkinglot plans & opportunities.

It is this: I have $100 from Gene, $65 from Apartment security money returnable when I leave, $50 loan from Merims, and $35 for a sold refrigerator—plus a week's vacation pay & week's regular pay ($70 together) totaling over $300 coming to me Dec. 12. I am driving to Washington D.C. with brother (to visit Pound if possible) see sights, see famous inimitable oriental painting collection in Wash. Then by thumb to Florida (stop in visit cousin in Miami for an hr., supper with Burrough's parents, Palm Beach, afternoon in Jacksonville with Bill's boyfriend Marker and Key West. There I will take a boat for $10 or a plane (my *first* airplane ride ever) for $20 to Cuba—one day in Havana to see famous sex orgies & sightsee if anything interesting. Then a cheap Mexican Freighter for another $10 to Merida, Yucatan (Mexico) then by bus to the Jungle archeological sites of Mayan civilization—which I've always been interested in and have been reading about and *must* see as Byron saw Ruins of Athens & Rome (& Egypt?)—the *wonder* of this trip (so cheap)—then by R.R. stopping off at various nearly inaccessible Jungle & River & Swamp towns, going sometimes by boat, sometimes afoot (if there's no other transport for 50 mile stretch (tho I doubt it) of lower mexico near Guatamala (where there are still Indian tribes that yearly worship ancient forgotten gods) then rejoining the old Panamerican Highway and continuing by cheap bus—thru famous colorful Oaxaca and then Mex City & then the West Coast, up to L.A. & Frisco.

This is a rare & marvellous trip I need to feed (& free) my soul from 10 years of N.Y.C. which I can afford to make—and as you must agree should make so when I see you I'll be able to talk for hours about not only N.Y.C. intellectual beauties but also manly savage solitude of Jungles we've never seen—will add to our store of souls.

This will take—? how long? Well I should be in Cuba a little around or after New Years or before, and in Yucatan by the 5th Jan. And a week there, or maybe 2 weeks—there are various lost

cities I must see—then to *Palenque* Ruins also very great. Then to
Coast Tehuantepec. Another week. Then to Oaxaca—where at
Monte Alban and *Mitla* 2 other civilizations left their ruins. Then
(after a week to Mex City—then to Lake Patzquaro—for a week of
rest and vernal beauty—loveliest area I ever saw (passed by last
time)—and then up the Coast past Mazatlan. Count till—the whole
thing should take around 2 months, wind me up in Frisco, hitchiking thru L.A. or whatever route I take) Somewhere in or before
March.

   Now will this so *important* pilgrimage fuck up the job supply
situation—and I dont want to make trouble for you before I even
get there?

   Perhaps Jack could get there before I and fill in? I finish this now
till he gets here to add his piece—of course (whatever the rest
of the letter will hold) please reply immediately or call me (collect)
at Oregon 3-4967 if there is a great rush—any nite after 12 N.Y.
Time—I'm sure to be home then—especially at say 6 A.M. N.Y.
Time—outlining the precise practical situation out there.

   I also enclose last summer's prophetic poem about the trip—in
hand M.S.S. to make it more real—also my typewriter is on loan.

   Remember in this—there is no *soul* rush—really—I will really
get to S.F. but now after being tied down in N.Y. all this time I
want to take a real faraway magical trip and it's such an opportunity that you should not make me come out there prematurely
before I get my true kicks from Yucatan if it is possible to avoid the
rush.

   Your letter was just what I wanted to hear & makes me exhuber-
ant—thank you Caroline, Neal, Jack Allen, etc—had horror of
some doomeful doleful hangup dumps negation of plans but thank
god no—I have a goal in my journies thru Chichen Itza.

   Send on the 4 page letter now, too.

                                              [no signature]

                                              New York
                                        Wed. Nov 25, 53

Dear Neal:
   Jack & I talked & the results are still unsure, but he probably
will go to California sometime after Xmas. He might possibly (I

doubt it for various reasons mostly my desire for short period of solitary travel) come thru Yucatan with me—but probably not.

He's out of favor & hope (at the moment—situation may suddenly change immediately for better such are the vagaries of publishing) for anything moneywise here except routine jobs, or R.R. here, & is thinking about work, so he will probably join us, maybe go there before I do—for work on Lot till I come, then R.R. or ship.

Meanwhile write me what precise parkinglot need situation is there.

Expect me sometime in *feb*. I think perhaps early in *Feb*. I will write more exactly in a while when my plans jell.

I will leave here Dec 12. Am sending a small Xmas gift.

Allen

Mérida
[Early Jan. 54]

Dear Jack & Neal & Carolyne:

I am sitting here on the balcony of my Merida "Casa de Huespedes" looking down the block to the Square at Twilite—have a big $5 peso room for the Nite, just returned from 8 days inland. Came by plane from horrid Havana & more horrid Miami Beach. All these tropical stars—just filled my gut with big meal and codeinettas & am sitting down to enjoy the nite—first rest I've had in longtime.

Saw Bill's Marker in Jacksonville—a sweet fellow who donated $12 to my trip on his own hook, very sympatico—but, and, I *must* say Bill's taste in boys is Macabre—(to say the least etc) he is so starved looking & rickety & pitifully purseymouthed & "laid"— french for ugly & with a disgusting birthmark below left ear—and skin the texture of a badly shaved haemophilliac—the first sight of him was a shock—poor poor Bill! to be in love with that sickly myopic pebblemouthed scarecrow! Had great long talk about mystical ignus personality & drank rum & stayed in big mouldy apartment in slums house that he owns.

In Palm Beach I called up the Burroughs family & was given big welcome—Xmas dinner & put me up at fancy hotel & drove me around town siteseeing and asked me about Bill, who I told them was "a very good & perhaps become a very great writer" which I think they liked to hear said, and was glad to say it in most Conservative Bob Merrims considering manner. Old Burroughs very nice, some of Bill's innate wisdom-tooth. Miami Beach I stopped over-nite for $1.50 & saw all the Mad hotels—miles of them—too much for the eye, the lushest unreal spectacle I ever saw. Also ran into Alan Eager at a Birdland they have there. Key West pretty like Provincetown, nothing happened there, Rode on Keys on Truck at Nite. Havana I won't talk of—kind of dreary rotting antiquity, rotting stone, *heaviness* all about & dont dig Cubans much even in Cuba—got lost penniless 20 miles out of town in small village & had to be sent home on train with man who bought me drinks—so sad, so hospitable, but I wanted to get away, can't dig his fate. Marvellous first airplane air vistas of the earth, Carib Isles, great green maplike Yucatan Coast maplike below with sinkholes in earth of limestone crust & narrow road & trails like antpath down below & little cities like mushrooms in pockets & hollows of afternoon hills, & windmills.

Stayed in Merida 3 days at this place, ran into 2 Quintana Roo Indians & drove in horsecarriage round city, met mayor's brother so got invited to big City Hall Ceremonies New Years day—free beer & sandwiches overlooking plaza on balcony City Hall; that Nite, New Years, formall dress—New York-Paris-London Society type "Country Cloob" (Club) Champagne free & french & english & german speaking industrialists & young Yucatan Spanish girls fresh from New Orleans Finishing School—all dressed in Tux & party evening dress at tables under stars—nothing happened I just wandered around & talked to people, then after went downtown & heard poor mambo in dancehalls & drank little & slept at 5 AM. Next day to Chichen Itza where I got free house next to pyramid & spent days eating in native hut for $7 pesos a day, wandering around great ruins—at nite take hammock up on top of big pyramid temple (whole dead city to myself as living in archeologists' camp) & look at stars & void & Deathheads engraved up on the stone pillars & write & doze on Codeinetta. Free guide from where I eat, & drink every nite before supper at Richman's Mayaland Hotel talk to rico Americans, meet 35 yr old Ginger B. all hung up on Yucatan songs & costumes, dumb, drag, talking bitch sad. Stars over pyramids—tropic nite, forest of Chirruping insects, birds & maybe owls—once I heard one hooting—great stone portals, bas reliefs of unknown perceptions, half a thousand years old—and earlier in day saw stone cocks a thousand years old grown over with moss & batshit in dripping vaulted room of stone stuck in the wall. A high air silent above niteforest—tho a clap of hands brings great echoes from various pillars & arenas. So then left for Valladolid—money allready running out—in central Yucatan & nite there with amigo speaking english who showed me the tower & I ate at his middleclass family house where his wife bowed respectful & a movie about ghosts—and next day awful miserable 10 hour train to town name of Tizinia for the oldest Fiesta of Mexico; most venerable Indians from Campeche & Tabasco on train with great sacks full of food & babies & hammocks; started on train at 4 AM morning rode till afternoon cramped noplace to stand, train ran off rails, hold-ups, arrive at really crowded small town middle of nowhere—with silly bullring and 400 yr old cathedral, mobbed by old indians, candles, 3 wooden kings old as the conquest they came to see (3 Mages)—the air of cathedral so smokey & so full of candles the wax on the floor was inches deep & slippery—thought I was the only American in town but later found a Buffalo optometrist on train back who said famous documentary film maker named Rotha was there with movie cameras—(I saw Rotha pix in Mus of Modern Art once)— trip back horrible—the *boxcars* with benches on sides & down center, wood, Mex-made & all crude, 110 people to car, people hanging on platform and even *steps* for hours—me too—so uncomfortable to sit it was insane, for 10 hours—and had left my codeine behind! (*no* have habit by the way only used 2 times) old women & babies falling asleep on my shoulder & lap, everybody suffering meaningless hourlong stops in the nite to change tracks or engines—

Had met priest at Tiyimin Cathedral who took me backstairs & smoked & cursed native pagan rite of the feast, & so went with him to his village "Colonia Yucatan" a lumber town a la Levittown or Vet housing project—& he drove me by jeep next day to forests of Quintana Roo & back—then to train & horrid ride. Then another day at great silent Chichen Itza—recalling a dream I once had about a future world of great plateaux covered with grass & levels & plaines of plateau leading to horizon with deep canyons between—so at Chichen is a vast building with grassy roofs on many levels of dripping stone chambers & wild sculptured ornament all round the sides—stood up & looked from top at jungle spread all around circle to horizon, dream actualized. Who came up but the optometrist, with his nice camera.

Came back to Merida today. Met bunch of Mex city painters on junket to study provinces & talked french & will go to a big gran baille (dance) tonite (Sat Nite)—& tomorrow look up Professor

Stromswich for info on Mayapan ruins—also must pick up letter
from Bill from Rome at Consulate & telegram perhaps with money
from home—down to $25 dollars, enuf to get to Mexico City but
not much more & want to see more Mexico south so sent for some
more $ from Gene. My Spanish is got to a point where I can find
out what I want easily but I keep making mistakes that
have cost me money from time to time—enough to wish I knew—
like I bought the wrong kind of hammock & so lost out 9 pesos the
other day—

Also in Merida a "homeopathic druggist" i.e. I dont know,
different from pharmaceutical druggists—name of George Ubo
been everywhere in U.S. & Yucatan & told me how to get everywhere on big 10 foot Map he has—So far everywhere I have run
across someone or other who showed me the town in English or
french or English-spanish mixture but have not met anyone
great—except one nite in the rich hotel in Merida last week, wandered into bar for 1 peso rich-man's Tequila and ran into a drunk
brilliant elderly spaniard who talked to me in french in great
world weary Monologue full of filth and Paris and N.Y. and Mexico
City & who was later led off by his bodyguard to be sick in the
urinal—later found out he was the richest man in the area Yucatan
Peninsula—famous character who married a whore 20 yrs. ago &
owns everything everywhere & gets drunk every nite with vener-
able looking Jaime de Angulo whitebearded spick international-
ists at the hotel—who were there that night winking and calming
him down—sort of an old evil Claude he was, full of misery & rich
& drunken disregard of life.

Mosquitos down here awful—all beds come with M-nets & I
have bought one for my hammock.

Jack, incidentally—they wont let you past customs in Merida
without health card. & all the indians have vaccination marks they
wear "proudly"—it's really a 50-50 necessity. Have had dysentery
& took pills and it went away, so no suffer. No such thing as a
natural man untouched by medicine around here—it's not for
touristas, tho it's a tourista routine—it is for everyone.

If I had more money, I found a way to get thru Quintana Roo
involving busses & narrow gauge mule driven R.R. and an afternoon walk 13 kilometers on rocky mulepath thru jungle—or else a
40 peso boat around peninsula—but cannot go cause too costly for
my purse. But will be fine trip for someone someday. Many people
all over ready to help the traveller—it's like a frontier—with
engineers building a road thru that never gets done.

Recieved a letter from Garver saying he's still in D.F. & will see me there.

The man here, head of archeology, name given me by Mus. Nat. History in N.Y.—turned out valuable—gave me pass to stay on Archeologist's Camps, free, everywhere there's a ruin I go. Great way to travel & see ruins. Write me note to Mex. City Embassy.

Love, Allen

P.S. Had a great dream—must go to Europe to make movie about Bill riding on trains from Italy.

Palenque, Chiapas, Mex.
Jan 18 54

Dear Neal & Jack & Caroline:

Since I last wrote I have been from Merida to Uxmal to Campeche (a port on the peninsula on the way) to Palenque where I am now.

I am beginning to really hate mexico & almost wish I were out of it us travelling with so little money, I am continually obsessed with saving it, and consequently making mistakes in spending what I have & building up great reserves of anger at whoever gets in my way—usually a mexican—when I spend it. As it is I have about 34 bucks left to get to D.F. on where (I presume) I have more waiting from the Telegram and it better be there—though with dear old Bill Garver around I suppose I won't become a public charge. However I ain't going to hit a lot of cities on the way that I wanted to— partly no money to get there (San Cristobal, Las Casas way down South Chiapas) or time & $ to find out how to get there—travel around here mainly by R.R. but I am sure there are roads. By R.R. it would take days & days to San Cristobal from here, which is only 100 or so miles away as bird flies.

Uxmal where I was last week is the 2nd most important Yucatan Roon but is the best to live at I think—more glory though less grandeur than Chichen Itza. Have much to say about Ruins but am more concerned with a typical paranoid incident occurring 10 miles out of Merida the day before I left—having nothing to do I got on a local bus to a small town 20 miles away where there was a small party (a Kermesse they called it —sounds French) advertised. On the way 2 young fellers picked up on me—at a time when I didn't really want to try to talk this rotten language anymore—it's too exhausting just to work out the necessities like food drink & transportation to carry on further trying to make self understood— (in a very bad mood tonite having trekked in mud for hours in a real jungle too hung up picking my way thru slime & thorn trees to get to see any jungle though it was there—and thirsty, little water around—and slightly disenteric, & with a lousy cold been with me 10 days) so as I say not wanting to try to talk no more spanish that day, just ride & see & eat tortillas, I got hung up—

The lights there went out (Jan 25 is today) and I have not had a chance to continue this letter till now) (a week later) and am not at Palenque & the story is half forgotten—be that as it may I got on the bus & got involved in dull conversation with 2 youths & got off bus half way to get drunk with them & went on to fair & returned at dark & was given over in the small halfway town to what intuition & all told me was the local queer who began singing songs of Corazon on this road at nite & I really did'nt dig the situation as he was a 35 yr old . . . child effemminite this mexican, an archtype of a kind—I'm sure Ive seen him somewhere—and I got a bus & returned home—Point is not understanding spanish I could'nt make anything of the drunken paranoia—much like Jack's Mexico.

Well anyway to get off this bum kick of incomprehensible story.

I was walking around Palenque & ran into a woman who grew up around here—the edge of the most inaccessable jungle area of South Mexico—who had returned 6 yrs ago after various carreers in the States, a professional Archeologist whose family had owned the Palenque site so that she knew it inside out. As result I am spending a week on her Cocoa Finca (or plantation)—have been here 7 days—don't yet know when I'll leave—located in middle of jungle a days horseback ride out of Palenque. Last week we set out on March, took jeep to path, then she, I, another girl (wandered thru forest on foot to Palenque from City on Pacific, a student, ugly) an old indian retainer & a boy being taken to live at the Senora's Finca—4 horses & a mule set out for 7 hour ride thru beautiful dark jungle—soldier ants, anthills, lianas, orchids, vast trees covered with parasite cactus & fern, big leaved plantan trees, parrots screeching and wild deep roar of howler monkeys in trees sounding like Tarzan Jungle. First time I ever rode a horse—on mucky path, full of little up & downhill wind, trees fallen over path full of hunky-like fungus growths, small streams—and always every few miles a small hill covered with stones which was a part of the City of Palenque (40 sq. miles)—the woman knowing from childhood all parts everywhere, and more, being a sort of mystic & *medium* type personality, as well as *learned* in the subject—

perhaps the person in the world most emotionally & knowledgably
tied to these ruins & this area—so that I found after a few days
talking, she had been on foot & plaue all thru jungles down to
Guatemala & in lost cities all places, some even she discovered,
had written books (her editor is Giroux)* & learned papers &
worked for Mex. Gvt. reconstructing Palenque & others, owned a
few cities in her great tract of land here (hundreds of sq. mi) *and,*
most important, was the only person in the world who knew of a
lost tribe of Mayans living in Guatamala on a . . . river who still
possibly could interpret codices & were specially on a mission to
keep alive Mayan flame—and she told me all sorts of secrets, beginning with outline of Mayan Metaphysics & mystical lore &
history & symbolism, that would have delighted Bill, who does'nt
know—that it is all still extant. This lost tribe apparently had
brought her up as child, being in area where her father owned
$3,000,000 dollar ranch here & having selected her for confidance.
Well all this is sort of corny and amusing but the curious thing is
that much of it is true in its most classically corny aspects. It is a
great kick to enjoy her hospitality in the jungle—she being starved
for ignu conversation tho she is not an ignu herself—& go out
everyday with machete and rifle in jungle trails, on 3-4 mile walks,
hunting, swimming in great clear little rock pools surrounded by
giant ferns, in crystal water, returning at nite in darkness when
jungle begins stirring, talking Mayan Metaphysics. We live in an
opensided room with continual fire for coffee & food at one end
tended by an indian, hammocks strung up across the room, a great
unexplored mountain right ahead looking very near—a few
hundred feet thru the brush behind the house are 6 native huts
with families—who work on the plantation, a sort of feudal system
of which she is queen & we are royal guests. Party includes a
young mexican Point 4 apprentice who is supervising the cultiva-
tion of the cocoa (which is chocolate.) I will leave here sooner or
later by horseback for 2 hours and then by Kayuko (a big tree
hollowed out for a boat) up a river to a R.R. town. Then by plane
for 80 pesos to San Cristobal, where I have decided to go after all.
Plane is cheapest way—there being no way to get across Ithsmus
except by 5 day roundabout rail or 5 day by horse, just as expensive, more so, cant afford—tho horses are only 6 pesos a day here.
At San Cristobal I meet Franz Blum who is a famous archeolo-
gist-Hal Chase in disgrace with Universities in states, an old lush
now gone tropical, who everybody says is the most brilliant man in

*Robert Giroux, Kerouac's editor on *The Town and the City.*

Mexico & lived with Sherwood Anderson & Faulkner in N. Orleans years ago before he came down here & discovered Palenque etc— he being now the foremost authority on indians & mayans & a friend of my hostess etc.

I am sending this by Kayuko ahead of me—will leave in a few days more. If you get this letter send me a note care of U.S. Embassy Mexico D.F.

Allen

Have no place on which to write & cant write comfortable so excuse this sloppy letter effort—cant concentrate & compose.

What is the Situation in Frisco—I am dawdling here & will dawdle in mexico as long as my money lasts—another 2 or 3 weeks perhaps? Then will go to yr cheerful household—I have many photographs too with me I will develop in Frisco—about 200 photos, maybe 25 interesting ones.

I had a dream: Everyone I knew killed (by knife) frightening series of murders as in a movie—Gene, Jack, Bill. Police called me in for questioning.

Tacalapan, Palenque
Chiapas, Mexico
February 18, 1954

Dear Neal, Caroline, Jack:

Well I am still here in the state of Chiapas & don't know for sure when I will leave, maybe next week maybe next month. Does'nt depend on anything for sure, just when I come out of a sort of retreat or limbo & push on for bright lights alchohol & sex joys. Here, I am on the brush field surrounded by big forest trees looking over typewriter past leaning thin palm to a great long green mount, a tropical Greylock nobody's ever been on, supposedly Mayan & enchanted with gold & an old Guardian and ruins near a white rocky bluff, triangle shaped, which can be seen on some days; and the contour of the mount changes daily, sometimes can be seen as being far far away, sometimes seems close up & detailed, especially in erie cloud light of dusk; sometimes seen as a series of ridges with huge valleys unknown between, which it actually is, tho looks daily most like one solid long green mount, name of Don Juan.

In daily walks thru jungle (or nitely) saw a huge rust reddish colored spotted blossom which when smelt apalls the mind with a fetid charnelhouse odor, stink of flesh manufactured by blind blossom on vine to catch flies.

Feb 19, 54

Have a beard, a goatee, black & moustachio, long hair, heavy shoes, ride horses, go fishing at nite in streams with natives giggling with focos (flashlites) & long stick with prongs to catch great crawfishes size of lobsters. Or go walking midday naked up a mile of rocky clear stream, bluey sky, with lianas & elephant ear trees and angel hair trees of platain leaves & giant saibol (mahogany) trees filled with monkeys, on bank or dank islands midstream, ankle or waist or neck deep walk. A few mosquitos.

And every hour or so get up from hammock and sit and idle with my drums, especially at dawn, at dusk, and during dark hours by fire before mosquito net is opened over hammock. Drums: smallest is 3½ feet, longest is 17 feet and stands on a vine and stick support for vibrations to hang free. I went out and tapped rubber trees for black hard balls to tip heavy foot long sticks with for proper bong. I play several hours daily, mostly very soft listening, and when a file of indians rides in thru the trails from Agua Azul, eden like little town in hills an hour ride away, I break out in african reverbrations which can be heard for miles around. Am known as Senor Jalisco.

I read the Cloud of Unknowing, anonymous 14th century handbook of abstraction & in this limbo have developed a feeling again for possibilities of sitting & with stark blankness concieving a familiar uncanny sensation which never comes to me whole, presumably too divine. Time spent here has been mainly contemplative of this fixed idea, and I had one day of excited agitation thinking I should go be a monk, but no need to do that, can develop anywhere and such agitations are passing. What hung me up on Cloud of Un. was the lovely and obviously true idea that a contemplative doesnt have to do anything but what he feels like, sit and think or walk and think, dont worry about work, life, money, no hangups, his job is to have no job but the unknown Abstraction & its sensations, & his love of it. I have a tentative offer if I want to stay here till August alone when owner of ranch goes off to make money in states & manage it passively, no duties, just be here & see nobody sets fire to house or steals cocoa. Probably a very small pay like 100 pesos mo, but perfect refuge and learn a lot. However want to get back to states & am lonely for someone to share pleasures with, wish someone were here to understand beauty of the drums, they're so big they would make Newmann for instance cream if he were not beyond the creaming state in his bald sun-burned pate age.

Plans: Every several nights I have a melancholy dream that I am embarking for the ancient parapets of Europe: passageways, captains, gangplanks, staterooms, bunks, huge decks cluttered with people in furs a la '20s or deckchairs, nite lunches, foc'sls, arrangements with family, breaking up of apartments, foghorns in N.Y. . Harbor mist near docksides, Front Street or Telegram street; and one night as summary I had a picture of N.Y. in color, in oval frame, enclosing Hohnsbean, Kingsland, Dusty, Keck, Anton, D. Gaynor or others, Durgin, Merims, was Cannastra?, a compressed proustian moment in oval frame of all characters in activity at a psychic party technicolor, all NY in one picture as You, Jack (are you there?) must have had many times over from road to road.

So, after waking up from four of these in two weeks I realized (especially after dream of Burroughs on Italian 2nd class train going to spain) that as soon as possible must go to live awhile in Europe—think of the marvelous facades & palaces of dank Venice alone for instance, which will be digged in spacious St. Mark's Square dusk by us among pigeons of Europe & Eyetalian beggars as in some slow silent stage presentation of Melancholy cloaked Byronic traveller passing thru in sad ballet. To say nothing of hollow old Catholic Rome, Prague! the very name conjures a mirage of centuries, the Golem, Ghettoes, stone kings and foun-tains of dark lions and grey cherubs, students drinking beer and dueling thru the night. And perhaps sweet Moscow. Then there is Paris. Paris! City of Light! ici mouru Racine! Here proust sipped his delicate tea, here Jean Gabin stared out over the roofs with his mistress crying in bed, glum. Memories, ancient waltzes, tristesse de la lune, all the tenderness of antiquity & the angel gentility of Civilization, with the Eifel tower and strange city mystics a la cocteau and Rimbaud and most the tearful reality of the old world places. Even wish to see Londres, London of great bells and bank-ing houses old as time, where liveth still in silence Seymour wait-ing for a winking eye from us undoubtedly.

As I sit here under the mountain at the moment of noon, sun white in that green high palm tree leaves, butterflies in the meadow, contemplating a voyage to the old world, having seen a ruin in the new, headful of abstraction and memory, there are sitting beside me 4 Gaugin maids conversing in spanish (I half understand & can follow) barefoot in bright storeclothes, with big safety pins in bosom of dresses for ornament, complaining about their ailments to the senora who has medicines,: codeine, barbiturates, W.C. Fields Wampole drink for the weary & worried, vitimins that would mystify and delight Burroughs. And last week a murderer, having avenged the death of his father (sister of one of these girls), young boy with bullet holes in hand and arm, came at dawn for refuge from law and help, and we operated, cutting open upper arm to take out bullet (I felt faint, watching her cut with a gillette double edged blade) and put him up for two days till rumors of a posse (just like frontier) reached us one night & we sent him to the woods to hide. Two weeks ago we had a meteor so grand, big as star of Bethlehem, illuminated blue and red the whole half horizon. Same day my first tremblor; which earthquake, I later found, had half destroyed the back-interior town of Yajalon (Ya-ha-lone), the church in ruins, lava coming up, a new volcano like Paracutin—though this is rumor, another man passing thru said the mountain top went to the bottom and the bottom went to the top—meaning a landslide? Quien sabe? however adding that the priest who was supposed to have perished screaming in the tottering cathedral 4 centuries old really was still alive though seriously wounded, as he had been konked by a single brick shook loose. As well as a perfect lunar eclipse I saw the nite I left Palenque.

I live among the thatchroof huts, eat tortillas and frijoles at every meal with mucho pleasure, amazing how a real strong taste for them can be developed, like for potatoes with eggs, meat, vegs. etc. I pass bannana groves & work in them for an hour or so weekly, cutting pruning, gathering the bunches, eat them fried and raw, daily also. And work a few hours or a day in the Cocoa grove, cutting, washing fermenting and drying Cocoa (makes chocolate)—washing particularly, very pleasant, with group of injuns barefoot each with a woven basket swushing the goey nuts around to rid them of guk, squatting in sunlite under hot greenery by rocky stream. Well not always a group of injuns, but often. & at nite I sit in huts by fires watching violin and drum, sometimes.

La Senora, in case I forgot to say last time, is a Giroux-Harcourt authoress, once wrote a best seller about Jungle ("Three in the Jungle") Ugh. Writing another about mystical mayans, interesting facts for Bill but she's a strange case, some good and some nutty and some tiresome about her; her best feature aside from real (tho perhaps indefinite mystic hangup) being pioneer type-operating - on - the - indians - grew - up - around - here - carries -

a - machete - & - runs - plantation aloneness,   real archeological
pro.

   Yesterday I laughed to myself with delight at the thought of
finally leaving here sometime and really making it to frisco; and
tho I will, and arrival in frisco is sure shooting barring unforseen changes in soul atmosphere here or there or seismic phen-
omena unwonted or civil states & wars unheard of here as yet (no
seen newspaper in 2 months) (me), I dont know when & it's like
a dream of Europe. I ordered my mail sent down here from D.F. &
other places so if you've written me, I'll get it this comming week.
Can be reached here: HOTEL ARTURO HUY, %Karena Shields,
Allen Ginsberg, Salto De Agua, Chiapas, Mexico. When I leave
mail if any will be forwarded and I'll write then anyway.

   Shutting up shop—man bit by bushmaster in next villiage &
must find horses in field rush with razors & antiviperina. But eat
first, we sent medicine ahead. Stupid corrupted blood indians who
play poor drums dont even know enuf to cut open & bleed snake-
bite. Older time real indians know savvy more lore.

                                                Croak.
                                                A. Groan.

                                                Yajalon
                                          March 4, 1954

Neal:
Carolyn:
Jack:
   Forgive me for not answering your letter about spiritualism
earlier. I recieved it in a kayuko in the Rio Michol travelling toward
Salto de Agua when we met a messenger with months old mail, so
I read it and a flippant letter from Claude & Burrough's messages
under the trees leaning back on my knapsack while the indians
rowed in green crockodile water. That Neal is religious is a great
piece of news: I always wondered what he would be like with some
overpowering Awful thought humbling his soul to saintliness. But
wait! I have been doing some magnificent deeds in the last week,
and now am sitting in awful dumps all gone wrong and will tell
you about it first.

   I got to Salto with yr. letter 2 weeks ago. To make a long story short, I hitchiked a plane ride into deeper Chiapas, Yajalon where all the earthquakes have been. I heard about Mt. Acavalna— Tzeltal for Night House? What does that mean—Refuge from Darkness, or Place to Suffer Darkness—casa obscura. A mystery. Acavalna (roll that name its Blakean on yr lips)—in the mountains beyond Yajalon—havent got time to tell you all the mayan sierra and mystery forest ruins details, nor the meaning of names— Tumbala, Bachahon, Lancandon etc. But Acavalna is in that direction. According to geologists source of the quakes—still going on here every day after 2 months.

So in Yajalon with 100 pesos and no toothbrush and dirty clothes on my back, nothin but a fountain pen stepped off plane empty handed—small mexican south town, 400 yr. church at end of 10 blocks long, 4 blocks wide, walled in by high mountains on either side, fantastic scenery—approachable by plane that crashes every 10 days or 3 days of mule inland from railroad town Salto.

I went to Presidente and said I was a periodista on vacation and wanted to visit Acavalna—no newsman ever been there, just one geologist climbed it 10 days before and reported nothing but a big crack in its front, said maybe no volcano. But 2 days later Instituto Geologica his office said maybe there was volcano, in papers. Much confusion, Yajalon frightened. President promised mule free & guide. Next day no mule, just guide, I started over La Ventana— mountain wall between Yajalon and Acavalna—till halfway up a kind mexican saw my beard and in midpassage gave me his mule to ride up (he continuing his trip down on foot—true courtesy of local road). I arrived in afternoon at Finca or Plantation named Hunacmec—was treated as honored important guest— we sent mule & guide back. Hunacmec is at foot of Acavalna. That late afternoon, was loaned hammock & blanket for cold air mountain, given guide & horse to go spend the night at Zapata—a celtal indian villiage lost in side of Acavalna where men wear white & women wierd black & pigs gobble yr. crap by the river, pushing you aside to get it before yr. finished. Meanwhile joined by 2 laurel and hardy Yajalontecans who ran up and down mt. after me to go along. Night—drums, primitive church, bamboo pipe, (greatest hollow primitive drums I ever saw by the way they make brilliant drums here) guitars, men on cedar logs around wall, women in black pool at center in front of alter lighting long sinister pagan candles in front of glasscase alter covered with bunting and 1890 german religious paintings containing dolls of Jesu Christi & bearded black indian saints, another drum hanging from thatch roof—entertainment for me—suddenly boom, stupendous under-

ground roar like the Subway of the End under years of concrete
pavement, and the whole mountain begins to shake, the thatchroof
adobe church creaking, tortilla sized adobe chunks falling by my
shoulders, women screaming and rushing out the door into the
black shaking night, me trembling for my stupid pride in comming
to dread Acavalna, Horror of the awful power under the mountain
making so much noise and moving so much, and building up the
noisy shuddering—then stopped, everything quiet except for dogs
barking and cocks crowing and women screaming. It was the worst
shake they had since Feb. 5, the first earthquake, and me on top
of the fucking mountain right there. Nobody killed or nothing.

Well to make a long story short again, next day at dawn we got
together an expedition of 54 men indians all beautiful and number-
less boys and dogs more, from Zapata, from Tzahala, dirty town
south, and Chiviltic, over the next mountain—everybody scared,
and we started a great high dreadfull climb under hanging stone
thru milpas, to the unknown forest at the top of the mountain to
see if there was a volcanic fissure, or ruins, as was rumored, or a
secret lake, also rumored. High cedern forest, we cought a mon-
key—they eat monkeys. Cant tell you how I enjoyed the situation—
curious my psychology but it was a perfect set up—I was the lead-
er, I organized and supplied the general power and intelligence—
and I was defered to, boys carried my morale (little bag) and my
food, special indian coffee and eggs for me—the rest drank ground
maize for lunch, they asked me questions, dozens of indians ready
to run up and down mountains to get me horses or carry messages
or perform any mysterious white man with beard wish. At same
time I was weaker on horse or mountain or locality know how, and
my weakness deferred to with the greatest love and chivalry. This
was the sensation I had anyhow. Well anyhow we got to the top—
two or three small noisy tremblors on the way (there were 20 a
day)—not exactly unknown, I should say as the geologist had got
there with a few indians last time. They were all afraid to go when
he was here, but this time all the men of all three villages who
werent sick or busy went with me—the point being to calm the
injuns all over the area who think a volcano is smoking on top. So
we got to the top & saw all the mountains around and found nothing and set afire for joke smoke a great cedar tree to scare chiapas,
came down and I sat in middle of a circle and took names and we
made a declaration to send to the indians and towns saying exactly
what's going on in the mountain—for there is immense rumor
innacurate of every kind all over around here—and stamped it with
official seal of the three villages.

Went back to Hunacmec thinking Id had a great trip into rarely
seen parts more obscure than where I've been all along, though I
know well of parts more obscure toward the Usumacintly—and
we must sometime with mule go travelling through these parts—I
know spanish now & a little bit of Mayan, pocitito, and I love
indians & get along with them great, really, I think I could go anywhere practically—but anyway, the next morning when I woke up
I found fourty indians sitting on my doorstep of the tileroof finca
house at the foot of acavalna. They were from La Ventana, across
the way, had got up and walked five miles before dawn to talk to
me, they wanted to know what we saw on the mountain—and
wanted me to come with them to the other side. There was a legendary cave, they said they didnt know it, but two men from the
village had been there years before, and the geologist didnt
believe them, and they wanted to see if the earthquakes had closed
the mouth. They said should come and spend the night at their
village and they would give me horses and guides to get back to
Yajalon next day. So I went along on foot, and we stopped at
another village on the way and they put me up on a horse in the
middle of them—a long line of fourty whiterobed indians filing up
and down the hills—till we came to the end of the mulepath—and
I got off horse and twenty men went ahead to clear a path, so we
climbed up the east side of the mountain through the brush, till
we reached great boulders of ancient volcanic rock, like the great
waste plain at Paracutin—climbing over these—mountain ready to
shake or explode or god knows what: then shouting ahead, they
found it. When I came out in the clearing I saw a hole in the side of
the mountain as big as St. Patricks cathedral, entrance to the great
legendary cave—first stranger other than indians ever there—
solving riddle of name of Mountain—House of Night—dark cave.
Indians have great poetic imagination for names—a mountain
anciently named house of night & forgotten why except for one or
two who nobody believes centuries later. Well this cave was there,
and I climbed over the brush and went in first—I had to do something brave to justify the honor—and we all started staring and
wandering in the mouth—suddenly another boom from the mountain, I sat down hard and waited but nothing happened, and there
was another innocent tremblor 15 minutes later when we were all
deeper in, and could hear stalagtites crashing down interior—the
mouth of the cave had caved in and enlarged in earlier quakes,
so it was very scary. Beautiful cathedral like stalagtite formations—it's an enormous cave, one of the big world caves—I
never visited caves before like Crystal cave, but this one is as big

I'm sure or bigger, it's just stupendous, and right now thinking of it, it's like some awful dream vision, that big you know—and full of Pulpit formations, and naves and arches, like a piranesi drawing dont you know, Pilasters & arks and giant dark religious figurations.

Well we drew up a declaration of La Ventana later & I returned to Yajalon and read the mayor my declarations. I became a local hero—the cave was legendary, I was the first to verify it officially, as I had the 40 La Ventana wittnesses & the seal etc. So they asked me to stay & write up my story for newspaper & inform the Geological institute at mexico & have them come down and see if the tremblors have anything to do with the cave (I dont know)—and gave me a room in the president's house and told the local restaurant to send the bill to city hall & everybody in town wants to talk with me & invites me for coffee & merchants sell me cigarett packages cheap & dont charge me for pineapples and suchlike.

Chapter 2
Treachery in New York

Meanwhile first thing I do is spend 30 pesos wiring Claude, giving him a scoop for his Mexican U.P—for mexican newspapers are full of Acavalna tho no mex newsman as I say has ever seen the place, just typical mexican rumors via the geologist about secret lakes that dont exist (the cave has a river)—and mail him the documents to make sure & write up 3000 words discribing trip, indians, night of quakes on mountain, discovery of cave. Asking him to have mex U.P inform the Geologist, etc so he can have the story first and me maybe a little money like 50 bucks say for expenses.

In this telegram I said went to the top unvolcanic and next day discovered legendary cave secret of name.

In the middle of this sentence my typewriter began shaking— and the room trembling back and forth, dust falling from walls, I'm in the president's house in Yajalon, another earthquake, a kind of shuddering sound, but not like in the subway up in the mountain. No damage, though they say a house fell down at the end of the street near the airfield, I'll go and see when I'm done writing.

and said to Claude in this telegram that Geologist dont know, etc. & discribed cave. I wait three days & I get back:
      UNVOLCANIC CONDITIONS KNOWN STATESIDE
      APPLAUD MAGNIFICENT DISCOVERIES GONE BRAZIL
      WRITE
which means, the ironic stupid bastard, that he misunderstood my telegram and thought that I thought I was telling him some-

thing new about the top of the volcano (whereas I was giving him my itinerary shorthand) & that the cave didn't register, or mean anything to him—and that he was going to brazil (his vacation is April 2 or something to visit De Onis) and wouldnt recieve my explanation about the cave nor the interesting discription in detail about what it's like in a primitive indian church in the middle of the night when an earthquake shakes the mountain. In short I am left hung up in Yajalon with no money to telegraph anybody about anything, all my sweat writing 3 days no carbon in air to no hands in N.Y. & all my adventure slipping from my hands into the anonymity which it so richly deserves. So I'm leaving this dump, I've got 10 pesos left and soon my welcome here will be worn thin. I wrote Von Harz to read Claude's mail from me and use what he can—but it will be a week before anybody in N.Y. gets the idea and meanwhile I cant delay informing the Mexicano Institute, which will give the story to the mexican press and maybe I'll get my name in the papers here but no chance of collecting any small $$$ if there ever was one—though to be sure I havent seen a paper for months & have no idea how absurd all this sounds in U.S. ears unless anybody has enough imagination to see the importance and news value, however minor, of the cave. Well, I have some money—20 dollars in salto, will return to the Finca for rest & to still my troubled irritated nerves & explore legendary mountain Don Juan there and wait for another 20 bucks in checks the stupid embassy in D.F. returned to sender with the rest of my mail— World telegram back wages they were. If I get that I'll have enuf money I guess to get out, and come to frisco right off the bat. Meanwhile if you get a sudden wire from me asking for 25 dollars please get it to me if you have to pawn the family jewels because it will mean I am desperate & broke. Incidentally anyplace I wire from, Salto if anywhere, will recieve money wired back—I add this glumly since the last time my family sent me money the U.S. bureaucracy tried to say there was no such place on the wireless maps. Write me if you havent since last.

Love

Allen

And if that damned cave hasnt been reported by the time you get this letter do something—wire Giroux or my mother in Pilgrim State.

P.S. Jack: Re a meeting—I wont be in Mexico much longer— dont have plans yet, waiting for money to get out—write & wait.

San Jose
April 23, 1954

Dear Allen;
   Was notified this day by Western Union that you had not called
for the money I sent you April 9th, so they have returned it to me,
minus fee, 3.83. Naturally I'm very worried for your health and
safety and wonder where the hell you are, here I was expecting
you to show up hot on the heels of you last letter, but suddenly my
money is returned and there's no, no Allen, no news, nothing.
I'm writing a note to US Embassy, Mex City (the jerks returned all
three letters I wrote you there) and one to Bill Bourghs in Tangiers
and for godsake allen, write him, I get practically daily letters from
him wailing over your desertion of him, he's desperate believe me,
you better write your father too, he's written here once long ago
and if I don't hear from you before the 1st week of May I'm writing
him to tell of your disappearence and at the same time, early May,
I'm getting my lawyer to advise me on how best to find you, wire
police at Salto De Aqua, embassy at Mex city, or what. So you
better contact me or I'm scouring mexico for you, in person if all
else fails, tho I intend to return to work next week, and if I don't
hear something soon I'll know your in Jail or on the trail, dead that
is, with buzzards long since digested your meat, if you they'd
eat, who knows?!! . . . well I sure don't and that is why I write
asking you to alleviate my condition.
                                    Thank you.
                                    Love, N.
P.S.: Jack suddenly decides to live away from here, goes to San
Francisco to live in 3 dollar room for week then even more suddenly returns to New York via bus and is home with mama now. I
lost parking lot job and was refused 300 bucks back pay which
can't collect. but things here are rosy and will be even golden
soon.

Salto de Agua
May 12, 1954

Dear Neal: Carolyne:

I am O.K. allright though at the moment broke though also at
the moment not in troubles. I sent you a wire today, as soon as I
could after I got your note.

Bill is all taken care of. He recieved a letter from me from
Yajalon on April 22 and also I wrote him again this week. He just
never got my letters & began imagining all sorts of things. He sure
is lonely or imagines himself such and I guess it drives him off the
road at times. I'd been thinking of getting to the continent and
making a strange movie called BILL IN EUROPE (all plotted out)
while he was going through all this feeling of rejection, just
psychotic. He had it with Marker, with some reason. However this
kind of need with which I cannot but sympathize & try to do something real about, though now no need as I think he's back to
normal, will be real problem. But of our friendship, so complicated now & in some ways difficult—made more so accidentally by
this gratuitous crisis—I hardly know what to do to straighten out
and think probably the loco elements too deep to resolve and so
must be put up with—too ingrained with the genius. My confidence to Bill always—though was relieved leaving New York to
have his intensity off my back for a period. However a creative
intensity which catalysed me to where I am now—much better off.
Well we'll talk. In some respects situation quite horrible you know,
a kind of evil which in other situations I would not dream of putting
up with or being cause or object of; in this case not really dangerous since Bill ultimately sane somehow & anyway I do not believe
in black magic—you know you get on with life & like a more
humorous & humane view of things that might otherwise be
deadly.

What happened to me was, I put my letter to you & left next day
for the plantation penniless and was stuck there for the month till
yesterday when I got to town on the way out with the Senora. I
wanted to get out earlier but she kept delaying—local problems,
sickness, storms making rivers & paths unmanagable, and finally
her lack of finances. Also I didn't dream they'd send back the
money order—they knew here perfectly well where I was. Well
they are mexican bureaucrats. She had money comming too,
royalties from Harcourt Brace, and they sent that back to NY the
day before we arrived here. Well I collected a 20 dollar order that I

had (I had meanwhile had to wait for papers transferring payment from another city so was unable to collect it before I went back to finca) and paid her off what I owed her from before, paid the hotel, and had practically nothing but your letters saying what happened. Meanwhile we were stuck here waiting for her money from Harcourt to be resent so we could get out. That arrived five minutes ago. We will thus leave, she loaning me money, again, tomorrow morning by train for vera cruz. I havent enuf $$ for the San Cristobal-Oaxaca route, nor has she.

Meanwhile I sent telegram to you today, not knowing how long we would be here waiting till just now, hoping it might by chance reach here before the train left. At the same time, forseeing the charming possibility of her money arriving first & being able to get out of here, I have made ironclad usable arrangements for Sr. Huy of the hotel here, great man and caballero & friend, pistols and horses & all, to recieve the money for me and resend it on to an address, probably the Mexico City Embassy, which I'll determine. I will be there before the time runs out. That should work. In other words if I'm not here to collect it will be immediately forwarded to where I can collect.

I leave here tomorrow. I should be taking a week or less to get to Mexico city via train to the nearest bus city. I have written the embassy meanwhile to keep my mail & will arrive there in time before they dump it—they wait a month. Ought to arrive there at least by the 20th. If you send money about the time I get train, it will reach Mexico city about the 14th. If you delay a few days because of poverty or absence and send it around the 15th—well if you send it after this letter reaches you, send it around the 16th or 17th to arrive there around the 20th. Send it direct to Mexico City if you have not already sent it I mean, too. You get the pitch, with all these dates? If you havent sent it send it to Mex City. If you have it will be forwarded there from here, I'll get it.

So anyway I reach Mexico City around or before the 17th to the 20th I guess. I dont know how long I'll be there. Depends on finances. In any case I'll stop over for a very short time, a week or less. I have some business there—to meet Tamayo & Covarrubias & Pelliser (Mexico Poet Laureate), to inquire at U.P. office if I can still make money out of Acavalna, one or two other things—see Garver, pick up mail, see Mexico city for a day or so talking mexican—what a relief to be able to get around *not* in a language fog entirely. All things considered your money should arrive there in the days I'm there. I pay back the Senora what I borrow to get there.

What do I do for money then—I'll have some left over—the exchange rate has gone up to 12.5—a miracle for me, I get half *again* the value of the dollar. Thus except for telegraph fees it's good luck the wire was sent back—it came before the exchange went up. The same money will stretch way farther. Too bad you are not here to enjoy this perfect ripe moment—it will be lost in rising prices in a few weeks.

Also however in his overconcern Bill sent his parents a wire to send me a little gold. Did it without my asking and also makes me a little uneasy, but however cant complain. Well they sent it and I never got it for I recieved a telegram today "DID YOU RECEIVE THE MONEY BILL IS WORRIED ABOUT YOU WIRE ME COLLECT//M.P. BURROUGHS PALM BEACH" God knows how they sent it and why I never got it and when they sent it. Well I wrote them—no international collect service, telegrams now 25 pesos, & anyway a waste of their or my money—fast so they'll hear immediately that it hadnt come they should check and resend by cheap postal order to the Embassy.

You see a great deal of my trouble has come from the difficulty of communications—your and Burroughs money I somehow cant get ahold of; also my World Telegram Check, still due, maybe waiting also at the embassy in Mexico City. If all three come together in Mexico City I will be in a fine position with about $80 dollars worth really $120.00. However if only one or two come I will be on thinner ice and so am not yet all straight. However in any case I have done everything by wire and letter to all parties concerned today to assure as far as I can that the situation will be rosy & golden when I get to Mexico City. If however all has collapsed in Mexico City—I cant imagine how—I will figure some way out thru Embassy or Garver or even—ah horror—my family. However I am beginning to feel Burrough's sense of outrage at bureaucracy. May insist that the Embassy send me home since it is much their fault.

Well enuf of this essentially dull money talk. Incidentally, one final note: if you have not yet sent money, send it by cheaper postal money order, to Embassy. As long as it arrives around the 20th.

Meanwhile hung up here in Salto waiting has cost.

########

All this month not wasted as two things accomplished. Visited ruins near finca and discovered first small clay head to be found there, connecting it with Palenque culture, first time. Also discovered extensive suburbs of some ruins further down river.

Second spent all month in what is the major accomplishment of trip, working 5-10 hours a day for weeks writing 8 page poem SIESTA IN XBALBA, better than green auto. I seem to be back on ball, art *developing* and real serious. All old forms of Empty Mirror poems now fallen together and synthesized in such manner that the casual fragments of thought utilized for short poems; before are now linked together in a natural train of thought, or images, some very strong and powerful, very much paralleling the development of an intense meditation lying in a hammok just thinking along—but here only the quintessential thoughts, the crises and explosions at end of train of thoughts, the crystals, the natural observations of palmtrees erie appearance followed by some poetic high abstraction—all falling together in a kind of perfect sequence like a wordsworth meditation—and best of all, the central thing, of course, naturally, and really fortunately, the locale—the ruins of Palenque and remembrance of others worked in artfully—so that it is in this new form, an approach such as the romantic shelly or byron, to the subject of the ruins of time—a subject otherwise impossible to write about nontritely. As well, using these particularly obscure and essentially pathetic, not classical ruins, a feat otherwise impossible to achieve, to make something sublime or approaching the sublime out of visit here. So that the central passage is a meditation on a carving of a skull I saw in Chichen Itza months ago. Will not quote here but bring the finished thing—still needs work—with me to Frisco. Xbalba, the area from Tabasco thru Palenque to Guatemala border, is the Mayan Area of Limbo, or Place of Obscure Hope, purgatory. I have been in Xbalba (pronounced—dig sound—Chivalva) all these months. Just found out 2 weeks ago. That Don Juan Mt. is the center. Never got up there by the way.

Will write at soonest opportunity. What unluck jack is gone. I delayed too long, for one thing. I didnt mean to but things ripened as they did & with Acavalna and the poem at the end of all this time I am satisfied. Ah but it will be sweet to see you at the end.

Love,
Allen

[San Jose]
6-8-54

Dear Allen;
   We countenance no further delay, so, if of bad thumb luck you
are attack, call us collect at Cypress 7-0295, San Jose, & I'll come
for you in my new car, But, since I may be working when you call
you might have to wait some where as long as 24 hours before I
arrive, therefore, go to expensive hotel in town where you happen
to get stuck & I'll pay Bills or bail you out or whatever. But, better,
just thumb on up & do above only in emergency, of course if you
get within a couple of hundred miles just call & if I'm not here
Carolyn will come in car to get you.
                                        Love. N.

*These letters complete an eight year cycle of absence & correspon-
dence. I arrived in San Jose, spent several months with Neal and
family, migrated to San Francisco, got a job, met Peter Orlovsky
[Allen's longtime companion], wrote "Howl," hitchhiked with
Gary Snyder north.*
                                        A.G.

Bellingham
Feb. 7, 1956

Dear Neal:
   Still running around Northern Washington (Bellingham) & will
take bus trip up to Vancouver Canada Friday. Held reading at
Univ. of Washington, 5 old ladies ran out screaming. Then went
out to Skid Road Seattle with literary professors. Weather is misty
but balmy—not at all cold hereabouts, nothing as bad as N.Y.C.
Returning thru Portland the 13th to give speeches at Reed College.
My rent at the cottage is not paid and I will borrow it from you if
you can afford it (probably be able to repay in 30 days after return).
Send me a note via postcard to A.G. c/o Robert Allen 8879 S.E. 9th

St Portland, Oregon & let me know if this can be done so—Don't
be afraid of $ loss, I'll either log, ship, or work Greyhound. What's
shipping in S.F.? Los Gatos? Hear from Jack?

> Love,
> Allen

> New York
> [Early 1957]

Dear old dearest Neal,

Here's Allen and Jack writing you a letter on a nice typewriter in
a big yellow airy apartment owned by queer D. H. on 15th street
and 6th avenue with a Hi Fi set, Chinese mattings, on the floor,
Picasso, big cats, and a Hi Fi set, and a view of watertank on top of
17th street garment center building with late afternoon smoggy
light shining thru windows high New York oldfashioned 1890's
building 10 blocks away over the rooftops.

Jack has a pretty girl who clings to him constantly so he has
taken refuge in R's apartment to type novels for which there is a
constant demand from thousands of publishers clamoring over the
telephone for our stories & poems. . . . Please send immediately
one huge metaphysical manuscript to circulate among the fairy
editors of Manhattan. How is your foot? Peter told us the sole of it
had been scraped off when you stept off a train in the dark at Lost
Jose. How is sweet Carolyn? God has forgiven her (tell her) so how
can I not? (says Allen). . . . Please tell her to forgive me. for that
night in her house. The money you owe me: since you are sick you
can have it for keeps, that's $125, but in half a year when we are
starving to death in Europe and Jack is chewing on Peter's left
foot for a morsel of nourishment (chewing on little Arab girl foots),
in case we need it, I will write you big demanding desperate
letters, please do not let us starve to death, please, otherwise the
money is yours. Peter got laid six times on Organo street in Mexico
and we all got big blowjobs and orgies with fairies one winter night
on the plateau in a big bohemian apartment in the slums . . . And
Garver is old and shuddery and bent over his room over his
loom . . . his karma has reduced him to the stage of a pitiful dolter-
ing junkey in a kerosene smelley room in the basement creeping
barefoot on a rug full of spilled coffee and lost goofballs soaked

with spilled shots and him with $200 a month in his underwear. . . .
We hung around Mex city for 2 weeks, I met Esperanza* finally,
found her a Madonna, as Jack says, we got high on the pyramids,
the clouds were hanging over Lake Texcoco in vast airy spaces, the
sun was shining over that, and Greg** and I got on our knees. . . .
"THE BLISSFUL AWAKENER RESUMED: Subhuti, should there
be among the loyal followers some who have not yet penetrated
into a realization of their true position and who must first suffer the
natural remorse owing to crimes and failures in some previous
time by being degraded to a lower domain of existence and should
they earnestly and loyally observe and study this scripture and
because of it be laughed at and despised and even persecuted by
the people, they will immediately penetrate into a realization of
their true position and they will at once pass through knowing.''
It's all about Karma, see?
I am now going to Europe with Allen, to see ole Bill in Tangiers,
and write in sunny Spain, and April in Paris, and see Seymour in
London, and read Finnegans Wake in the Dublin library, and visit
Celine (got his address) and if I make a lot of money within next
five years I will get a Mercedes-Benz and drive right up your drive-
way, and give you the key, but dont wreck my new fenders.
Going to see my Maw in Florida, my new address there is 1219
Yates Avenue, Orlando, Florida, but within a year she and I will
come back and live in little Long Island pad again, with piano like
Ozone Park. . . . I love NY very much, it is really great, exciting, . . . I am having ball . . . . . sweet little girl I have with soft lips
and soft skin and pretty dark eyes and sings in bed with me . . . . .
says she loves me but I having trouble teaching her. . . . Saw Jerry
Newman who is still great cat and has bats. . . . Everything
fine. . . . Only trouble is I have headache from everything too much
wild. . . . Will write to you from Europe . . . . Allen says he loves
you, and that goes for me too . . . he says forever and ever and
always will and will be your husband in Paradise (he says) . . . and
he'll come back to coast and see you soon as back from Europe . . .
and court you again, he says . . . . . We saw Dusty who is still same
. . . . . I dont know what to say to Neal, says I . . . . . Peter, says Al,
if he were would send his sweetest and most Russian regards.

---

*Esperanza Villanueva, the woman upon whom Kerouac based the
central character in his novel *Tristessa.*
**Gregory Corso.

Lafcadio* is getting his hernia fixed in hospital this very moment.
Flowers,

Jack

Allen

c/o U.S. Embassy

Tangier, Morocco

April 24, 1957

Dear Neal:

Still here in Tangier, Peter & Bill also. Jack left 2 weeks ago by
boat for Marseilles on southern coast of France to hitch north to
Paris, where he must be by now. Got a card from Gregory who's
there, saying that he was trying to get job writing pornography for
Olympia Press which published Genet. You heard I guess that my
book was siezed by customs.** Our plans are still in the making. I
expect we will leave here the middle of May, next month, and head
north thru Spain to madrid or Barcelona and stay there a month,
and look for work. Money situation is very bad. Absolutely urgent
that you send me $100 or $125 before May 5—to reach me before
then. Bill in debt trying to support us (and beginning to rebel
against it) and we have been out of money for the last week and
will be out for another—camera and typewriter in hock. I didn't
think I would need what I lent you so soon, but I really do need it
now, badly. We won't be able to leave Tangier to go to Spain to
look for work unless I get it. So please don't fail me, if you have to
hock the Phonograph or whatever there is hockable. Need the
money here by May 5—a cashier's check from any bank prefer-
able (you go to bank, give them money, tell them what name to
make check out to, mine, they give you check, you mail it here—
that kind of check can be cashed immediately. Private check takes
too long to clear.) Please act on this at once.

I get up at dawn to watch the sun rise above Pillars of Hercules.
(Gibraltar mt & corresponding Afric shore are Piliars of Hercules).

---

*Lafcadio Orlovsky, younger brother of Peter.

**Copies of the book *Howl*, published by City Lights in San Fran-
cisco, were confiscated as obscene, resulting in a much-publicized
trial.

Havent used much T. The way they do it here, everybody smokes,
all the arabs, all day, young kids and old . . . bearded grandpappys
in white turbans & brown robes, is, they mix the kif and tobacco,
finely ground tobacco, and also with another dash of what seems to
be snuff, just snuff, and they carry around a little pouchful in a
small leather pouch about the size of a small changepurse. The
pipe is about a foot long, the bowl is a little clay cheap bowl that
fits on the bamboo pipestem—you can buy the pipestem, plain for
30¢ a fancy painted one costs 50¢—and the clay bowls you buy
anywhere, at tobacco stands or openair pushcarts—I notice in the
market most of the pushcarts that sell pepper, tumeric, spices,
also have a little box of these minature pipebowls for sale—2¢
each, they break all the time and are replacable. So they sit down
for a glass of mint tea and little music over the radio in this cheesy
one-table tearoom with a big brass urn in niche in dirty concrete
wall in some hole in the wall in the casbah; and light up a pipe or
two or three—or else just setting down in their robes under a tree
or by a fence downtown to rest, squatting—but they don't get
high, they just get a buzz off this mixture, and they smoke maybe
25 to 50 pipes a day, a continual buzz—sort of like smoking
straight tobacco cut with a little tea, they use it for tobacco smoking not for tea purposes. They dont dig getting real high, just
makes them sleepy or dizzy like drunk, bugs them—Bill's boy
Nimoun took a few pipefulls of our straight greenish brown sweet
smelling "Egyptian Hashish" & pushed it away with a sour
look saying it was "too sweet", he just didnt like it, none of them
do—no amount of argument or trial will convince them—they
apparently dont want to get really high as a rule—it gets in the
way. Other way of taking it is to make it into Majoun—cake-candy
type. Mix finely chopped Kief with caraway seeds, cinnamon,
honey, nutmeg, mostly Keif, heat it till it's stickey & should
harden a little like fudge (tho Bill's drunken-made rapid wild
chopping tea spilling all over the floor, clouds of cinamon in the
air, boiled fast—winds up consistency of stickey shit). Get high on
that lasts all night, off a tablespoonful, takes a few hours to work
but feels like peyote a little, except no nausea—just strong slow
fine tea high.

    That seems to be all report for moment. Met Jane Bowles, wife
of novelist named Paul Bowles, she's limp & speaks arabic & is
cool & shy & intelligent like Joan. Interesting English cockney
Hunckey-like ex thief now with TB on the lam from Britain, a
friend of Bill. Latest Burroughs magnum opus which Jack typed

up* is 100 pages of fragmentary fast action routines & (mostly
about different situations in which you could get hanged and
come—automatic reflex when neck snapped) & stream of conscious pictures, a revelation called The Word or Word or Word
Hoarde as Jack insists on "I'm going to let loose my word hoarde
like a great load of crap been waiting around inside me for 43
years" or words to that effect.

Send me $125 dollars immediately as per above instructions.
Write letter also. Leaving here by middle next month for sure,
probably for Madrid. Peter had asthsma is better. Anson due for a
visit next month from Venice, probably join us in Madrid.

Love, as ever
Allen

Madrid
18 June 1957

Dear Neal:

Gone thru Spain & now am in Madrid digging Prado Museum—
El Greco & Fra Angelico & Breughel & Bosch—nothing like a little
culture. Peter got awful hives from something he et, we had a
doctor—Living on $2-3 a day between us & headed for the Riviera
& then Ansen's in Venice. See you later.

Love
Allen

Vienna
[Aug.-Sept.] 1957

Dear Neal;

Been all over Italy, climbed Vesuvius & saw Pompeii & Capri &
saw Auden on Ischia (he's blind talker like Bill B.)—left Venice &
Ansen 2 days ago, now in Vienna—cant go to opera, no ties—
alas, they kicked us out—both still in beat dungarees (Peter in

*Naked Lunch (titled by Kerouac).

corduroy)—tomorrow we go to Munich, after that, Paris. Drinking lots of cheap beer.—How are you, wonder-child?—Alas to see you on the streets of Vienna or digging a Venice someday—When we're all rich we'll have a party on Lunar airplanes & dig the paris of the Moon (with Lafcadio) Write us c/o Amer. Express Paris, France. Love Allen People friendly here (Peter's words) Dig Time & Life mag. Sept. issues for articles on Allen & Jack & SF Poetry scene—Gregory Corso in Paris, he meet Genet—but Genet turn him down—he don't like americans who cant speak French Love Peter

Send us money! Yes? No? too.

[Paris]
Dec. 3, 57

Dear Neal & Carolyn:
Saw your picture in Life Neal, you were in the Court room looking in on how Allens Howl was progressing, just the side of your face with your hair back, yes it was you, Gregory just discovered it & told us we all said together Ha Neal was there seeing how things was going. And so I will write you now, have been meaning to but so much odd things happening here that time flicks like a coin in the air. We have a small room for 35$ mo. got gas & cook in, the hot water only runs four days out of the week, french are cheep & Oh so poor like us. Gregory & Allen are in the room now & two french seceteraiers are with us, we all may have a ball in a few hours, Gregory wants to go out & get some tee, the girls like it, we gave it to them the last time they were here. They are literaly, read a lot & went to college & speak some english. Allen wants to make it with girls now he wants his hips to rumble like only you can do with a girl. And also the great astounding news of the year is that Burroughs wrote us the other day saying he wants to make it with girls only, he had enough men & boys, now wants wommen, ant that great? Paris is all grey, you walk out in the street, clouds overhead make all Paris look grey ghostey like. Got a letter from Jack today, he is in Florida & will come to NYC in three weeks, has been drinking a lot & writting a play about you & other things. He may come to Paris in April, has been writting Poetry also with some strange lines that he will write you. soon.. Its been over a

year since I've seen you both & I wonder how the childern are
growing. Your a real Daddy now & you a real Mama. I'll bet you
have another twins.

I think the last time I wrote you was from Veniece where we, All
Allen & I stayed two months at Alan Anson's apt. & what a dissny
land that was. I fell in the Grand Cannal with my straw hat on &
cig. in mouth. All the art there had us hipmotized. We cooked
Ansen big mixed up meals wile he sat in other room making it with
young italan boys. We were there when the heat wave broke out,
we drank all the time, slept all day & walked out around Vienece at
night at the time there was big fire works in the sky & all the boats
on the water, thousands of people there durring the summer.
Gregory is telling both the girls to rub his back, they do it specking
french to themselves fast Gregory laying between perfummed girls
getting his back rubbed. No sex yet, latter.

Then we left Vienece headded for Austria whare we went to
Vienna to dig 15 Brougal paintings Whare we saw the whole world
on his canvasses—hes great to dig on too—we tried to go into
Opera to see Don Juan by Mozart but had no ties around necks &
they wouldent let us in, so we go out side & put our handkerchiffs
around our necks but they still wouldent let us in. We walked all
around eating cheep food & how good it was, plenty of different
kinds of frankfooters with wierd color of mustard. the off to
Germany we went whare we stoped off at Munich to see consentra-
tion camps called Dachow with black ashes all about the small
brick buildings whare fire furneses & gas chambers—Allen knew a
girl who lived in Munich she put us up & drove us around to all
Hitler used-to-be speach giving & ralling the people togeather.
There was a big bear gardinds almost a mile big whare all kinds of
people stay all day & throught the night drinking from big gallen
beautiful desined mugs of bear, bear. Germany rich & all the
people nervous looking. We stayed there for only 4 days. Saw one
good jazz spot called the owl. One thing interesting is that of the
young german people there the girls are far more better looking &
hipper dressed too, wile the young men all look tired & warn out.
Then we came to paris on the overnight train. Or rather we got into
Paris at 12 Oclock at night & walked the paris strets all night in ex-
citdness. Paris so big & so crowwded, buildings high & roof-tops
many with chimmenys the place of trees. Paris is Paris Neal, I
cant describe it to you, so for give. But we only stayed in Paris ten
days & then we went off to Amsterdam, Holland whare Gregory
was & so went to see him. We all lived in his room there & went
around town meeting literaily people gregory new. Saw 105 Van

Gough's (Allen just now came back to our room, he went to see a sick junky girl who is trying to kick habit.) I counted 51 crows in his last paintings. Holland cheeper then paris to live in, one gilder is a dollar. Thousands of bikes cralling around there. Would see wodden shoes every so often. Jazz very bad there. oh did I for get to tell you I shaved off my beard & my face looked smaller. I broke Allens cameria so cant send you any pictures. Also saw lots of Rembrants in Amsterdam. God Europe has been a education for us, I never expectied I would see so many paintings of all the great masters.

Vermeer's paintings that look like three-d paintings with great chlairity. Almost visited Rembrants toumb but the church was closed. No snow in Europe so far. We stayed in Amsterdam for three weeks eating rich black seeded bread for days & rich milk. Gregory has been writting lots of mad poems. His book of Poems will be comming out City Lights store soon, dont forget to see them. Come on Neal just drop us a post card, a small post card so that you dont have to write much on it—adress here is % American Express, Paris, France. Do it, just a small post card with a few words signed Neal, OK?

Gregory has been Paris six months poor living off rich girls when ever he can get them, but they keep leaving him.

Things are happening, Allen arms around girl pouring streams of poems made up in mind, Gregory quite with his girl, they grabing each other, I spray perfume on them & continue writting to you. Its a not-to-small room here with a painting on the wall by gregory. We just to day bought some scarce books, one The Thief's Journal by Jean Jenet thats difficult to get, do you know it? Oh yes one of these days we will go to the outskerts of paris and see Louis F. Celine. Allen just finnished a story to his girl saying "the worm is a bigger bird than the Vulture." But will write about Celine after we see him—

Dear Neal—Gregory speaking. Yes of course now I know you were right about Astrals because I have come to flash realization that Time is illusion in only that illusion is by-product of Time— Time being the horse and the track—the track always wins, but man does not place his 2 bucks on the track—you, my friend, did offer me a fortune by placing my bets on your choice—I did not follow you—I was an ass—but reason I did not follow you was because I felt that you inspired in me a shot at what number illumes before me. The number lost. I lost. I will never forget the lost. Not that I lost 30 dollars, but that I lost your power that you so kindly bestowed upon me. I now ask you to forgive me and give me

another chance. I will soon have 20 thousand francs—I want to go
to the races—please advise me how to bet—what I win will go half
to you—or if you order it so, I will continue to bet until you say
stop. I mean to say that I will tell everyone I encounter your
wisdom of the race—I will implore them heed, thus they too what
they win will pay tribute to you—you will be a millionaire in no
time because you deserve to be—What I learn from Jack & Allen
and my short life with you is that you are wonderful human being—As I write this letter I am happy to remember that you were
kind to me and liked me—the mad no brakes car ride—the track—
your home and television—your suddenly transformed actions
when you were in your RR garb—your love of women—your sad
face—our great conversation in McCorkles shack when I first realized your mind—I love you—

Gregory

Peter again: the latist thing with me is I will have to go back to
NY & help get brother Juluis out of bug hause, sad to leave Paris
at this time when Allen may get chance to go to Russia. Jack will
be comming to Paris again tho not definate. I wonder what you are
doing in spare time, will send you some poems I wrote soon. We
just bought Jenet's Thievs Jurnal which is great in parts—so long
energy inthewest, by-by Carloyn—hope you drop us a line.

Love to you all
Peter

Dear Neal—Love—I'll write too in a week. Why dont you tell us
your alive?

Allen

*In April 1958 Neal was sent to prison for possession and sale of
marijuana. He was in San Quentin for two years.*

[New York
Jan 10, 1959]

Hollo Dear Carolin:
Heres a letter that only now seemed to have time & feeling to
write.
We got your letter today & what you said about Neal—he a
speck amoung 5000 inmates—is that what he deserves & gets for
all he did—what can be done—Allen may be able to get that
Laywer who defended his poetry ban wile back to come into the
picture.
Lucky that Neal is strong all around so that he can take care of
him self—but god, me in there, a weeping helpless babe, lost,
tortured, beaten up, raped beyond reason and everything—I was,
when a boy, with my brother, becaues of poor parents, put in
prison like home for wandering boys, that they had to keep us
togeather locked up and compleatly seperated from the pack of
other youngsters who were vicious—but knowes his way in prisoin
—so thats one good thing. I think I sent you & Neal picture post
card when in europe, did I?
Allens in the other room reading paper, we got a 4 room apt.,
Gregory is in other room sleeping, its 6 Oclock now & hes been out
all day chaising girl & going to the paper publisher. The weather
has got a warm color on the street, I just came back from china
town walking thro the Bowery. Howes your children? You must be
working to keep everything going in that big house? You dont have
to answer my questions, I just wanted to say Hollo to you & Neal
& wave Hollo to the children. The prision is a big scarry thing—I
got a job in Mental Hospital but lucky I feel swing with that but a
prision is too tough for me. Also Jack just yesterday came in from
Northport & is around the corner with his new girl friend, Doty.
Because I got to work & have so many famiely problems I dont get
to see him when hes around & thats not much—he's well set up
with his mother & is alone a lot dreaming or writting or a flower he
touches in the garden. He is very calm & piecefull in Northport but
its when he comes to the city that too much comotion flies around
he gets drunk to fast & argues, but hes got a good independent
strong body & minded girl friend whom Jack respects.
My younger sister is learning to be a baby nurse in New Jersy,
shes the only one & me who have so far gotten out of famiely
mental hospital poor welfare hold. She, Maire meets Gregory
when she was last here on her off days & said to me "hes,

(Gregory) is like Jery Louis.

We also got a black cat that came with the apt., allen thinks its a 2 generation symises all black & acts like one, active jumpy thing, allens goten to be able to immitate its voice so they talk togeather at times. Since Gregorys got back from europe, a mo. ago we have never had so many art pictures all over the walls, post cards & drawings, in fact here I am in the kitchen & next to my shoulder is christ laying out body & three robed sad real faced women & on the window sill above my head is three picture cards, cezanne bridge & two egyption murels of birds. We all have been working on this movie*, Jack wrote the script to, its being shot in a loft of a painter. Thats what also I wanted to tell you. The movie is about that time we all were in you house & the Bishop came in with his mother & sister was it? Theres a painter whos acting as NEAL & Gregory is acting as jack & I is I, & allen is Allen & a good looking actriss is acting as you Carolin. If it goes over well you will get to see in art theator in Frisco some whare. Allen will tell you all about it when he sees you. He will be in SF on May 1st & will see you & you, if you have time can go to poetry reading he will give. There are a lot of funney things in the script, the movie has not been edited yet so cant tell how it is but have feeling we acted as bunch of dry hams. The fellows shooting it feel it will go over well. It would of been great if the original all of us could of been in it, you & Neal & your young son. who if you remember rushes out of his bed room into the living room just when the Bishop is about to leave with famiely, into Neals arms. The Bishop we got here is altogeather different then the one in SF. This guy here is a thin, painterfellow.

I will hope allen cando somthing for Neal, this laywer who defended him might be of help 1. to clarify what Neals sentence is & how long & what lupe holes there are for Neal to get out faster. I got your letter here on the tabol here now—and I feel the same way did about being lousy correspondent (Your spelling). No Allen has not published any of Neals writting yet & he wont if Neal dont want to, like you say (but if you dont mind I'll sign my name to the bottom of this writting of Neals & pub. it myself) (just joking, I wouldent do that). He may in time strike happy medium as you say, I wonder. Whats this about a portrait, do you paint? When I first read your letter this morning I got scared when you said "He's on maximum security at S.Q.— — — Cal. hysteria about narcotics". But if Allen could find a confident & daring laywer &

---

* *Pull My Daisy*, filmed by Robert Frank & Al Leslie. —A.G.

powerful one somthing might be done for Neal, somthing to find out anyway. I go to visit my brother in Mental hosp. & it takes attendants 45 min. to dress him up presentable to go out side walk-ing, hes been there 5 years & that ugly hospital has helped des-troyed him. His name is Julius. I call him Jullss some times now. No dont get excited about the penal system, the child-ren need you lots. I dont think Jack is comming out with Allen, Gregory might tho., Jacks a real tree baby. What are you acting,? "one of my theatre groups—"???? Dont worry, about approaching allen, hes still the stupid shmuck & only getting balder & still has dirty dungrees (pants) (I support him you know & buy the sope) He will want to get away from that pile of crowd out there and so will came, or I should say may want to get away from them & come to stay at your place for meditation rest. He has a cuple of places to read out there and about. Say do you know Robert La Vigne, hes a very good painter living at 12 Polk St. hes a good painter, Allen & I know him well, hes gone thro lot of phasses of kinds of painting & medium.

Its a shame we cant write Neal, I wish I could but like it is cant do. Allen just said "shall we send her $10.00 bucks" "Sure" I say, & he says "she probably needs it, New Years present". And now Gregory just woke up—dark out side & they are talking about some play and I must go to sleep now cause I was working the night before and feel sickness comming over me.

> So heres solong for now untill, untill a wile, say five years when I then brake down and get sick again & write you again only then Neal will be out & he will be next to you reading this letter
> so good night

> hollo Al hinkle & his geography trees with A's

> Love peter
> [Peter Orlovsky]

Dear Carolyn:
    That was Peter, this is me. I haven't sent yr letter back because wanted to make a copy, will soon (tho I keep saying that) or bring it when I come. U of C invited me to read there, will give me round trip fare & $100, & SF State Poetry Center invited me also, another hundred $, & probably a few other colleges. So will be there May 1

or earlier, and stay a few weeks. I wonder if I can, am in a position, to do anything for Neal, when I am there, I do not know, I'll try—perhaps a bigtime type Lawyer, god knows how these things work—or some sort of representation from Ruth Witt Diamant. But we'll discuss that. Perhaps I'm being silly. Formal official address while I'm there will be % Prof Tom Parkinson, 1001 Cragmont, Berkeley, Cal. Tho I'll probably get cheap hotel room same Hotel Bway & Columbus $7 a week. So have forms sent to Parkinson, me % Parkinson. I don't know if I'm considered officially Nice Person out there or Juvenile Delinquent but with professorial address it ought be OK. See if you can get Neal to fill out forms for me to visit—and write if possible. I'm not clear if writing is or is not allowed once forms are filled out.

Reporter from the NY Post doing sympathetic 12 part literary story on "Beat writing" been interviewing me & W.C. Williams & going out to Calif this week to see Gary Snyder, Ferlinghetti, poets there, etc. will probably look you up. I assume anyway he's sympathetic within the limitations of journalism. See him if you wish, or not. He might eventually if his story is sincere enough be able to help—he sees Neal as sort of a martyr, given bad deal by Wicked Opinion, Law. Reporter's name is Al Aronowitz.

We are making an experimental movie, maybe it'll be good, or funny. Even getting paid ($18 a day for 5 days work) acting. First money I've worked for since SF. Harder to act than I thought, more wearying. Names & situations are all changed, man playing Neal is great painter Larry Rivers—you know of him??—had a spread in Life last month. Young hawknosed fellow, paints, plays Sax, won 34,000$ on quiz program has photograph mind, now acts too & writes some, has grown kids, wives—sort of renaissance man, Italian style. Movie takes place in Loft in NY, painter's loft. I walk around with my finger in Peter's ear.

OK—let me know about the forms—love to Neal, & al H & wife if you see them. Tell Neal I hope see him soon. Well, that's 4 months, not so soon. Finishing new book of poems, main long poem about my mother 50 pages long* & higher & wilder than howl.

As ever
Allen
X X X

---

*"Kaddish"

FACT SHEET
*On behalf of Neal Cassady, for Parole Board Appeal, for use
of lawyers, journalists, family, etc.*

A. G.

[1 July 1959]

Neal Cassady

A47667 San Quentin—been in jail since April 16, '58, sentenced
July 3, '58 5-Life   2 counts posession & sale of marijuana—
Judge Carpanetti.

Public Defenders for him: Robert Nicco first, & sympathetic,
(charge dropped). A Mr. MacNamara second, & sluggish.

Probation report made by Wallace Takeguchi with minimal
examination of Neal Cassady & no information about his literary
character & career.

Convicted on sale; but tho he used marijuana quite a bit was in
no sense a professional pusher, probably gave it out socially. Refused to talk about connections, so cops were annoyed with him.
Not out on bail for months before trial & didn't have lawyer. Probation report was ugly & Judge Carpanetti denounced him as a
double-life monster on stand before sentencing.

Married—Mrs. Carolyn Cassady, 18231 Bancroft, Los Gatos.
Has ranch style house, 3 children. Wife presently on Welfare—
(Santa Clara County A.N.C.—Aid to Needy Children). She's
sympathetic & wants him out.

Worked around 10 years steadily as Brakeman & Conductor
on Southern Pacific Railroad. S.P. Union voted him his seniority
back whenever he gets out & can come back to work. SP management probably hire him, with union assent. His friend Albert
Hinckle (an SP conductor who doubles as Geography instructor at
SP State College) knows this scene—Andrews 6-7695 (San Jose).

Letters recommending early parole already in from James
Laughlin 333 6th Ave NYC (Laughlin Runs New Directions and
offered to publish Cassady writing); Ruth Witt-Diamant, San Francisco State College Poetry Center Directress (affirming his literary
reputation   &   value   to   community   etc.);   and   Larry
Ferlinghetti of City Lights, offering to publish a book of Cassady's

& also offering a job at City Lights. More letters due in from Grove Press in NY & various professors at U.C.

He's an old friend of Jack Kerouac & Ginsberg (known him since 1945) & fellow writer. Howl is dedicated to Cassady, Kerouac & Burroughs. Kerouac's On The Road had Cassady as the main heroic character, so an early picture of him can be got there. He's since settled down has wife family house steady job etc. New Kerouac book called Visions of Neal (titled Visions of Cody) will be published in Dec. by New Directions—consists of adventures and tape recorded literal conversations together.

Kerouac credits Cassady with having done the first advanced spontaneous prose style narrative which put Kerouac on to his own literary style, & taught him how to write modern prose modeled on natural speech, in certain Western rhythms.

None of Cassady's mss. have been published, most consisted of long letters (up to 40,000 words) of autobiographical narrative. Some of these have been lost. A selection of early letters by Cassady is being prepared by Kerouac for publication in an anthology of modern prose & poetry that Kerouac's been assembling for paperback publication later this year—Avon Press, N.Y. Cassady is writing in San Quentin (with typewriter sent by Kerouac) but since his subject matter is intimate & personal—confessional Dostoyevskian autobiography, in detailed & (proustian) style, it would be unwise for him to pass his mss. thru official hands. Probably be censored there for subject matter might get him in trouble re parole considerations. Outside of smuggling mss. out, therefore, there's no way of getting new material from him while he's in the can.

Cassady has already a considerable literary reputation in SF among local writers, since his identity as Dean Moriarty in the Kerouac book is well known. He was the subject of a study by the NY Post, as a literary hero; and his name is mentioned & discussed in respectable literary magazines in Germany, France, Denmark etc. A month ago there was an article & discussion of his literary role in the Paris Express, with a large picture of him & Kerouac. He's taken quite seriously & is well known as a U.S. literary figure in Europe. Which adds poignance to his obscurity & imprisonment here.

At the time of his arrest he was considerably depressed & made no attempt to get a lawyer & defend himself adequately—told his wife not to try raise his bail, so was not out before trial at all. As far as can tell, he did not at the time think that the sentence would be so lengthy serious, & so was negligent in securing his rights & outside aid.

Unless some reasonable intervention is made, or representations of the situation to the Parole people, his parole, which comes up in October will be mechanically passed over for another year. When Parole board does finally reconsider his file, it will be Oct 1960 and even then there is no security against their setting a lengthy sentence. Depending as they are on an inadequate & lurid Probation report, he may be in San Quentin for years.

Gavin Arthur, who teaches a Saturday morning Comparative Religion course at San Quentin, knows him & is sympathetic & would help; as presumably would Eichelman, the Protestant Religious Chaplain at S.Q., who is acquainted with him.

Cassady has a long interest in oriental religious devotions & is quite Faithful, in an original fashion; it's his main interest.

He has a beautiful soul, & is a great & secret author; his family life is getting balled up; his job is waiting for him; continued incarceration is completely meaningless & quite horrible.

                                            Allen Ginsberg
% City Lights Bookstore
261 Columbus

                                            [San Francisco
                                            2 July 1959]

Dear Carolyn:

I am still (dammit, hung up here in SF. Finished my record LP tape for the most part; and now hanging around following up leads on Neal. The situation so far is that I've got letters recommending parole from Ferlinghetti, Witt-Diamant (SF Poesy Center) & J. Laughlin of New Directions; they are in hands of Harry Wainright (Flood Bldg SF), a lawyer sidekick protege of Erlich: he'll try to reach proper authorities w/them. Also thru friends on Chronicle exploring ways to reach & convince perhaps Carpanetti; the DA; or State Senators. Slow work following various tenuous leads. Can you call Al Hinckle & tell him to reach me—am staying at Beach Hotel on Broadway (above Ann's 440 club) rm. 27—EX 2-9250; or messages at City Lights. Need to talk to Al abt. RR letters. But he can't seem to contact me, in town. Main problem has been the takaguchi probation report—any way of your talking to Takaguchi & explaining he made murid mistake? That may be a possibility later, if can be done, I dunno. Meanwhile I'm in town for another week then must leave, going broke & NY affairs hanging etc. All fine otherwise. Peter says Hello. Jack moving soon to Fla. to get away. okokok—Later, Allen

[San Quentin]

Dear Friend Allen:
 NEAL CASSADY, A-47667. 10-25-59.
 Since I'm already well past 90, and not just emotionally either, any trade you intend taking out must necessarily be retroactive and, as you perhaps gathered by my "Caroway dropping seeds instead of (poverty-happy) you" hint, it best be in pins; but quickly. else this, being my very last card, may well be the only time you will hear from me, until Eastertide at least: so remind as I thank you, all Postal Money Orders are C/O F. P. Dickson, Warden. Nice to know about H. Huncke, isn't that 1933 Side Show piece the very one he spoke about doing while in 1947 Texas Bayou Bath? or did the distraction of nibbling fish nipping flesh fool my hearing then, or cause exact memory to fail now? Is Big Bill B. having any new work published? Tell poor women-starved me the inside on Arly Francis & Margie Mead—or, fearing the older one is really R. Benedict's lover, just Arly. Always thought Greg needed something. maybe the Hydra*, Hap. is it, may it prove lasting—& what did he use? Disagreeing with Varda: "Gin. so decadent, is Magnif." I remain
                                                N.

---

*A visionary experience of "skinless light."—A.G.

Dear Allen, Et al: CASSADY A-47667
The lights have failed in the cell-Block so am writing this last S.Q.
line in semi-darkness, making my scribble excusable for once.
Assuming I get thru this 787th straight nite behind bars, just as i
assume you missed the Chile—got your great letter from there—
Earthquakes & are still alive, I shall leave here in the morning &
go to a job at Con. Lithograph Corp & my home at 18231 Bancroft
Ave., Los Gatos to begin a 3 yr. parole.

                                        Love to all—Write,
                                        Neal

THE
SIXTIES

170 E 2 St N.Y.C.
Dec. 4, 1960

Neal: Merry Xmas

Forgive my silence—Enclosed a note from Hunke as of 6 months
ago . . . —I will write you—Peter and I were up at Harvard* last
week eating synthetic mushrooms—very high—*The Revolution
Has Begun*—Stop giving your authority to Christ & the Void & the
Imagination—*you are it,* now, *the God*—I will have babies instead
of jacking off into Limbo—all's well—we're starting a plot to get
everyone in Power in America high—Hurrah!—I flipped my lid
last week at harvard & rushed out stark naked to telephone Jack &
wake him up—he's always wanting to die—I stopped vomiting up
the Universe last week—my book Kaddish (all Death Death Death)
(hymns) is done & will be out in a few months. How are you? and
Caroline & the Babies? I love you in Life's sweet July. I am a
horse's ass as always. What kind of money work you doing? Why
dont you write again to communicate the holy news to the world?
They need that many lovers of wisdom to tip their mit & make a
break—you are *needed*— stop hiding yr light in a bushel. I'll sit
down & write you a long gossipy letter soon as I can. Always,
always,—

Allen

July 6, 1961
c/o U.S. Consulate
Tanger, Moroco

Dear Neal:

Left NY. March & spent month in Paris & month on Riviera
Cannes & St Tropez, broke, till rich friend sent us (me, Peter, &
Gregory Corso) by boat to Tanger to see Bill Burroughs. I came
across Strait of Gib. today to cash exchange loot from City Lites
check, then back tonite. Been here a month, going inland to
Marrakesh touring with Paul Bowles. All is well dearie & how are
you & the Folks? I'll write again sometime. Too much else for a

---

*Visiting Timothy Leary.—A.G.

postcard but it all addes up to Love,—

Allen

[Tangier
Aug. '61]
Allen Ginsberg US Consulate Tangier Maroc

Dear Neal:
  Get hi & dig the walls of the desert city on reverse. Been here with Paul Bowles for a week—Maddest city anywhere, everybody ahead—vast labyrinthine markets covered with bamboo against the sun, looks like Arabian Knights scenery, gleaming cnadles & hooded beggars and lamps for sale. There's a big main square bigger than Times Square where snake charmers acrobats, great spade drum-and-dance troupes, fortune & storytellers & gamblers pitch for coins in the middle of big circles of rubes everybody smoking kif—and the heat gets me all confused & zonked too—at nite we go up on roof & drink & smoke tea and look at the stars & listen to the Muezzins calling from Minaret towers across the city. How are you dear Neal & how's Carolyn & the kiddies? Burroughs is all hung up on Magic lately. Peter & Gregory are waiting in Tangier.

Allen

1086—Marrakech—Les Remparts et l'Atlas enneige

American Express
Calcutta, India
Oct 8, 1962

Dear Neal:
  When'd I last write? I forgot—hear about you occasionally from Jack long ago, more recently Ferlinghetti & Nanda Pivano. Ferlinghetti says he has your First Third mss & would publish it, I guess that'll be nice. I don't remember—he says he has 116 pages—all

that—& says the end has complicated sphagetti sentences he cant understand. Dont change it if the sentences make sense on any level, that's my opinion. I hope you do publish it. Can you write more?

Secondly, enclosed find an old poem of mine 1957* I looked at here & cut down a little. Please look it over & let me know if it's OK to publish using your name in it like that. It's very romantic idealistic but does be what i really felt when I wrote it & always feel anyway so, if it aint "mature" even yet still I dont care. I'm putting together a book for Ferlinghetti City Lights & will include it as is if I have your OK. Better send it to me in writing so you cant sue me in Eternity.

How are you? All sorts of strange & horrible things have happened the last 2 years—strangest thing for me was what Burroughs is, doing,—real impersonal no-man inside it seemed—we all met (Gregory Peter Ansen Me Bill Paul Bowles) in Tanger a year ago & Bill made me feel I never knew him. Said he was trying to get out of his body & as such was cutting off from all attachments. Seemed like he was making it too.

Anyway since then I been thru Greece, Palestine, Kenya & now here in India since Feb—great scenery—last night went with some Fakir friend to the burning ghats (place on ganges where corpses are hindu burned) & there Tues & Sat nite is Ganja nite, everybody comes out & shouts Boom Boom Mahadev! to the stars as they lift up to blast red clay pipes—sit around near ganges with saddhu-saints halfnaked with long wierd hair and ash-smeared bodies everybody high six feet from a corpse burning, half the shoulders & head of a businessman being turned over to the center of the coals, smoke rolling over the potsmokers heads. This is the classical Bengali Tantrik scene for meditation, in the burning ghats, & using pot, with big sedate rituals, everything legal, groups of friends meet twice weekly in burning grounds, bring incense & flowers & candy for ritual distribution to the smokers, and a few wierd saddhus who sleep live on the grounds for meditation doing snakey dances to the blindman's drums & going from group to group collecting candy & free drags from pipes—it's a family outing scene—very respectable here.

Living in Mohammedan hotel downtown calcutta the last 4 months, now it's Durga-kali Worship holiday weekend, like Xmas, statues of 10 armed goddess killing Buffalo Demon set up in tents all over town & crowds out at night banging gongs & drums &

---

*"The Names."—A.G.

visiting the images to pray & dance & sing & get high—Tuesday
officially everybody drinks Bhang (Cannibis in almond flavor milk)
& goes down to ganges to throw the Statues in the water.

Met some wierd saints on streets, but no guru. We (Peter here
to) know a lot of people, poets & businessmen, go round on streets
in indian clothes & I got long black hair down to shoulders & a
beard & peter long blond hair, we sure look looney. But everybody
here also looks looney so we pass unnoticed more than if we were
in slacks & U.S. hair.

You working in Tire repair place or something? How's Carolyn
& hows family. Your kids must be nearly my age by now. Write me
& say if its okay to publish poem &, at least that, & let me know
what's up. Oh, also I got letter from Bertrand Russell 2 weeks ago
he says the Radar networks & atomic networks are all faulty &
gonna explode it's a "matter of mathematical statistical proba-
bility" unless we do something. What you think?

Love
Allen

P.S. If you don't write, please ask Carolyn to write me about the
poem, by one or 2 days. I have to instruct Ferlinghetti to put it in or
take it out of book now in proofs.—Allen

[Enclosed in letter]

Fragment 1957

Time comes spirit weakens and goes blank apartments shuffled
　　through and forgotten
The dead in their cenotaphs locomotive high schools & African
　　cities small town motorcycle graves
O America what saints given vision are shrouded in junk their
　　elegy nameless hoodlum elegance leaning against deaths
　　military garage
Huncke who first saw the sun revolve Chicago survived into
　　middleage Times Square
Thief stole hearts of wildcat tractor boys arrived to morphine
　　brilliance Pickford table midnight noon to take a fall
arrested 41 times late 40's his acned skin & black spanish hair
　　grown coy and old and lip bitten in Rikers Island Jail
as bestial newsprint photograph we shared once busted, me scared
　　of black eye cops Manhatten
you blissful nothing to lose digging the live detectives perhaps
　　even offering God a cigarette

I'll answer you Huncke I never could before—admiring your
    natural tact and charm and irony—now sad Sing Sing
whatever inept Queens burglary you goofed again let God judge
    his sacred case
rather than mustached Time Judge steal a dirty photograph of
    your soul—I knew you when—
& you loved me better than my lawyer wanted frightened rat for
    official thousand buck mousetrap, no doubt, no doubt—
Shine in Cell free behind bars Immortal soul why not
Hell machine can't sentence except itself, have I to do that?
It gives jail I give you poem, bars last twenty years rust in hundred
my handwork remains when prisons fall because the hand is com-
    passion.

Brilliant bitter Morphy stalking Los Angeles after his ghost boy
haunting basements in Denver with his Montmartre black beard
Charming ladies man oft for a purpose I heard great cat Shakes-
    pearean sex
first poet suicide I knew sat on park benches watched despair his
    forehead star
my elder asked serious advice, gentle man! international queer
    pride broken to pre-death cigarette gun fright
Love a young blond demon of broken army nemesis his own mad
    cock for the kids sardonic ass
his dream mouthful of white prick trembling in his head—woke a
    bullet in his side days later in Passaic
last moments gasping stricken blood under stars coughing intes-
    tines & lighted highway cars flowing past his eyes into the
    dark.
Joe Army's beauty forgotten that night, pain cops nightmare,
    drunken AWOL through Detroit
phonecalls angels backrooms & courtsmarshal lawyer trains a
    kaleidescope of instant change,
shrinkage of soul, bearded dead dreams, all Balzac read in jail,
late disappearance from the city hides metamorphosis to humancy
    loathing that deathscene.

Phil Black hung in Tombs, horsefaced junky, dreamy strange
    murderer, forgotten pistol three buck holdup, stoolpigeon
    suicide I save him from the grave

Iriquois his indian head red cock intelligence buried in miserous
    solitaire politics
his narcissistic blond haired hooknosed pride, I made him once
    he groaned and came

Later stranger chill made me tremble, I loved hopeless years,
he's hid in Seattle consumed by lesbian hypochondrias stealthy
communion, green bullfighters envy age,
unless I save him from the grave, but he won't talk no more
much less fall in my arms or any mental bed forgiveness before we
climb Olympics death,

Leroi returning to bughouse monkishness & drear stinky soupdish
his fatness fright & suffering mind insult a repetitious void
"I have done my best to make saintliness as uninteresting as
possible"
and has succeeded, when did I last write or receive ambiguous
message jokey hangdog prophetic spade

Joan in dreams bent forward smiling asks news of the living
as in life the same sad tolerance, no skullbone judge of drunks
asking whereabouts sending regards from Mexican paradise
garden where life & death are one
A postcard from eternity sent with human hand, wish I could see
you now, it's happening as should
whatever we really need, we ought get, don't blame yourself—a
photograph on reverse
the rare tomb smile where trees grow crooked energy above
grass—
yet died early—old teeth gone, tequila bottle in hand, an infantile paralysis limp, lacklove, the worst.
I dreamed such vision of her secret in my frisco bed, heart can live
rest of my, or her, desire—love.

Bill King black haired sorry drunken wop lawyer, woke up trembling in Connecticut DT's among cows
Him there to recover I guess, but made his way back to New York
shuddering to fuck stiff Time girls,
Death charm in person, sexual childlike radiant pain
See his face in old photographs & bandaged naked wrist leaning
melancholy contemplating the camera
awkward face now calm, kind to me in cafeteria one sober morn
looking for jobs at breakfast,
but mostly smiled at roof edge midnight, all 1920's elegance
reincarnate in black vomit bestriven suit
& screetchy, records *Mahagony* airplane crash, lushed young man
of 40's hated his fairy woe, came on Lizzie's belly or Ansen's
sock in desperate orgies of music canopener
God but I loved his murdered face when he talked with a mouthful
of rain in 14th St subway—

where he fell skull broken underground last, head crushed by the
    radiant wheel on iron track
Farewell dear Bill that's done, you're gone, we all go into the
    ancient void drunkard mouth
you made it too soon, here was more to say, & more to drink,
    but now too late to sit and talk
all night toward the eternity you sought so well so fearlessly
    in so much alcoholic pain with so much fire behind yes with
    such
sweet manner in your heart that never won a happy fate thru what
    bleak years you saw your red skull burning deathshead in the
    U.S. sun.

Mix living dead, Neal Cassidy, old hero of travel love alyosha
    idiot seek train poems, what crown you wear at last
what fameless reward for patience & pain, what golden whore
    come secret from the clouds, what god bidden for coffin &
    heart someday.
what will give back your famous arm, your happy catholic boy eye,
    orphan torso shining in poolhall & library, intimate sperm-
works with old girls downtown rockabelly energy,
what Paradise built high enough to hold your desire, deep enough
    to encompass your cock kindnesses, soft for your children to
    pray, 10 foot iron wheels you fell under?
what American heaven receive you? Christ allow sufferings then
    will he allow you His opening tinbarrel Iowa light as Jeru-
    salem?
O Neal that life end we together on knees know harvest of prayers
    together,
Paradise autos ascend to the moon no illusion, short time earth
    life Bibles bear out eyes make it dear baby
stay with me Angel now in Shroud of railroad lost bet racetrack
    broke leg oblivion
till I get the shining Word or you the cockless cock to lay in my
    ass hope mental radiance—
It's all lost we fall without glory to empty tomb comedown to
    nothing but evil thinkless worm, but we know better
merely by old heart hope, or merely Desire, or merely the love
    whisper breathed in your ear on lawns of long gone by
    Denver.
merely by night you leaned on my body & held me for All & called
    me Adore I wondered at child age ten I
wandered by hopeless green hedges, you sat under alley balcony

garbagestair, ache in the breast Futurity
meeting Love for Love, so wept as child now man I weep for true
    end,
Save from the grave! O Neal I love you I bring this Lamb into the
    middle of the world happily—O tenderness—to see you again
    —O tenderness—to recognize you in the middle of Time.

Neal, Carolyn—please reply—fast—whether this is OK to publish
in a book.
                                  Allen Ginsberg
                                  American Express
                                  Calcutta, India
Oct. 8, 1962
Durga Puja!

                                    [San Francisco?]
                                      1963

Neal—
    Claude called me here from City Lights—he's at Colombo Hotel
around corner from C.L.*—I taking bus up—I'll try to contact you
before weekend's over—perhaps come down to that party in Palo
Alto—in any case dont worry we'll be in contact—Lovely Claude to
care so & fly so far—Lovely Neal to be here & me to Be here and
all—
                                    Love
                                    Allen

*Phone call earlier that year [1967] (after Feb. S.F. Be-in), I'd
invited Neal to come with me to Europe, if we could meet in N.Y.
I was negligent about arrangements and went alone, so never
received the following messages.*
                                    A.G.

---

*City Lights Bookstore.

[San Miguel de Allende, Mexico]
4-12-67

Dear Allen; Comrade!
SERIOUS—TOP SECRET—DO THIS!
After 28th in New Mexico, (Invite: if in Phone book or at your
Lecture there—ask audience—Bob Adams—Ask if he's friend of
me & Mannerly) Take bus to Dallas (Dallas, Tex.) on 29th, be in
Dallas Tex. 30th late or early. 1st May so can, *you must* meet me.
(May 1, noon) at JFK Ass. site (by bookstore). Write at once.
                                        Love,
                                        Neal

Address is: Kathy Van Leeuwen
San Francisco 49,
San Miguel De Allende.
Gto. Mexico

[San Miguel de Allende
April 67]
Cassady (c/o Diane Sward)
Lista de Corrso
San Miguel de Allende
Gto., Mexico

Dear Poopsie—comrade—etc.
Again a change—decided against Dallas. Get on the plane or
train and come down to San Miguel de Allende. There's a train
that leaves El Paso every day around seven at night and takes
thirty hours and leaves you at a town called Celaya at some incred-
ible hour in the morning. If you come by train let us know when so
we can meet it. If we don't meet the train just take a cab from
Celaya—it will cost about 60 pesos ($5) to San Miguel.
Or you can take the plane to Mexico City and take a bus from
there to here (4½) hours.
You can find me at Dian's house at 4 Murillo—and stay here too.
Then we can figure out what to do from there. But its better than
that. I got big plans—just stick with me—and really want to see
you—

No need to make it immediately after the 28th—I can wait another week or so—but I'm going to stay here until you get here even if
its June because you've got to save me—if not mentally and physically—at least financially—

Really I'll stay until you get here—won't take no for an answer—

Enclosed is a card so you can let me know what's happening.
Will be in Vera Cruz for a week—then back here by around the
26th—

I'm counting on you al—we'll talk when you get here . . .

Love & Hurry on Down Allen.
Neal
(Himself)

P.S. I wrote jack a card.

P.P.S. Don't get rioted & get your hairless head bumped. heh,
heh,

N.

EPILOGUE

Letter to Carolyn
from Allen
& Poem "Los Gatos"

R.D. 2 Cherry Valley NY 13320
Feb 19. 1970

Dear Carolyn:
A few months quiet home & been typing old notebook poems,
enclosed a page from Los Gatos, I guess notes the time Ansen
came thru on greyhound bus, (& gossiping about old school chum
mentioned Cogswell, whom you didn't know), & Neal drove
Kesey's bus down. How & where are yr children tonight?
Jack's funeral very solemn, I went with Peter & Gregory & John
Holmes in Holmes' car, saw Jack in coffin in Archambault funeral
home on Pawtucketville St Lowell, some name & funerary home
from Jack's own memory—& pallbore thru high mass at St. Jean
Baptiste Cemetary—Jack in coffin looked large headed, grim-
lipped, tiny bald spot top of skull begun but hair still black & soft,
cold skin make up chill to finger touch on his brow, fingers wrinkled, hairy hands protruding from sports jacket holding rosary,
flower masses around coffin & shaped wrinkle-furrow familiar at
his brow, eyes closed, mid-aged heavy looked like his father had
become from earlier dream decades—shock first seeing him there
in theatric-lit coffin room as if a Buddha in Parinirvana pose, come
here left his message of Illusion-wink & left the body behind.
Sad I didn't call you before, but too much woe, life & business
on my desk till this dusk. Take care of yourself.
OK—as ever
Allen

Los Gatos

Years later, house repainted,
    blue swimming pool full,
husband returns mumbling and sweating prophecies
admirers, lovers, cocksuckers aghast,
    novelists listening in velvet shirts
speed freaks & swamis waiting in a painted bus—
Wife talks thru newspapers in spiritual Californiaese
decades later again, movies roll on, blond baby boy
    enters french doors sports-jacketed
        moslem neck charm leatherthonged to breast,
    dark daughter whispers in her longhaired date's ear
        at the barbecue oven,
Alan Ansen returns from Greece a day
        surveying antique America,
Wayne Cogswell's an insurance man & plays chamber music at
    leisure,
the husband raves on, Egyptian lifetimes pass
        thru his lips at the fireplace
& th' elderly lady guest returns from Bedroom
        television
with News: shooting's started in the Gulf of Aquaba

June 4, 1967

                        Allen Ginsberg

Afterword

Any stupidities about John Clellon Holmes, Marker, Mannerly, embarrass me now, as well as opinionation & egoism of Teen & Twenties, but I'm not in position to censor myself or others here. The letters are printed exact to their time, one paragraph removed to protect living sensibilities, and some typos corrected, some footnotes added. The letters speak for themselves, regarding love and inquisitiveness and constancy. Tho some aspects of affection & dependancy on my part (& Neal's) seem hysterical or false faced or self defeating, there does seem to be a depth of good intention toward each other ("What's the cosmic score now . . . ?" "You've got to save me") that survived erotic infatuation, absence, jail, world wandering, marriages, disillusionment. "Look for a miracle—" "I wish I could see you in a timeless world in the sunlight."

We saw each other a lot in the Sixties on Ken Kesey's magic bus—After a long 1967 trip down from Bellingham, Washington (where the three of us taught together in an English Composition class) Neal & I spent a night naked together with his present girl in a motel on Van Ness in San Francisco. His skin was cold, chill, sweaty & corpselike—the chemical cast of excess weeks amphetamine—and irritable. I think it was the first time I ever got out of bed with Neal voluntarily, in despair myself finally, & walked the street, pondering over the miracle of deathly fate that had overtaken my youthful idealism in romance with him.

Allen Ginsberg
June 3, 1977

Index

BOOKS BY ALLEN GINSBERG

Howl (City Lights)
Kaddish (City Lights)
Reality Sandwiches (City Lights)
Indian Journals (Dave Haselwood/City Lights)
First Blues (Full Court Press)
Bixby Canyon Ocean Path (Gotham Book Mart)
Sad Dust Glories (The Workingmans Press)
Visions of The Great Rememberer (Mulch Press)
Gates of Wrath (Grey Fox)
Allen Verbatim [Ed. by Gordon Ball] (McGraw-Hill)
Improvised Poetics (Anonym Press)
Empty Mirror (Corinth)
Gay Sunshine Interview [Ed. by Allen Young] (Gay Sunshine)
Airplane Dreams (House of Anansi/City Lights)
The Fall of America (City Lights)
Planet News (City Lights)
Iron Horse (Coach House Press)
The Yage Letters [With William S. Burroughs] (City Lights)
Chicago Trial Transcript (City Lights)
Mind Breaths (City Lights)
Angkor Wat (Fulcrum Press)
TV Baby Poems (Cape Goliard)
Journals Early 50s/Early 60s [Ed. by Gordon Ball] (Grove)
*As Ever: The Collected Correspondence of Allen Ginsberg &
    Neal Cassady* [Ed. by Barry Gifford] (Creative Arts Book
    Company)

BY NEAL CASSADY

The First Third (City Lights)
As Ever (Creative Arts Book Company)

BY CAROLYN CASSADY

Heart Beat: My Life With Jack & Neal (Creative Arts Book
    Company; Pocket Books)